D0049037

The Evangelicals You Don't Know

The Evangelicals You Don't Know

*Introducing the Next Generation
of Christians*

Tom Krattenmaker

ROWMAN & LITTLEFIELD PUBLISHERS, INC.
Lanham • Boulder • New York • Toronto • Plymouth, UK

Published by Rowman & Littlefield Publishers, Inc.
A wholly owned subsidiary of The Rowman & Littlefield Publishing Group, Inc.
4501 Forbes Boulevard, Suite 200, Lanham, Maryland 20706
www.rowman.com

10 Thornbury Road, Plymouth PL6 7PP, United Kingdom

British Library Cataloguing in Publication Information Available

Library of Congress Cataloging-in-Publication Data

Krattenmaker, Tom, 1960–
The evangelicals you don't know : introducing the next generation of Christians / Tom Krattenmaker.
pages cm.
Includes index.
ISBN 978-1-4422-1544-3 (cloth : alk. paper) — ISBN 978-1-4422-1546-7 (electronic)
1. Evangelicalism—United States—History—21st century. 2. United States—Church history—21st century. I. Title.
BR1642.U5K74 2013
277.3'083—dc23
2012047053

Printed in the United States of America

To C., with love and respect

Contents

Acknowledgments

For the title of this book and so much more, credit is owed to John Siniff. John created and for many years edited *USA Today*'s long-running "On Religion" commentary series, the platform for most of my pontifications on religion in American public life. It was John who crafted those words "The Evangelicals You Don't Know"—not for this book, but as a headline for a column of mine that he published in 2008. The headline beautifully captured the essence of that particular piece, which was, in retrospect, the seed from which this book grew. When my book editor and I brainstormed title ideas for this volume, it did not take long to realize we already had it in hand— thanks to that excellent headline by John Siniff. I also owe thanks to John for his advocacy, his belief in me when I was totally new on the scene as a commentator on religion in public life, and his tough but superb editing. (John has since moved on to a different position at the paper.) John under- stood my stand as a writer who strived for even-handedness and a generous understanding of the other side, or sides, and he held me to it whenever I strayed.

I am also grateful to someone who supported and influenced me well before I started writing columns for the nation's largest general-interest newspaper. When I first encountered Steve Dunning, I was a new, part-time master's degree student at the University of Pennsylvania, and Steve was teaching a seminar that had caught my eye while I perused the course cata- log: "Religion in Public Life." I wanted in. The seminar fascinated me, provoking endless questions and ideas, and left me wanting more. I quickly decided to concentrate my future coursework on this subject, doing much of it, including my capstone project, under Professor Dunning's direction. Uncomfortable though it was at the time, I thank Steve Dunning for calling me out on my assumptions and biases and helping shape me as a writer willing to try to understand and respect the "other"—especially, in my case, the evangelicals.

Special thanks go as well to Sarah Stanton at Rowman & Littlefield for doing so much to launch this book when it was in its formative stages. When I initially approached her I had little more than a half-baked idea and some promising material. Her ability to see the potential, and to guide me toward a clearer approach and sharper argument, made all the difference. Kathryn Knigge worked diligently to birth this book at the other end of the process. All my thanks to her and the others at Rowman & Littlefield—Jon Sisk, Sam Caggiula, and many more—who have supported my work through this project and the one that preceded it.

My wife, Carolyn, deserves enormous thanks and appreciation. She not only contributed her excellent editorial skills to this book, but, more important, she has provided constant emotional support, tolerance of my recurring writer neuroses, and much-needed irreverence and perspective for a husband who is known to get a little too worked up at times. Thank you, C. No "trang gun" necessary at this point (I think).

I extend my deepest appreciation to the many evangelical Christians who have gone out of their way to help me with this book and my column-writing, and who have invariably treated me with kindness and hospitality. They are too numerous to name on this page. But that's all right. You'll meet most of them in the book.

And, finally, I convey heartfelt appreciation to the readers of this book and my columns. Thank you for supporting my work. More important, thank you for caring about the important issues surrounding religion in our public life. As Norman Lear once said, the conversation about religion and spirituality is "the greatest conversation going—and I want in." I want in, too, especially the part about the way this all plays out in our changing culture and politics. Evidently, some part of this conversation draws you in as well.

In we go.

Tom Krattenmaker, January 2013

Chapter One

Replacing Styrofoam Jesus

Leave it to one of the young church members to see a deeper symbolic
meaning, to divine a prophetic message, when the *King of Kings* Jesus statue
at Solid Rock Church in Monroe, Ohio, was struck by lightning and inciner-
ated in the ensuing conflagration.

A young man named Kevin Jones, wearing a T-shirt and a troubled expression as he spoke to the television newspeople, had rushed to the scene
shortly before midnight when he'd caught word that the iconic Jesus statue—
the sixty-two-foot-high likeness of a triumphant Christ with his hands raised
to the heavens as though signaling a touchdown, the sight so familiar to
drivers on the nearby interstate—had been reduced to nothing but its bare
wire substructure.

"It's a sign from God," Jones said, shaking his head grimly, sounding
more like a wizened old prophet than the teenager he was. "We need to learn
something. As Christians, we're not doing something right."[1]

As statue designers and builders, the church certainly needed to learn a
thing or two. It came out in the news reports that the *King of Kings* statue, for
all its might and glory, was made not of stone or metal, as you'd expect of a
statue, but of wood, Styrofoam, fiberglass, and resin—"all highly flamm-
able," as one news report noted.

Ironic that a church with a name that conveys solidity and durability—
faith like a "solid rock"—advertised itself with a Jesus statue that proved to
be so combustible at its core. The *King of Kings* was not, to put it mildly,
quite as formidable, quite as destruction-proof, as names and appearances
might suggest.

1

To those reading the demographic trend lines and tea leaves and monitoring the shifts in the cultural tides, it seems the young church member was on to something when he mused about Christians "not doing something right," on to something far weightier than schemes for making any replacement Jesus statue a little more fire-resistant and lightning-proof. The story of "Styrofoam Jesus," as one blogger dubbed the statue—its imposing size and triumphant pose, its gargantuan presence along a heavily traveled interstate, its surprisingly high levels of susceptibility to destruction, the freaky fact that this image of Jesus was *struck down by lightning* as if a target of God's wrath—can teach you a lot about what's been happening with religion in this country. It can teach you a lot about what's happening, and what's to come, in the unfolding story of Christianity in America.

In my neighborhood, you won't see any eye-grabbing Jesus statues. You won't spot a steeple or hear church bells chiming on Sunday morning. There's nary a church building to be found among the loft condos, art galleries, boutique shops, microbrew pubs, chic eateries, and ubiquitous coffeehouses that make up Portland's Pearl District. One of the few "churchy" things you'll see is the sandwich-board sign that appears outside the ultra-green Ecotrust Building to advertise the services that Pearl Church holds in rented space inside.

Remember when radio evangelist Harold Camping was drawing massive media coverage a few years ago in the run-up to the apocalypse that he was prophesying? A good joke circulated in my Facebook circle about post-Rapture looting parties, where the unsaved could snatch up the earthly goods left behind by all those lucky Christians swept up to heaven. In the Pearl, I realized, the post-Rapture pickings would be slim.

In the condominium building where my wife and I live, the elevator carried notice for a while one recent April that the property-management company would be closed that coming Friday. To calendar-savvy elevator riders taking a quick but cursory glance, the message might have triggered surprise: "Oh, they're closing for Good Friday?" But as the reader would discover just a few words later, the management company was closing for a different reason that Friday. No, it was not about remembering the Savior's execution on the cross and anticipating the celebration, two days hence, of his resurrection. The closure, the sign noted, was in observance of Earth Day. "We apologize," the notice said, "for any inconveniences this may cause."

Ask an old-school Christian or a sociologist with an eye on the religion trend lines, and he or she will tell you that the change afoot in American religion is more than an "inconvenience" to those with a traditionalist's view. Let the notice in the elevator herald the ending-in-progress of the age when Christianity was the default in our culture—the consensus—and when Christian piety infused the air we all breathe. Consider it a sign of the continuing emergence of our new "post-Christian" age.[2]

My neighborhood is an extreme version of the post-Christian paradigm, a place where the future has arrived a little sooner. But close observers of the culture will tell you that we are in the midst of a cultural transformation of massive proportions that will leave few zip codes unaffected. As revealed by the terms used to describe it—postmodern, post-Christian, post-capitalist, post–culture wars, post-this, and post-that—we don't know yet what to call this new age that's dawning. We just know that the old context has burned through most of the gas in its tank and is now running on fumes.

We can see and name the signal characteristics of the new thing, even if we haven't conjured a good title for the sum of the parts. Ambiguity, diffuse and decentralized authority, access to riches of information and perspectives beyond previous generations' dreams (and nightmares), rejection of grand know-it-all narratives and ideologies, an insistence on heeding the practical and particular that is on the street and under our noses—these are some of the characteristics of this new paradigm, and they have startling implications for politics, for philosophy, for the arts, for economics. And, of course, for religion.

Speaking at the annual Q gathering (the signature conference of next-generation evangelicals), an influential Texas pastor and nonprofit leader had this powerful observation about the cultural shift and its effect on evangelical Christianity: Postmodernity, he said, has knocked the "wind out of the church—has put the church on its knees."[3]

On its knees. Not a bad position for a Christian church movement when you think about it—a position suggestive of prayer. It's a position conducive to humility, too, as is another situation in which American evangelicals increasingly find themselves and their faith movement in the new millennium: sharing space, influence, power, and prerogatives with people of other religions, and of no religion.

Among media people (present company included), it's tempting and all too easy to get carried away with nascent trends and fads, to dramatize their enormity and profundity, only to see them blow away with the next wind. But if we are to believe the best-informed agents and observers of this cultural moment, this change on the religious and cultural landscape is a fad like

Everest is a hill. In her influential 2008 book *The Great Emergence*, longtime religion editor and expert Phyllis Tickle argues that the paradigm shift under way in North American Christianity is no less an upheaval than the Great Reformation that hit Europe five hundred years ago. Tickle calls it Western Christianity's twice-a-millennium "rummage sale," where it unloads those ideas and approaches that have outlived their usefulness and relevance and makes room for a new way of being Christian in the world.[4]

Visit one of the evangelical worship services happening under this postmodern influence, in venues from living rooms and pubs to rented school auditoriums and grimy city streets, and you'll begin to see what it looks like in action: wildly variant formats that feature art, propulsive rock music, smart use of technology, and ancient spiritual rites. You will see believers eschewing locked-down doctrinal declarations and political battles to tend to the specific and the local—epitomized, often, by serving the disadvantaged and down-and-out in one's own city or neighborhood. You'll find Jesus lovers refusing to march in the lockstep formation of the culture wars and, while lessening their devotion to Jesus by not a single jot or tittle, forming partnerships and friendships with unsavory types like liberals, atheists, and gays—people whom their evangelical elders, like the Pharisees of Jesus' time, would only shun. You will witness members of a religious camp criticized for outsize certitude and superior attitudes humbling themselves to kneel in front of homeless people, to wash their feet.[5]

As I have found in my travels and conversations, the new current is sweeping up even some no-nonsense evangelicals who would seem otherwise disinclined to throw around pretentious-sounding terms like "postmodern." How else to explain a rugged-personality type like the evangelism director of Athletes in Action, a man whose early career and ministry planted him squarely in the middle of the old school of aggressive evangelism and Jesus-or-hell theology, inviting this left-leaning, secular-talking religion columnist from the People's Republic of Portland to join him on a megachurch stage for an evangelism training seminar? How else to explain his interviewing me, in a sympathetic manner in front of a hall full of ardent missionaries-in-training, about perceptions of evangelicals and ways they might get along better with those outside their subculture?

Spend time with people like this Athletes in Action evangelist-in-chief, Doug Pollock, and you quickly start to see that the inventions of the new evangelicals are born of necessity. You will hear that the old ways are simply not working. You will hear them admit that their engagement with the rest of

America has been fatally one-way, as in "We talk, you listen." (Or, as frequently happens, "We talk, you tune out.") You will learn that despite all the evident advances of Christian conservatives in the public square over the past thirty years, religious diversity is growing, the culture is no closer to the God-sanctioned ideal, and younger Americans, even those with hearts pure for Jesus, are voting "no" with their feet and rejecting their elders' megachurch and politicized models of evangelical Christianity. More and more, we hear that the traditionalists' Christian heyday is over, that Christians can no longer take it for granted that their faith and culture will enjoy a dominant place in the United States.

In the spring of 2009, the cover of *Newsweek* magazine broached an astonishing proposition: "The End of Christian America." You might see counterexamples all around you. Yet it seems undeniable that a post-Christian era is upon us. You can find confirmation of it even from those working most strenuously to resist the tide. Albert Mohler, president of the Southern Baptist Theological Seminary and a leading voice of traditional conservative Christianity, laments, "The most basic contours of American culture have been radically altered. The so-called Judeo-Christian consensus . . . has given way to a postmodern, post-Christian, post-Western cultural crisis which threatens the very heart of our culture."[6]

The changing tune of next-generation evangelicals—their complicity in the upheaval and the peace they are making with it—have not gone unnoticed by the old guard. Many of the traditionalists, suffice it to say, have not been pleased. What, they ask, do stewardship of the environment and the elimination of nuclear weapons have to do with winning souls for Jesus? Where is the younger believers' resistance against the normalization of homosexuality? Where are their condemnations of women who have abortions? "Who in the next generation will be willing to take the heat," Focus on the Family founder James Dobson wondered out loud, "when it's so much safer and more comfortable to avoid controversial subjects?"[7] Before his death, Moral Majority founder Jerry Falwell expressed his own displeasure with the new form of evangelical expression. "The so-called emerging church movement," he wrote, "was formed out of frustration with dead and irrelevant evangelicalism. The problem is that it has decided to modernize and re-create the church so as not to offend sinners. This renders virtually meaningless the life-changing message of the gospel."[8]

More likely, history will show the opposite—that the new-millennium evangelical generation, those advertising their different ethos with their tattoos and soul patches, their denim and sneakers, their quieter voices and more attentive ears, were the Christian believers who devised and implemented the correctives needed to keep the two-millennium Jesus Movement *alive* for another go-round. More likely, they are breathing new vitality into what Falwell calls the "life-changing message of the gospel." And challenging a lot of non-evangelicals' set ideas in the process.

My engagement with evangelical America—as a half-in, half-out participant for part of my college years, and as an *all-in* observer, interpreter, interlocutor, chronicler, and constructive critic in my writing life—has been long and winding.

While writing my columns for *USA Today*'s "On Religion" commentary series, I have gotten to know evangelical America like few other secular- and progressive-leaning writers. I have not held back from criticizing evangelicals for misdeeds that demanded a response. In particular, I have challenged overt political manipulations of faith for unholy political objectives—abuses that were reaching their crescendo as I began my career as a religion-in-public-life commentator in the days of the Iraq invasion and the 2004 presidential election. In view of what's happened with the Christian Right in the years since—its discrediting in the eyes of large swaths of the public, the rejection of its tactics and tone by a younger generation of Jesus followers, the deaths and retirements of some of its most iconic standard-bearers—it seems astonishing to remember that, not long ago, evangelical Christianity seemed to have taken over the country, from the White House to the statehouse to the school board in community after community. Christian rhetoric was being marshaled by an evangelical president to justify an aggressive war against a Muslim country, and triumphant Republicans were drenching their national convention with talk of George W. Bush as the man chosen by God to continue leading a good-versus-evil crusade against Islamic terrorists and American liberals (with the half-serious assertion that "GOP" had come to mean "God's Official Party").

In many respects, things have changed for the better between then and now. It is much too soon to pronounce the Christian Right dead. But its approval ratings in opinion sampling are astonishingly low. Think of the status of its icons and ideology today relative to 2004. Jerry Falwell, founder of the Moral Majority—deceased. James Kennedy, famed televangelist and chief proclaimer of the incessant "Take Back America for Christ" rhetoric—

deceased. James Dobson, onetime head of Focus on the Family and unofficial Republican presidential kingmaker—gone, replaced by a man of a younger generation and a tone and temperament a world apart. George W. Bush, the war president who rode high on Bible rhetoric and military glory before his house of cards collapsed in his second term—gone from the public stage. And the conflation of Christian piety and right-wing politics—not gone, but muted, more discredited now, closer to the political margins and backwaters than it's been for decades.

Not to cheer anyone's death or demise. But much of the change that I'd hoped to see has been happening. How heartening to discover that I was not the only one disturbed by the aggressive misuse of religion in the public square and determined to call a foul. How encouraging to learn that many Christians—many *evangelical* Christians—were as offended as I, and even more determined to expose the wrongs and correct course.

Job done, it might seem. Time to don the jumpsuit, land the fighter plane on the metaphorical flight deck, and unfurl the "Mission Accomplished" banner.

Not quite.

The story of religion in American public life has been changing, but it still captivates, still compels me to watch, listen, and write. It's no longer righteous indignation that drives me, but fascination, even inspiration at times. For this chronicler, the story about evangelicals in America has been shifting from all that is stale and galling to much that is new and uplifting.

Evangelicals rescuing girls from sexual slavery in Asia. Evangelicals rejecting American consumerism and embracing "downward mobility" in solidarity with the poor. Evangelicals invoking crucial themes of the Bible and insisting on political reforms that will extend hospitality toward the strangers in our midst known as "illegal immigrants." Evangelicals insisting that if the term "pro-life" is to have any credibility, it will have to apply to human beings outside the womb, outside of the churches, and outside of the national boundaries. Evangelicals admitting that they have no monopoly on truth and beauty and conceding that there is much they can learn from people outside their camp. Evangelicals, young evangelicals in particular, practically *pleading* for an end to the Christian Right's liberal-bashing and gay-damning and obsessive pursuit of political power via tactics and rhetoric that sound, all too often, like hate.

Young Americans reaching a stop-you-in-your-tracks conclusion about the "faith" modeled by their country's highest-profile Christian leaders: "un-Christian."

In headlining a column of mine that told a small part of this story, my editor at *USA Today* crafted an incisive phrase for these expectation-defying Jesus followers. They were, as the headline put it, "The Evangelicals You Don't Know."[9]

When he conjured that headline, my editor was obviously playing off the usual stereotypes and simplistic media story lines, the negative perceptions of evangelicals that prevail among secularists[10] and the religiously liberal. In those circles—the circles in which I reside for the most part—these indeed are the images that rush to mind when one hears that word "evangelical." As *New York Times* columnist Nicholas Kristof notes, "In these polarized times, few words conjure as much distaste in liberal circles as 'evangelical Christian.'"[11] But what does that term "evangelical" actually mean?

As Kristof implies, "arrogant right-wing nut job" would be the answer many a secular progressive might blurt out. This is the impression they have formed from the evangelicals they have gotten to "know" from politics and media portrayals or, perhaps, from strained conversations with people in their lives who have embraced the evangelical creed and worldview. But there is much more to know about that term "evangelical" and the people to whom it applies.

What makes a Christian an "evangelical" in modern America understanding is possession of all (or most) of the following: faith in the authority, even the divine perfection, of the Bible as the ultimate source of truth and wisdom, straight from God; a "personal relationship" with Jesus Christ, as it's popularly termed, meaning a sense of devoting oneself to, depending on, and continually receiving from the figure at the heart of Christianity; a belief that Jesus "died for our sins"—provided that people accept that gift by believing in him as the divine son of God; a seriousness about the reality of heaven and hell, and the need to accept Jesus if one is to reach the former and avoid the latter; a belief in the universality of Christianity as the reigning truth for all humanity, trumping all other religions and philosophies; and, as naturally flows from that universality, a commitment to doing what the root of that word "evangelical" implies: evangelizing, making Jesus known to all (or as many as possible) so that they, too, may share in that gift of eternal life.

Unfortunately, that term "evangelical" has come to be associated with the following labels and descriptors, too: anti-choice, anti-gay, anti–women's rights, anti-science, anti-liberal, pushy and arrogant, judgmental, quick to shout, and disinclined to listen. You can attribute a great deal of this to politics, to the fact that conservative, Republican political action and rhetoric have become perhaps the most conspicuous public manifestations of the evangelical faith.

"'Evangelical voters' have now been sized and squeezed into a homogeneous political bloc," writes Wes Granberg-Michaelson, former general secretary of the Reformed Church in America. "These folks have views on the political right wing, trust in robust American military might, believe that wealth is a blessing to be protected by tax policy, want society to be inhospitable toward gays, oppose any form of abortion, feel that 'big' government is always malevolent, and assert that American individualism is the divinely sanctioned cornerstone of the Republic. Apply the label 'evangelical' to a voter and you can expect these political responses.

"The problem is that it's simply inaccurate," Granberg-Michaelson rightly declares. "One size doesn't fit all when in come to evangelicals. . . . You can always interview someone who will validate the stereotype. But there are other millions who don't. Yet no one seems to notice (or care)."[12]

Count me as one who notices. Count me as one who cares and who is keenly interested in the millions of evangelicals who defy the stereotype. Count me as one who has experienced a reality articulated by Florida evangelical pastor Joel Hunter (based, intriguingly, on his dialogue with the Muslim militant group Hezbollah). "The enemy," Hunter says, "is never as scary or threatening up close."[13] Or even your enemy, as I have found.

Many of the people and projects described in this book fit, roughly, a category you might call the "new evangelicals." That is a term you'll see often on the pages that follow, mixed in with variations like "new-century evangelicals" and "new-paradigm evangelicals." Who are they?

Part of the answer is that the characters in this book are generally Caucasian. Not to deny black churches the attention and credit (and criticism) they warrant, and not to imply that African American, Latino, and other nonwhite evangelicals are not participating in the course corrections necessitated by the changing times. But the transformations and correctives described in this book are generally seen in the ranks of white evangelicalism, a tradition that has largely been distinct (and, sadly, separate) from the black Protestant experience in America and that finds itself today with distinct challenges and imperatives for change.

In addition to being white, the new evangelicals chronicled in this book are generally, but not exclusively, young adults and adults in early middle age. Sharp-eyed readers will notice, too, that a disproportionate number of the central figures of this book are male. This parallels an unfortunate reality about this new evangelicalism (and the old one, too)—namely, that the movement is largely led by men. By showcasing several women in the coming chapters, I hope to encourage more to step forward, and more men to accept their leadership.

As might be expected of a movement and a moniker so new on the scene, there is no set definition of "new evangelical"—of who is qualified, and who is not, to wear the label. Nor is there an agreed-upon set of qualifications.

Religion scholar Marcia Pally, in her 2011 book *The New Evangelicals: Expanding the Vision of the Common Good*, concentrates on figures like the aforementioned Hunter; Richard Cizik, the former vice president for governmental affairs for the National Association of Evangelicals, who resigned in 2008 under heavy criticism for voicing support for same-sex unions and who would go on to co-found the New Evangelical Partnership for the Common Good; and Jim Wallis, longtime leader of the progressive evangelical group Sojourners.

Michael Cromartie, vice president of the conservative Ethics and Public Policy Center and director of the center's Evangelicals in Civic Life program, believes the "new evangelicals" more deserving of attention—the *real* new evangelicals, if you will—are Southern California pastor and mega-selling author Rick Warren and Focus on the Family President Jim Daly (as well as prison ministry leader and traditional-values champion Charles Colson, who died in 2012). These are figures with more visibility and clout than Pally's subjects, Cromartie argues, and who retain real conservative bona fides even as they nudge the public expression of the faith in new, nonpartisan directions.

This book uses a "big-tent" definition—a tent large enough to fit both Pally's and Cromartie's "new evangelicals" while also providing plenty of room for others: people like *unChristian* coauthor and Q conference convener Gabe Lyons, Portland-based "Seasons of Service" innovator Kevin Palau, and Seattle-based author and impresario Jim Henderson, an ex-pastor and ex-evangelist who exemplifies a network of believers who have jettisoned the cultural trappings of conventional evangelicalism but who can't quit Jesus, who can't shed the impulse to follow Jesus and "take him public," as Henderson likes to put it.

What makes the new evangelicals *new*? You will find the answer in the following chapters. Suffice it to say for now that they are Christians who are rooted in the orthodox beliefs of evangelical Christianity and who are fiercely devoted to Jesus—yet are largely free, or becoming free, of the cultural and political baggage that has made evangelicalism appear, often, to be just another voting bloc or culture war army.

From what religious perspective do I write this book? I am not an evangelical Christian (although more than once I have been mistaken for one on account of my being willing to say and write positive things about this group of Americans). Fitting for one with my first name, I am something of a doubting Thomas in my own religious/spiritual life. But while I am not a conventional believer, I do have a religious and spiritual dimension to my life. I have been to many a church, and even a few synagogues, mosques, and temples, along the way. I have an intense fascination with religion and its encounter with the eternal cosmic questions, and I maintain a friendly respect for committed believers—so long as their devout faith does not devolve into superiority or a club for bashing those who believe differently. As for Christianity, whether Jesus is literally the son of God or not—whether it's a fact that he died for humanity's sins or not—I cannot shake the idea that if his example were truly followed, and his teachings widely implemented, this world would be a vastly different and better place.

And, finally, to whose attention do I wish to bring these "new evangelicals"? I make this introduction to those who don't yet know these new-paradigm Christians but who would likely benefit from an updated notion of who they are and what they are up to, and who are open to some good news about this large and influential sector of America. Secular progressives, the spiritual-but-not-religious, liberal religionists, anyone with a concern for the common good and an open-mindedness about allies for the cause—these are the readers for whom this book is intended. Those with a hard grudge against religious people and evangelical Christians in particular—these are the people whose view I would like to respectfully challenge, whose view of religion in America I aim to complicate.

So, too, I hope, will the subjects of this book, the members of the movements and networks I describe, find value on the following pages. I have found that it can be fascinating and highly useful to see how one's own community looks from the outside, to the eyes of a curious and open-minded observer. When you're making an earnest effort to accomplish something good, it's encouraging to learn that someone is noticing and appreciating what he sees.

In the view of pollster and author David Kinnaman of the Barna Group, the rising generation of evangelical Christians has reached a fork in the road and is in the process of making a no-turning-back decision about which route to take. "The next generation," Kinnaman writes, "is caught between two possible destinies—one moored by the power and depth of the Jesus-centered gospel, and one anchored to a cheap, Americanized version of the historic faith that will snap at the slightest puff of wind."[14]

Or, we might add, that will instantly burst into all-consuming flames when lightning strikes, metaphorically and otherwise, as happened to the massive Jesus statue at Solid Rock Church in Ohio, and as is happening all across this land as evangelical Christianity finds itself rocked by its fast-emerging new context.

Yes, about that Styrofoam Jesus. . . . Let it serve as a sign of the times that the leadership at Solid Rock Church learned a lesson from the statue's quick incineration in 2010. No, they did not dispense with the notion of having a large Jesus statue, as some critics suggested they should. In short order, they announced plans to build a new Jesus statue—but out of sturdier, more durable stuff this time. In September 2011, just a few days after nationwide observances of the tenth anniversary of the 9/11 attacks that defined the first decade of the century, the steel framework for the new Jesus statue was assembled; by the following autumn, the statue was completed.[15] The replacement Jesus statue is slightly smaller this time—about fifty feet in contrast with the sixty-two feet of the original "Touchdown Jesus"—and made of nonflammable materials. The hands, rather than shooting upward as if to signal a touchdown, extend sideways now, palms forward as if to invite and beckon. An added feature: the lightning-suppression system.[16]

On the pages that follow you will read about evangelical Christians who are likewise concerned about the lightning storms that threaten their faith movement and who, because of some ominous clouds on the horizon, are rethinking, reworking, and rebuilding their movement into something that can last in a new century—crafting a lightning-suppression system of a different sort, you might say. You will read about the Jesus followers who have ventured out from behind the walls of "The Church"—the institutionalized, codified Christian subculture that has emphasized conservative politics, doctrinal correctness, and the separation from secular society—to connect with the rest of us. You will meet such people as Portland's Kevin Palau, the son of a famed evangelist who has responded to the city's progressivism and religious skepticism not by retreating and condemning but by connecting with the local culture, taking cues from it, and bringing forward a service-oriented representation of the gospel.

You will get to know something about the Christians who are striving to re-create the church for the new time and new context, to make sure the Jesus they lean on and proclaim has more at the core than Styrofoam. Like, for example, Philadelphia's Shane Claiborne, a bearded, long-haired evangelical activist who lives among the poor on the city's ravaged north side and who, in his speaking around the country and in his books and articles, pleads with his fellow Christians to live their lives in ways that make them and their faith a blessing to their fellow communities and fellow citizens—not an irritant. There is a silent majority of young evangelicals, Claiborne writes, "who love Jesus with all that they are and are not willing to use our faith as simply a ticket to heaven and ignore the hells of the world around us. There is a new evangelicalism that loves Jesus and wants to change the world."[17]

I can practically hear the words of caution and protest coursing through some readers' thoughts at this point—especially the thoughts of the religiously liberal, who have been on this service and compassion track and promoting many of these allegedly "new" insights for decades. Why should the emerging subculture of evangelicals get all this positive attention—all this ink—for something that many other religious people figured out long ago?

Unfair though it may be, the tide change in evangelicalism *is* big news. Those of us with a journalistic train of thought are always drawn to that which is new and counterintuitive. It's big news, too, because of the sheer size and clout of the community where this story is happening. The new evangelicals form a growing subset of an evangelical movement that comprises somewhere between a quarter and a third of the population (depending on how you count) and that has enjoyed a level of visibility and sway disproportionate to its numbers. Changes occurring on this team change the game itself—change it for everyone. What happens in evangelical America promises significant ramifications for American religion, American culture, and American politics, and whatever our stake might be, we are wise to keep up. For those reasons and others, these new evangelicals and their faith movement are worth getting to know, and reconsidering.

"Make no mistake; we are caught in another faith's crisis." So writes Jason Pitzl-Waters for the Patheos.com website.[18] By "we," the writer means the growing cadre of Americans who are not conventionally religious, who belong to no church and no faith tradition. As the writer correctly suggests, how this change shakes out, and how evangelical America comes to terms (or blows) with those of other persuasions, will go a long way toward determining the tenor of the emerging times. Pitzl-Waters has this astute suggestion for his fellow non-Christians: Treat these religious fellow citizens in a way conducive to a peaceful outcome. Extend a hand, I might add. Clear out a place for them to land. Let them know that this need not be a fight to the end, that they will not be ridiculed and shunned by non-religious progressives solely because of their religious beliefs. Getting to know them is an eminently sensible first step that might make all the subsequent steps that much easier.

The book before you is, I believe, an introduction that is overdue. Given how much we have in common once we take a moment to re-examine our stereotypes, given how much needs to be done and how much good we can accomplish together, the progressive and secular people on my side of the tracks would do well to become acquainted with these new evangelicals. They could be your next best friends for the fight—for the environment, for the poverty-stricken, for the enslaved and abused.

The new evangelicals, Gabe Lyons assures, are not interested in political power plays. They are, rather, "restorers who will work with anyone to see goodness go forward in the world and evil pressed back." These "next Christians," as Lyons calls them in the title of his 2010 book, "are socially conscious, grounded in their gospel commitment, and optimistic that when their faith is practiced according to the ways of Jesus, it is complementary to cultural reforms that value all human beings, all human flourishing, and all spiritual traditions."[19]

This, from an evangelical Christian leader who grew up in Jerry Falwell's church, who got his college education at Falwell's Liberty University?

These newly emerging evangelicals might surprise you in all sorts of ways.

Meet them.

Chapter Two

Jesus' Favorite City

When he first heard the proposition from the representative of the church leaders committee, the liberal mayor couldn't quite process what his ears were hearing.

"Ken, I've told you before," Portland Mayor Sam Adams responded. "We don't *have* any money."

The "Ken" was Ken Weigel, a pastor at Imago Dei, a thriving evangelical church in the city's southeast quarter. Despite what the mayor thought he heard, the minister was not calling to ask city hall to fund something. Nor had he phoned to harangue Adams about his unabashedly liberal politics or well-known sexual orientation. "No, Mayor," Weigel corrected, "we want to *give* money to you, to the city."[1]

Adams was, as he later put it, completely disoriented. The Democratic mayor's faulty listening could be forgiven in view of what evangelicals have come to be known for in many progressive circles: their condemnations of liberals and gays, their allegiance to the Republican Party, their disdain for government and the "godless" public schools. Now the evangelical church leaders wanted to make a gift to the liberal city hall?

They did, and they did—a $100,000 Christmas present, as it were, comprising donations collected at two dozen evangelical churches. Adams and the city commissioners decided to devote the money to a program aimed at reducing the alarmingly high dropout rate in the city's strapped public education system.[2]

Later reflecting on the episode, Adams said he often encounters incredulity similar to his own when he tells people about the gift to the city from the

Portland evangelical community. "When I talk to other liberal mayors around the country," Adams said, "the response I get is, 'Did they really? *Really?*' I say, 'Yes, and we're better for it.'"[3]

Encounters like this, and the larger phenomenon they illuminate, are the reason why there's now one more entry on the long list of nicknames for this city at the confluence of the Columbia and Willamette Rivers. Rose City, Bridgetown, the People's Republic of Portland, Stumptown, Portlandia, PDX—these all have a reason and a story, as does a new one you hear from time to time at the now-common intersections between the evangelical churches, city government progressives, and Portland's disadvantaged people: Jesus' favorite city.

As is clear from their winks and grins, the Portland leaders involved in this stereotype-busting friendship between the evangelical churches and city government are mainly engaging in wry playfulness when they toss out that "Jesus' favorite city" line. Those who have played some of the lead roles in this surprising play—people like then-mayor Sam Adams, City Commissioner Nick Fish, locally based international evangelist Luis Palau and his son Kevin—are not so foolish as to claim that Portland has achieved perfect virtue and enlightenment, or that the son of God whispers sweet compliments in their ears: "You're number one, you're number one."

Portland has its problems, to be sure: race inequities, for instance, poorly performing public schools, and a scarcity of good jobs that can make it difficult to live in a city renowned for its "livability." The "Jesus' favorite city" tag might seem blasphemous to people with a traditional view of what constitutes a godly city. The Rose City sports an ultra-secular reputation and voting tendencies as blue as the Columbia on a clear-sky July day. Regional land and transportation planning is so progressive that conservative pundit George Will once likened the Portland ethos to a disease, worrying in one of his columns about it "metastasizing" to other parts of the country.[4] Church? People steer clear at rates matched in few other cities. A survey released in 2012 by the Association of Statisticians of American Religious Bodies found greater Portland the least religious of all U.S. metropolitan areas of a million people or more, with just 32 percent of residents identifying themselves as religious adherents. By contrast, the figure was 74 percent for Salt Lake City, the area found by the survey to be the country's most religious.[5]

Yet there has to be a kernel of truth in that "Jesus' favorite city" notion, one that might be instructive for others around the country looking for compelling new ways to bring the faith forward in an increasingly post-Christian culture. As evangelical leaders of Weigel's and the Palaus' ilk would say, as the thoroughly convinced liberal ex-mayor would echo, what *wouldn't* Jesus like about people from supposedly opposing camps tossing aside their differences to do right by the city's least fortunate? Why *wouldn't* the Jesus of the New Testament smile upon a community where the church people eschewed power, prerogatives, and self-righteous piety and instead led with their hearts—who served the city and its people? Just because it was a good thing to do?

Rarely will you see a newspaper or magazine cover photo capture a cultural moment in such perfect strokes.[6] Picture it: Standing in the background is one of the most famous American evangelists of the passing era. Luis Palau exudes a grandfatherly air with his white, combed-to-the-side hair, his V-neck sweater and collared shirt. His face is out of focus like a receding memory. In front, very much in focus, is the face of the evangelist's forty-something son. Kevin Palau jumps out of a shadowed foreground so dramatically that all but the right side of his face is off the page, as if the subject has mostly left this worn-out age and entered the indeterminate time to follow. The eye pierces you with earnestness and alarm. It's clear that the son is serious about something—serious about Jesus, as the readers learn inside the covers of Portland's *Willamette Week*—and even though he is generally a smiling, mild-mannered man when you meet him for coffee or lunch, as I have often done, Kevin Palau seems a little disturbed in that cover shot, too. As you learn if you talk with him, what disturbs him underneath his earnest, friendly countenance are the wrongs that have been committed in Jesus' name by many who position themselves as his most devout followers. What disturbs him is the bad name the faith has increasingly borne as a result.

That face in the photo also looks determined. As I've come to learn, Palau and growing numbers of idealistic Christians around this country, young in age or young in outlook, *are* determined. They have their minds set on pulling American evangelicalism out of its late twentieth-century rut and turning it into the jaw-dropping, life-changing, world-altering force they believe it ought to be.

Think of it as Evangelism 2.0. Nowhere will you find a better example of it than in Portland, in the work that Kevin Palau and others have undertaken to expand the mass-evangelism model perfected by the Palau organization in the 1970s, 1980s, and 1990s and to migrate it in a direction so disarmingly counterintuitive that even Portland's cynical alternative weekly *Willamette Week* could devote a lengthy cover story to it with remarkably little criticism or snark.

With Kevin Palau playing the role of organizer, matchmaker, bridge-builder, and promoter, the evangelical churches in the greater Portland region—a community that had previously been more inclined to compete than cooperate, and that had virtually no relationship with city government—have joined forces for a constellation of sustained service projects mobilizing thousands of volunteers, all in coordination with, and with access provided by, liberal city hall. Called the Seasons of Service, the annual campaign consists of free medical and dental clinics; public school beautification and mentoring efforts; shelters for victims of sex trafficking; drives to provide the homeless with food, clothing, shelter, and counseling; and other good works.

Witness one of these projects in action, and you will see that the church people are going well beyond feel-good dabbling or hit-and-run public relations stunts.

For one participating congregation, a permanent, committed relationship has grown out of what was supposed to be a one-and-done day of service at Portland's Roosevelt High School, where family incomes trend as low as the graduation rates. Since then, the congregation at Southlake Church in suburban West Linn has "adopted" the school, or its students, more accurately. One church member with a big name in these parts, former Portland State and pro-football quarterback Neil Lomax, volunteers as assistant coach of the football team. A pair of church staff members—their salaries paid by Southlake—have taken up full-time residence at the school and spend their time operating a "clothes closet" where students can pick up a new used hoodie or pair of jeans (not to mention toothbrushes and soap), helping support extracurricular activities and counseling students, and coordinating a complex network of mentors and volunteers operating at the school. The service-givers have all taken a no-proselytizing pledge.

Equally impressive are the medical and dental clinics, one of which I scouted on a Saturday morning in 2010. Mobilized by a Christian nonprofit called Compassion Connect and working in coordination with the Seasons of Service, church volunteers transformed a Christian school campus in a suburb east of Portland into a large and bustling medical complex for a day. Trained volunteers in matching T-shirts performed intake with hundreds of patients and directed them to different areas of the school, where nurses and doctors of varying specialties were waiting to see them. People in need of dental care boarded buses for short trips to a satellite location where ten dentists were deployed. The gymnasium was set up as a community resource center, with dozens of tables dispensing information and advice on everything from Head Start to sustainability to the Pregnancy Resource Center of Greater Portland. An estimated three hundred or more "guests"—a term preferred over "patients"—would go through the clinic that day, a large percentage of them Latino. They walked off with prescriptions and pharmacy vouchers, with new glasses and dental fillings, with free meals under their belts—even a free haircut if they wanted. Altogether, some forty-seven churches were represented in the volunteer corps manning the clinic that day. [7]

Down one hall, a prayer station operated—one of the few conspicuous reminders that this was, after all, a church undertaking. Tellingly, though, the prayer station was entirely optional, something the patients could easily bypass—which most of them did, from what I observed. A visitor with a cynic's view of evangelical Christians might have done a double-take. Weren't the patients going to be subjected to a get-saved pitch in exchange for the free care?

"We don't feel like we have to preach or hand out gospel tracts," Milan Homola, executive director of Compassion Connect, the man overseeing the operation, explained to me. "We believe we're communicating strongly without words." [8]

"No strings attached." That's the phrase you'll hear Kevin Palau emphasize repeatedly when he describes what the Seasons of Service campaign is conspiring to do. Sure, he hopes the church community's service to the city might change some people's minds about evangelicals. It's not as though they're hiding their faith. "If you give me the opportunity and you want to hear," Kevin Palau says, "I'll happily tell you about how Jesus Christ changed my life. Man, I'd love to tell you about that. But I'm not going to shove anything down anybody's throat."

What prompted and inspired the Portland-area evangelical community to the Seasons of Service, to this no-strings-attached, no-proselytizing form of engagement, will tell you a lot about these fast-changing times.

"Many years later, it still fills me with a kind of dread," Kevin Palau recalls. A slender man whom you'll normally find in jeans and an untucked shirt at the innumerable church and coffeehouse meetings that make up his days, Palau is recounting an epiphany of sorts, the moment when he knew there needed to be a new model for representing the gospel in a shifting American culture. The moment came in 1996 at a largely empty college basketball arena in Chicago where the Palau organization was giving an evangelistic presentation to a couple thousand people, most of them already Christian, as Kevin tells it.

"It was not a crisis of faith in terms of 'I'm not even sure that there's a God anymore.' It was a crisis of, 'Does this approach even meaningfully work anymore in the Western world?'" Kevin Palau recalls. "You'd look out into the audience and say, 'This is 99 percent evangelical. We're preaching literally to the choir.'"[9] Where were the unconverted, the ones for whom the message was really intended?

When you're the son of a famous evangelical figure, it often goes without saying that you will follow your father's footsteps in some fashion. So it's been with many of Christianity's best-known icons: Billy Graham and son Franklin; Oral Roberts and son Richard; Pat Robertson and son Gordon (who succeeded his father as CEO of the Christian Broadcasting Network)[10]; Jim and Tammy Faye Bakker and son Jay (although the heavily tattooed Jay Bakker has taken his ministry in dramatically edgier directions, preaching a gospel of affirmation and acceptance of gay people); and the Palaus, with Kevin and two of his three brothers going to work for their father's ministry, Kevin becoming president in 2010.

Be clear that it takes some pretty big feet to fill the footsteps of Kevin Palau's father. Raised in Argentina before venturing to Oregon as a young adult, a man who maintained a strong presence in South America over his many decades of success in the United States, Luis Palau has often been described as the Billy Graham of Latin America. While it's true that he has preached to many millions in Central and South America, the title fails to do him justice; Luis Palau has been big in North America, too. By some reckonings, he might be second *only* to Graham in the pantheon of high-profile American evangelists of recent decades (not counting the ubiquitous televangelists).

Visit the Luis Palau Association offices in Beaverton, a suburb just west of Portland, and you'll see walls adorned with impressive mementos from a career that has been truly major league. Framed photos capture the effusive evangelist preaching to throngs of seven hundred thousand in Guatemala, nine hundred thousand in Buenos Aires, three hundred thousand on the beach in Fort Lauderdale, Florida. Attending many of these crusades as a boy, watching his charismatic father witnessing to the assembled masses, Kevin Palau felt a kind of awe—and, before long, a realization that he would probably have a meltdown if he had to be the one up there preaching. As he would later reflect, "My gifts aren't preaching in front of big crowds. I'd be scared to death."[11]

Kevin Palau indeed did go into the family business. It wasn't as the evangelist on the stage, however, but as the in-house strategist—and change agent. This differently wired Palau was able to enter and stay in the family business, with conscience clean and dread at bay, only by finding a way to *change* the family business. Not radically or abruptly, and never with Jesus left behind, Kevin Palau has taken the ship his father built and nudged it in a different direction.

And all the while, he has been figuring out the answers to the vexing questions facing the faith movement in which his family and he are so deeply invested: How do you start a conversation about Jesus with a society growing less and less interested in what you have to say and the manner in which you say it? How do you get on the same wavelength with a culture less and less tuned in to the messages and mores that have been evangelical Christendom's stocks in trade? And, especially fascinating for an enterprise that *is* all about conversion, how might the church itself need to change if it is to make Jesus known?

The respected religion scholar Rodney Stark, himself a Christian, has written persuasively of a tendency within Christianity over its two-thousand-year history to lose its way when it strives for, and achieves, temporal successes like wealth and political power. Think of Western Europe, where the church's dominant, government-sanctioned status has correlated with periods of arrogant abuses of power and, jumping to the present, listless participation and empty pews. Think of the Catholic Church today—an institution beset by crisis because of its all-too-human insistence on protecting itself and, ironically, its reputation at the expense of human decency and compassion for the victims of sexual predator priests.

Given the demographics, dominant status is not a "problem" that's going to afflict America's white, conservative Christianity much longer.

First, consider the race dynamics in the United States: The Census Bureau reported in 2012 that, for the first time in history, white babies no longer make up the majority of births in the United States. The births of minority infants—African American, Asian, mixed-race, and, especially, Hispanic—

have broken the 50 percent barrier, meaning minorities are becoming the majority.[12] Welcome to the post-white era.

Second, consider the religious identification dynamics: "Millennials," the generation that has come of age post-2000, are significantly less religiously affiliated than the generations preceding them.[13] More important, they are significantly less religiously attached *than preceding generations were at the same age.* That second point bears emphasis because it refutes the oft-heard retort from older, conservative Christians who scoff at these trend lines and maintain that the declining religious affiliation metrics are a mere flash in the pan, that millennials—in particular, those raised in evangelical families—will turn out to be just like previous generations: less religious in young adulthood but certain to return to the church and its conservative values when they mature and start families. Given the trend lines, there simply is no reason for confidence in a mass return to these churches and their teachings when these millennials age deeper into adulthood and family lives. "I don't expect these younger voters to wake up all of a sudden when they're thirty-eight years old and say, 'I was for gay marriage before, but now I'm against it,'" says Republican political strategist Matthew Dowd.[14]

Whatever is afoot appears to be much more than the follies of youth. Despite the prominence of religious believers in politics and culture and a Republican presidential primary race that featured several faith-touting evangelical and conservative Christians, the Associated Press reported in 2011 that "America has shrinking congregations, growing dissatisfaction with religious leaders, and more people who do not think about faith."[15] The news report cited fresh research from Duke University researcher Mark Chaves, who reported a "softening" of Christian faith in America, and a polarization that has seen nominally religious people migrating toward the no-religious-affiliation category, leaving the still-religious camp to the most intense believers.

As if to put flesh on the bones of statistical data, tales circulate in the news, in blogs, in conversations, of megachurches scrambling to stanch what writer Brett McCracken has likened to a gusher—a gusher of young people leaving the church. "As a twenty-seven-year-old evangelical myself, I understand the concern," McCracken—author of the book *Hipster Christianity*—wrote in the *Wall Street Journal* in 2010. "My peers, many of whom grew up in the church, are losing interest in the Christian establishment."[16]

Do not take this to mean that the rising generation of American adults is not attracted to spirituality, or that America is on its way to becoming the

Land of the Atheists. As has been confirmed numerous times by pollsters, the vast majority of Americans profess high rates of religious belief even if their affiliations with churches and denominations are waning, and they say their faith influences their engagement with issues, with politics, with the public life of their country and community. The number of professed atheists and agnostics remains conspicuously low. Today's under-thirties, according to polling by the Pew Forum on Religion & Public Life, are just as sold as older adults on concepts of life after death (75 percent), heaven and hell (74 percent and 62 percent, respectively), and miracles (78 percent). And young evangelicals are just as likely as their older co-religionists to view the Bible as the word of God (88 percent).[17] Moreover, as Public Religion Research found in a 2011 poll, 56 percent of Americans consider it important for a presidential candidate to be a person of strong faith. This isn't just a Republican phenomenon; 51 percent of Democrats surveyed believed it important for a presidential candidate to have strong religious beliefs.[18]

Again, that pairing of seemingly incompatible trends: large numbers of Americans expressing high regard for faith, God, and spirituality, juxtaposed with unmistakable declines in participation in the institutions through which Americans have traditionally channeled their spiritual yearnings. And mixed in with all of that are increasingly evident shifts in culture and beliefs that portend particular worries and vulnerabilities for the old-guard keepers of the evangelicalism we've come to know these past several decades. It's at this level of the discussion that one begins to sense how the spirit of a dawning postmodern age poses dire challenges for those invested in the "Christian America" status quo.

In the age of the Internet—the age of virtually unlimited access to other perspectives and people and seemingly unlimited challenges to evangelical Christendom's old nodes of authority—three-quarters of church-affiliated young adults concede that there is more than one true way to interpret the teachings of their faith.[19] This reverberates right to the core of an evangelical faith movement that has always emphasized that its truth is the *only* truth. Moreover, fewer than half of young evangelicals take the Bible as the literal word of God, a significant difference from older evangelicals.[20] Seemingly every month, new voices within evangelicalism are challenging iron-clad orthodoxy with their books and public statements, posing seemingly heretical questions about such matters as the nature and existence of hell, the reality of human beings springing from an actual Adam and Eve, and the implausibility of evolution being an atheist scam and of the planet being only six thousand years old, as the "young-earth" creationists insist.

In the meantime, religious diversity and pluralism are clear-and-present realities that, with each passing year, are becoming harder to deny and more useless to ignore. Long gone is the time when Americans' encounter with religious "diversity" was the experience of living on a street where the family to the left was Catholic, the family to the right was Presbyterian, the family across the street was Lutheran, and the family two streets over was Jewish. Now in the mix—even in the supposedly homogeneous suburbs—are followers of faiths outside the Christian (or "Judeo-Christian") box: Islam, Buddhism, Hinduism, Sikhism, and others. Americans are facing a new reality posed by the opening of a mosque or Hindu temple in their community, or by learning that one of the most famous sports celebrities of our time, golfer Tiger Woods, did not turn to Christian faith for solace and self-improvement in his time of scandal and personal crisis but to his Buddhist tradition. There was once a time when Americans were more or less on the same page when it came to faith; now, increasingly, they are not even holding the same book. As Barack Obama accurately states, America, for better or worse, "is no longer just a Christian nation."[21]

It's not that these "world religions," as we view them between these shores, are stealing Christians. The growth of those categories stems from immigration. What's draining Christendom is the category whose popular-vernacular tag reveals both the drift from Christianity and the unpopularity of atheism: "spiritual but not religious."

The American Religious Identification Survey finds a steady decline in Christianity from 1990, when it claimed the allegiance of 86 percent of American adults. By 2000, the figure had declined to 77 percent, and by 2008, the figure had dropped an additional percentage point.[22] "The ex-Christians do not seem to have joined new religious movements or other world religions," state the operators of the ReligiousTolerance.org website. "They mostly left organized religion entirely."[23]

The most robust growth category? Not affiliated, which has more than doubled from the 1990 figure of 8 percent to an attention-grabbing 20 percent today.[24] The growth of this group—the rise and broadening impact of the "nones," as they are often called—profoundly changes long-standing equations in American culture and politics.

Christians are still making up some three-quarters of the population—isn't that quite a lot? Certainly, but those with the most complex understanding of the landscape point out that, for many Americans, "Christian" is more a vague identifier of their family's tradition than a commitment to orthodox Christian beliefs and life paths. Evangelicals, the Christian subgroup of which many secularists are most aware (and most leery), make up a quarter or more of the American population, the exact percentage varying from poll to poll.

"There was a time when Christianity was at the center of society," writes Gabe Lyons, a leading spokesperson for the emerging generation of Christians. "Most people grew up attending church. Christians held influence in the public square and were viewed as credible in culture. America was still thought of as a 'Christian nation.' Not so anymore."[25]

Being known as a Christian conferred advantage to one—indeed was often *expected* of one if he or she was to be accepted in social, professional, and civic circles. In many spheres today, revealing oneself as a Christian can have just the opposite effect. Now, it is far from a given that the new person in your neighborhood or office considers herself a Christian. "Not belonging, not showing up for worship, is an option that doesn't attract the neighbors' opprobrium these days," religion scholar Mark Silk writes, "and many Americans are availing themselves of it."[26] Jon Meacham is right in declaring that we are witnessing the end of "an America shaped and suffused by Christianity."[27]

In the several years following Meacham's trenchant observation, the evidence of its accuracy has abounded. Aware of the shifting terrain and with an eye on the long-term future, some of the most venerable evangelical organizations in the country have undertaken corrective measures that would have seemed unthinkable just a few years before. The board of Focus on the Family, for instance, parted ways with founder and leader James Dobson, who just a few years before had been dubbed a "kingmaker" in Republican presidential politics but whose hostile rhetoric about gays and liberals had become increasingly problematic. In his place was installed a new leader, Jim Daly, whose calling cards are his friendly smile and his deemphasizing of divisive politics. The famed Campus Crusade for Christ, meanwhile, shed not its leader but its iconic name—a name that had become increasingly inaccurate and alienating (inaccurate, because the organization had grown well beyond the college campuses that were its original playing field; alienating, because nothing reminds people of the darker side of Christendom's history than the word *crusade*). Although something of a head-scratcher, the new name—simply "Cru"—at least avoided those troublesome connotations.

Kevin Palau has been in the midst of his own process of refiguring, reimagining. As he and I have discussed in many a conversation, no longer can a gospel promoter outside of the Bible Belt count on his unconverted listeners having at least some baseline familiarity with the Bible and respect for its authority. No longer can an evangelist rely on the promise of heaven and threat of hell holding some sway over people. What does it take to pique people's curiosity, spark their thinking about the possibility of the Christian life offering something special—something *more*? What does it take to show them, at the very least, that Christianity is more than the unattractive reputation it bears in many circles, more than angry opposition to abortion and gays?

As a first step in the evolution of the Palau evangelism model, Kevin Palau and his younger brother, Andrew, persuaded their father to add action sports and Christian rock music to the mix and turn "crusades" into "festivals." Consider the sports and music to be honey for the younger people who might otherwise want nothing to do with an evangelism event. But even though they expanded the audience and diversified the demographic, the exhibitions by big-name skateboarders and concerts by popular Christian rockers would prove more of a toddler step than a giant leap forward.

More significant, the Palaus were gradually working community-service elements into the festivals. Few could have predicted at first that good works would become central to the Palau approach. Bear in mind that evangelical Protestants have long been suspicious of overreliance on deeds, either as an expression of the faith or as a pathway to salvation. The point has always been proclamation, conversion, receiving Jesus into one's heart—coupled with a trust that inside-out transformations would follow, for communities as for individuals. How far could an evangelism organization go with service before it became something other than what it was created to be—a channel for the promotion and proclamation of the gospel?

Kevin Palau wasn't satisfied with the one-off service projects attached to the festivals at first—more sideshows than featured events. As he looked out across the landscape—Portland being Portland, he did not have to look far— and listened to the unflattering portrayals of evangelicals among the unconvinced and unconverted, the evangelist's son was dreaming and scheming not just about tactical adjustments but also about a strategic tour de force. What if service played an ever bigger role, the "good news" being shared by deed as well as word?[28]

The Palau son made his first moves inside the evangelical church community, with both the edgier "emerging" churches sprouting around the city and the more traditional churches in the suburbs. Let's come together, he urged, and show Portland we're here and we care. Let's have the city see what Christians are for, not what we're against. Let's serve the community, he urged, on a coordinated, *sustained* basis.

In addition to the churches' disunity and their dim reputation outside of evangelical circles, Kevin Palau had something else bothering him: the barrier between the evangelical community and city government. No surprise, this. Since the late 1970s, many of the biggest names in evangelical Christianity and, seemingly, the majority of their fans and followers, were marching shoulder to shoulder with the Republican Party and its increasingly severe anti-government ideology, exhibiting little but disdain for institutions of government, and for the liberals who so often populate the city halls and city school systems of mid- and large-sized cities. Christians in relationship with these godless liberals? Heresy!

Not to Kevin Palau. "We realized," Palau would later reflect, "that we hadn't built much of a relationship at all with our city leaders. [Evangelicals] had been on the sidelines, coming from that 'critiquing culture' standpoint. But we were not getting engaged."[29]

What to work on, and how? To find the answer, Kevin Palau and the rapidly unifying evangelical church leaders did something stunningly simple and shockingly rare in a time when evangelicals have been known for always having their own answers and solutions to well-nigh everything. They asked then-mayor Tom Potter what the city most needed. What could the church community do to help?

City hall could scarcely believe its ears. In a panel discussion held at the Q conference several years after that first Season of Service, Kevin Palau quizzed Sam Adams on his reaction to the evangelicals' initial olive branch and service offer.

"Anxiety," Adams responded, tensing up his body for comedic effect and drawing a big laugh from the audience. Adams, who was a city council member at the time of the first entreaties and who would become mayor not long after, elaborated on the risk and the dilemma posed by the offer, pointing out that as a public servant he had to carefully guard against an inappropriate fusing of church and state. "In a city that's so liberal," he said, "people are very on guard. I've taken criticism. 'Are you sure they're not going to proselytize?'"[30]

Despite the city's nervousness about this new suitor, Adams was swayed by a factor even stronger than his anxiety about proselytizing: desperation for whatever help the city could get.

"Like a lot of cities, we're suffering through the recession," the mayor said. "We don't have enough resources. . . . It was a question of whether a city as liberal as Portland could pull this off in a way that both partners felt good about. It had never been done before. The anxiety was around the potential for this to turn into missionary work as opposed to community work."[31]

Another participant in that Q panel, Ken Weigel from Imago Dei, noted that the church leaders had their own questions. "When it came to cleaning up a park or a school, we really didn't think there'd be much opposition," Weigel recalled, his shaved head, goatee, and untucked black shirt posing a striking contrast to the suit and tie–clad mayor. But, he wondered, would the city trust the church people and let them participate in the decision-making and strategy plotting, or would they treat them with suspicion and condescension?[32]

Adams had this worry, too: having seen again and again how even the best-intentioned volunteers often slack off and fail to follow through, he was not convinced the church people could make good on their promise. "I didn't know if they could deliver," he said.[33]

The plot element that Adams did not mention in this panel conversation, but that hung over the early stages of the Seasons of Service courtship in intriguing ways, was the new mayor's well-known sexual orientation and—more dramatic still—the fact that Adams, the first openly gay man ever elected mayor of a major American city, had begun his term under the cloud of a well-publicized sex scandal involving allegations of an inappropriate relationship with a much younger man. Was this really someone the evangelical Christians could do business with?

The following weeks, and months, and years revealed the answer. The church community did not make an issue of Adams's sex life. They warmly applauded him at the Seasons of Service kickoff events that I witnessed. Luis Palau stood shoulder to shoulder with the mayor on various church stages and altars, the two of them celebrating their partnership and declaring their shared commitment to making things better in "Jesus' favorite city."

To be sure, some diplomatic maneuvers were necessary to prevent any key differences of opinion and persuasion from derailing the enterprise. Planned Parenthood had often been in the lineup of agencies offering services and resources at recurring "Homeless Connect" events held by the city to assist the homeless. In planning for a special running of the event in conjunction with the first Season of Service—with the churches now involved—organizers realized that would be problematic. Because of Planned Parenthood's association with abortion, its presence would be difficult for the more conservative members of the church community to abide. As *Christianity Today* reported in an in-depth feature on the Seasons of Service, the parties quietly worked out a deal that enabled them to concentrate on what they shared—their commitment to helping the homeless. The church forces agreed to leave out any anti-abortion materials or advocacy and the city agreed to leave out Planned Parenthood. [34]

Adams had wondered when first approached by the evangelical community: Would the church people keep their promise not to proselytize? For that matter, would they even show up in the numbers, and over the sustained period of time, that they had promised? The answers came: yes, and yes.

No easy feat for a religious movement that is all about public proclamation, a movement of believers known for talking about Christ as naturally as breathing, the first four Seasons of Service came with no reports or complaints of inappropriate evangelizing. And the Portland-area evangelicals indeed put their money—their hands and feet, more accurately—where their mouths were. In the first year, the Palau organization reported a turnout by 550 churches (plus sixty-eight nonprofit organizations and business) and twenty-seven thousand volunteers, an army that took on roughly three hundred community-service projects. [35] In the end, more than one hundred thousand people thronged to a Palau festival on Portland's riverfront to celebrate their faith and the success of the first Season of Service.

Kevin Palau has seen another of his fondest wishes coming true. Over its first four years, the Seasons of Service attracted extensive and positive media coverage, including in-depth features in *Christianity Today*, evangelical America's periodical of record, and *Willamette Week*, Portland's edgy alternative weekly—two media outlets that could scarcely be more different. There was glowing coverage, too, in *USA Today* and *Reader's Digest*, the latter naming the Seasons of Service as 2008's best group service project in the country. [36]

Beyond the media, other cities were watching, too. It's easy to imagine what conflict-weary, change-minded evangelicals might have said to themselves and one another as they heard about the bridge-building going on in that great unchurched mecca in the Pacific Northwest: *If Portland can do it, why can't we?* Over the next four years, Kevin Palau and his team, working with local church leaders in their respective areas, initiated similar service campaigns in several other cities—Phoenix, San Diego, Little Rock, and Sacramento, among them—spreading compassionate service and church-city partnerships like a blessed contagion.

Palau takes pains to emphasize the "both-and" nature of the enterprise, stressing that the no-strings-attached service comes in addition to, not instead of, the evangelism festivals for which the Palau organization has long been known. It's telling, too, that Kevin's younger brother, Andrew, has taken up the preacher/evangelist mantle of his father, making the family something of a microcosm of the dynamic around a changing evangelicalism in American culture. In a real sense, the Palau family has come to model, and bridge, the traditional and the new.

The Palau Association—and he himself, he emphasizes—"are still very much about wanting to share the message of Christ," Kevin Palau stresses to me. "We're not embarrassed about evangelism. Our festivals still feature Dad, and now Andrew, preaching to a crowd from a stage. We don't try to hide our desire to see people's lives changed by Christ. We are wildly enthusiastic about loving and serving the city with no strings attached, and we are wildly enthusiastic about telling people about Jesus."

"It's not about us 'fitting in' or following cultural trends," Palau concludes, "but trying to better follow Christ."[37]

When I hear some of my secular friends, colleagues, and fellow Portlanders react to the Seasons of Service, when I see reader comments beneath the articles that I and others have written about it, I am reminded that not everyone is on board. Some ask: *Isn't this just a ploy—a sneaky way for the church crazies to get some positive press? Is it really appropriate that we're allowing them to force their noxious ideas on the kids in the school and the poor people they're interacting with?* "I don't want these people in the school or anywhere else," one reader said in response to an *Oregonian* column I wrote on the work Southlake Church is doing at Roosevelt High School. "Haven't they done enough damage with their warmongering, money-stealing, and self-righteous behavior? Apparently not. Why should they be trusted?"[38]

Along with the deep distrust, one hears a politically grounded critique. This service to the unfortunate might look nice, the argument goes, but isn't it complicit in the ongoing shredding of a public safety net for the poor—a shredding that these same Christians have helped carry out through their support of Republican politicians and policies? I recall one liberal minister friend of mine waxing most negative about Night Strike, a Christian serve-the-homeless campaign that, while not officially part of the Season of Service, is perfectly in sync with the spirit. Why should we applaud these evangelicals for caring for the homeless, my minister friend asked, when they contributed to that very homelessness by voting for George W. Bush? As other politics-minded skeptics have also argued, the Christian service modeled by the Seasons of Service gives cover to the conservative project to shrink government and leave care of the disadvantaged to churches and charity, which are not equal to the task. Wouldn't all this evangelical energy be better used for creating more just *systems*, a more just society and world, rather than putting Band-Aids on gaping social wounds?

As a non-evangelical who leans progressive in my politics, I can readily understand the distrust, the skeptical responses. They are (partially) valid. Who could blame people for nursing resentments and harboring doubts about evangelicals, given the culture wars we've endured, given the media fixation on aspects and representatives of evangelicalism that often make reasonable people's skin crawl? With its field of vision limited, the secular progressive crowd has gotten to know only a certain type of evangelicalism and only one aspect of its public expression. Think Sarah Palin. Think Rick Perry. Think James Dobson.

The evangelicals I've gotten to know in Portland would not recognize themselves in these portraits. While reporting on the Night Strike group, observing the volunteers' preparations, pep talks, and prayers before they hit the streets to meet the homeless and bring them supplies, I heard them cracking joke after joke about their supposed Republic politics—as if the notion were the most laughable thing they had heard all day. I have been struck by the number of evangelicals who criticize the church's entanglement with the Republican Party as a colossal mistake and who believe the church needs to disentangle itself from that party, from *any* political party, and keep partisan politics at arm's length. Their response to the idea that they are part of a right-wing conspiracy to install the church where the government safety net ought to be? A stretch—an exercise in overthinking something that, to them, is simple and natural: they see a need, they jump in to meet it. As Night Strike leader Marshall Snider often puts it, "We're just here to love on people."[39]

If that's naïve, it's a naïveté to which Snider will likely plead guilty. As will Kevin Palau. As will Shane Claiborne, the evangelical activist who has fostered a community of Christians embedded with their mostly poor neighbors in ravaged North Philadelphia, creating their own "Jesus' favorite city" of sorts. Better naïve than resigned, they will tell you. Better hopelessly idealistic than cynical.

To those disinclined to give any benefit of the doubt, I would pose this question: Isn't it a positive development to see our evangelical fellow citizens engaging society's least fortunate, getting to know them and their stories, rather than hunkering behind the walls of ideology and church subculture? I am convinced that these experiences cannot help but affect one's understanding of the broader phenomena of homelessness, abuse, poverty, inequity, even fostering political evolutions among the people having these encounters.

In addition to the surprising partnerships and stereotype-breaking strategies and tactics evident in the Seasons of Service, there is this intriguing question: Why would Portland, this secular mecca in the faraway Northwest, emerge as the place where evangelical Christianity is flying its brightest colors? Why would the People's Republic of Portland become the site of such evangelical innovation and an object of such fascination among the country's new evangelicals—a place that the larger church would want to emulate?

It was no coincidence that Gabe Lyons, leader and organizer of the annual Q conference of next-generation evangelicals, decided to hold the event in Portland in 2011, in an indie-rock concert venue at the edge of the more-secular-than-thou Pearl District that I call home. As Lyons explained at the time, Christians can learn from what's happening here.

Although Portland is hardly the only place where evangelical Christianity is evolving and making new friends in the process, there is little doubt that the Portland story represents the front end of a deep-change trend that is taking Christianity into its new future, or at least one of its possible new futures. The focus on Portland makes eminent sense when you realize that the Rose City is a place where the shift to a post-Christian America is a little further along. Juxtapose that with the hope-inducing city-church dynamics around the Seasons of Service, and you begin to understand why Lyons and his co-believers do not bemoan the end of "Christian America." If this is what the cultural shift can inspire in the church, they say, maybe a "post-Christian" culture is a good thing for American evangelicalism.

It might seem, at first glance, that Portland's Jesus followers are successful in spite of the city's great secularism. More likely, it's *because* they share the city with so many of the unconverted and unconvinced that the Rose

City's evangelicals have been, to use the sports cliché, at the top of their game. "The church thrives," says Milan Homola of Compassion Connect, "where it's most in need of adapting."[40]

In the Bible, Jesus speaks of a dynamic in which the first shall be last and the last shall be first. Like the prodigal son from another cherished passage in the Bible, this pearl of insight too often has been lost by evangelical America—but is now in the process of being found. In their quest for influence, status, and political power, Christianity's most visible and aggressive champions have spent their energy the past several decades striving to be first, fighting to win a culture war, winning mainly Pyrrhic victories while propelling their faith movement downward in the hearts and minds of the changing mainstream of their society. Public opinion surveys show that most Americans have the dimmest of views of the Christian Right and all it represents.[41] Could it be that forfeiting this competition is exactly what is needed to restore the credibility of the church and make it a widely appreciated, positive contributor to the greater good? Could it be that in sacrificing temporal "victory" evangelical Christianity will regain its soul?

The new evangelicals are answering with a resounding "yes." And they are doing so in a manner that that brings hope not just to evangelical Americans but also to the many non-evangelicals who share this country. If evangelical Christianity continues on this new path, if it comes to look more and more like compassionate service and humble goodwill-mongering, and less like a campaign of hostility and judgment against those with different beliefs and ways of life, it cannot be long before Americans of all faith persuasions, including the growing category of "no religion," come to better appreciate Christians and the good things about their religion. We can even envision a day when good-hearted action-takers of whatever religious persuasion, or of none, come to see in these evangelicals potential new allies and coalition partners with whom they can work for the common good—not enemies to be feared and loathed. As one *Huffington Post* reader declared in a comment beneath a column I wrote, "It's nice to see Christians behaving like their book says they should."[42]

Of course, to see this story unfolding, one has to know where to look. You certainly won't find these characters in the big-media coverage of national politics. Judging from the race for the presidency in 2011 and 2012, it's the same old, same old that we have seen for decades: Republican contenders courting the "evangelical vote," emphasizing their piety while promoting arch-conservative policy prescriptions that evince little concern for the people Jesus called the "least of these," and progressive media outlets offering alarm-sounding exposés of the creepiest aspects of the faith of evangelical candidates of the Rick Perry or Michele Bachmann type, with headlines like "A Wingnut and a Prayer."[43] Be aware that this is not all there is. And be assured that more and more evangelicals are rolling their eyes with the rest of us when Rick Perry asserts that evolution is "just a theory that's out there"[44] or mounts a showy prayer event to kick off his presidential campaign.

What's also happening—albeit with far less visibility—is a gathering movement of Christians dedicated to being and bringing a kind of good that most everyone can appreciate. Claiborne, the Christian activist from Philadelphia, describes it well when he declares that the best way for Christians to make people know about Jesus is simply by doing "fascinating things."

"The more I have read the Bible and studied the life of Jesus," writes Claiborne, "the more I have become convinced that Christianity spreads best not through force but through fascination."[45]

That's what they're doing in Portland, the unchurched mecca that has become an epicenter, a best foot forward, in the remaking of evangelicalism for the new time. Fascinating things *are* happening. And heads are turning.

Chapter Three

All Bait, No Switch

"We've won."

So states Jim Henderson, with all the enthusiasm of a person announcing he is on his way to a root canal appointment, as he sits in a coffeehouse with me on a rainy April day and shoots off, staccato-style, one paradigm-bending observation after another about the evangelical movement to which he belongs (more or less). From the way Henderson deadpans his victory declaration, you know that this Seattle-based author, instigator, subversive, impresario, and atheist-befriending "recovering evangelist" is really talking about a loss.

"Everyone knows that we have a voice now," Henderson continues. "Tony Perkins [of the ultra-conservative Family Research Council] gets interviewed on CNN whenever they need a 'Christian' perspective. Great. Congratulations. We had to put on a show for everyone to get to this point. So what? Now we're losing 'market share,' and many people think we suck."[1]

It's not that Henderson has anything against "shows," against creative projects that capture people's attention and tweak their preconceived notions. He is, after all, the Christian who inserted himself into the playful drama of the atheist who put his soul up for auction on eBay; it was Henderson who placed the winning bid. As one of several next acts, he produced a live staging of the huge-selling Christian spirituality book *The Shack*, featuring the book's author, Paul Young, in a form of performance Henderson calls "interactive spectacle art."[2]

No, Henderson does not have a problem with showmanship—just the kind of show that the main branch of publicly applied evangelicalism has been putting on since beginning its full-force re-engagement with politics and culture in the 1970s. What the mass media–consuming public has seen from evangelical Christianity has often seemed like a play with three acts— Anger, Judgment, Insularity—restaged and reenacted over and over. Henderson likes to surprise. It tells you something that when he won the eBay bidding for the soul of atheist blogger Hemant Mehta—"The Friendly Atheist," as he bills himself—Henderson's game was not to convert him. Henderson's aim, rather, was to become partners with Mehta in the search for fresh insights and perspectives. The pair embarked on a series of church visits and public dialogues aimed at building understanding between Christians and atheists and helping churches make necessary course corrections. "I owe many of my insights to my interactions with atheists," Henderson explains. "They have helped me grow closer to Jesus and more honest in my faith."[3]

Henderson's short spiky hair is white, and his age is north of sixty, but this is a "young evangelical" in nearly every other sense. He's got a handle on the popular vernacular. He talks fast, grins amusedly, and exudes a caffeinated enthusiasm about whatever ideas and projects are bouncing around in his agile mind at the moment. Henderson's quest, like that of so many of his younger co-believers, is the invention of new ways to be publicly and persuasively Christian in a fast-changing cultural context. Conventional wisdom teaches us that invention is invariably born of necessity; ask Christian change agents why they feel such urgency to rethink and regroup, and they'll tell you there's no choice: It's either that or stand by and witness Christ's slow fade into a cultural afterthought.

When he was younger, Henderson channeled his passion for Jesus into the enterprises that generally occupy entrepreneurial evangelical pastors— chasing souls and starting churches. I sometimes hear non-Christians ask, grumpily, why evangelicals can't keep their beliefs to themselves. It's like asking firefighters not to fight fires or race car drivers not to race cars. Evangelicals *evangelize*. Sharing the faith, proclaiming the "good news," proselytizing—call it what you will, this is what evangelicals do, and they get it from the Bible. "Make disciples of all nations," a resurrected Jesus tells the eleven remaining disciples in a verse commonly known as the Great Commission, "baptizing them in the name of the Father and of the Son and of the Holy Spirit, and teaching them to obey everything I have commanded you."[4]

As he went about this business of spreading the faith, of sharing with other people the gift of eternal life, as evangelists are wont to phrase it, the younger Henderson started to hear something he didn't like. It was the sound of his own voice as he pressed the gospel on would-be converts, and the sound of his own thoughts about who these people were to him. What they represented, he realized, were potential notches on his evangelism belt rather than fellow sojourners and prospective friends. Like a guitar-strumming performer who keeps singing notes out of sync with the chords he's playing, Henderson was hearing a grating dissonance between the gospel he deeply believed and the way his behavior was representing it.

He was manipulating conversations to set up a pitch. He was listening only to the extent it could reveal an argumentative opening. He was closing himself off to learning anything from the person on the receiving end of his pitch. He was overly certain that he stood in the light and they were in the dark. He realized, in sum, that he was doing unto others what he would never want done unto him.

"Finally," Henderson recalls, "I told the people in my church, 'I don't like evangelizing, and I know you *hate* it, so I've decided that I'm formally resigning from witnessing. You're all free to do so the same. I love Jesus, you love Jesus, and we all want to connect people with Jesus. But we're gonna have to figure out new ways to do it.'"[5]

Henderson's gradual epiphany and subsequent project—think of it as "post-evangelism"—frame the dilemma, challenge, and opportunity faced by the new evangelicals in post-Christian America. On the tactical level, there is nothing remarkable about this. It's as old as American evangelicalism, a movement that has always emphasized witnessing and has always been entrepreneurial and adaptable in finding ways to get people's attention and speak on their terms. But talking to people like Henderson clues you in on the reality that what's afoot now is no mere tactical adjustment. The game in which the Jesus sharers are engrossed has undergone something more profound than a few rule changes. It's as if they'd been playing baseball for the past three hundred years and now, suddenly, they're told the game is soccer. Time to ditch the bats and mitts and stop running a prescribed path around a diamond-shaped set of bases. Time to start using heads and feet and running in new, improvised patterns.

Why is traditional Protestant Christianity—despite centuries of ascendancy in the world's most powerful and influential country, despite surface appearances that might trick us into concluding it reigns supreme—suffering what gadflies like Jim Henderson term a loss of market share? Why has the game changed?

Look at your computer, and you'll begin to understand. It would be hard to exaggerate the immensity of the cultural impact of the Internet, a phenomenon that is both the perfect symbol and mightiest accelerator of the cultural paradigm the philosophers call postmodernity. At the core, the difference between the modern and postmodern world is the location and transmission of *authority*. Nothing since Gutenberg's printing press has spread authority from the few to the many like the Internet. Until very recently, power and authority resided in a finite number of hands such as big media outlets, corporate suites, university leaders, seats of government, presidents, pastors, and preachers. Religious authority—authority over what to believe and how it applies to our lives—has been contained in a discrete set of church leadership offices and their interpretations of the Bible, interpretations that in more conservative circles have tended toward the adamant, unambiguous, and unquestionable.

In the age of the Web, of Facebook, of Twitter, authority, power, and truth are becoming more fluid and diffuse, harder to locate, and less amenable to nailing down in the manner of Martin Luther, the man who literally and famously nailed his ninety-five theses to a church door in 1517 and thus sparked what became the Protestant Reformation. "We know more," says religion-and-culture scholar James Davison Hunter, "and as a consequence, we no longer trust the authority of traditional institutions who used to be carriers of moral ideals."[6] Or of *religious* ideas.

The Internet is, of course, a complex of networks, with a seemingly infinite number of "doors" to which we might nail things—or that we might open. No one is in charge. There are few controls. Very little (except the ability to attract an audience) is standing in the way of anyone becoming judge, arbiter, exegete, preacher, and publisher—of becoming his or her own seat of authority, in a tangled web of others doing just the same. It is in networks, increasingly, where truth is negotiated, discerned, defined, and changed—and changed again.

For evangelicals coming of age in the new paradigm, communications technology is "facilitating new patterns of learning, relating, and influencing the world, as well as changing the way they think about church and Christianity," writes David Kinnaman, president of the Christian opinion-research organization the Barna Group. "Technological access allows them to experience and examine content originating from non-biblical worldviews, giving them ample reason to question the nature of truth."[7] Young adults "are more likely to consult the Internet than their pastor about a religious question," Kinnaman adds (chillingly, some would say).[8]

The world looks remarkably different through the lenses of postmodernity. Like the Internet, it's messy, ambiguous, full of brilliant ideas and projects and possibilities, and spiked with harmful nonsense that almost makes one wish we could put the genie back in the bottle. This is the water in which religion now swims. The impact of this changing cultural context is especially profound for movements and bodies of belief, like evangelical Christianity, that tend to trade not in nuance and questions but in one-size-fits-all proclamations and conclusions.

Theologically conservative Christianity, an enterprise characterized by its determination to establish and proclaim clear, nonnegotiable truth about the issues most central to human existence—truths that apply not just to the proclaimer and his flock but also to the whole world—finds itself shouting its straight-up, black-and-white, final-word propositions in a context where "truth" is gray and finely grained and people innately sense that everything is more complicated than it might first appear. The religious truth assertions, and the usual manner of making them, simply do not connect the way they once did. The new Christians, steeped as they are in this emerging culture and capable of hearing the rhetoric of conventional evangelicalism with non-converts' ears, know that the message does not resonate with outsiders. It doesn't even resonate with *them*. It appears to be answering questions that society is not asking, in language fewer people understand, and ignoring the questions that *are* burning in people's consciences.

It's telling that the signature annual conference of the new evangelicals is called simply "Q." Think of it as an extended "Q and A"—minus the "A." "We don't want to project answers," Q convener Gabe Lyons explains, "to questions that people aren't even asking."[9]

Do not expect a simple (self-)righteous verdict if you ask a postmodern evangelical if, for example, it's a moral outrage for a woman to have an abortion. Polling data suggest there's a good chance this younger Christian indeed does oppose abortion. But instead of an unambiguous and condemnatory "yes"—the religiously correct answer for which evangelicals have been known in this country—you might have it pointed out for you that one should be careful not to pile stones on a particular woman who had an abortion. You'll hear that she probably had a complicated set of reasons, that we should know someone's "story" before passing judgment. You're likely to hear that there was a man involved in the equation who bears his share of the responsibility for the abortion.

You will find similar conversations about the other divisive issues of the day—about gay rights, the exercise of American military muscle, the supposed inferiority of other religions, the degree to which punching one's ticket to heaven is the point of being a Christian.

You will hear, as Lyons seems to suggest, not just different answers to evangelicalism's standard questions but also entirely different questions.

Evangelical writer Jonathan Merritt, a compatriot of Lyons and the author of two books before he hit the age of thirty, recalls evangelizing house-to-house as a youth. As soon as the door would open, he was ready: "I'd like to ask you a question," he would say. "If you were to die today, do you know for sure that you'd go to heaven?"[10]

In a 2012 article in which he recalls those youthful experiences, Merritt cites recent public-opinion research that proves the folly of such efforts.[11] As it turns out, "Am I going to heaven if I die tonight?" is simply not a question people are generally asking on a regular basis, and not something high on their list of daily worries. Nor, in the view of more and more evangelicals, is acquisition of "salvation insurance," to use the dismissive term of art, even a good reason to become a Christian.

"Americans ask themselves many questions," Merritt writes. "They wonder how they can build a strong family and nurture a healthy marriage in a world where both seem to be in increasingly short supply. As society fills with airbrushed fakes and facades, they want to know how to live a life of authenticity. Many desire to know how to make an imprint on the world that can outlive them. And they are looking for a vibrant, personal spiritual encounter with God—perhaps without the baggage of institutional religion. But many efforts to evangelize don't address such things. Could it be that the decline in Christian conversions is due, in part, to misguided evangelism efforts?"[12]

What burning questions *can* Christianity productively address? Merritt endorses the provocative set posed by the Christian writer Andrew Wilson in his 2012 book *If God Then What?*[13] Among them: What's wrong with the world? What's the solution? How did we get here? What is possible? What really happened on the fateful day in the year 30 AD when Christians believe Jesus rose from the dead? And why does it matter?

When it comes to answers, standard evangelism has generally hinged on the declaration of "spiritual laws" and logical arguments meant to take hearers from A to B to Z—to the decision that Christianity's claims are true and that Jesus is the way. Evangelism of this post–World War II vintage has organized itself around carefully sequenced biblical passages and interpretations, and it has presented, as if to a jury, the "evidence that demands a verdict," to quote a line popularized by the high-profile, old-school evangelist Josh McDowell.

In this new world, an evangelist can cite Bible verses and spiritual laws all day and accomplish nothing. What good are scriptural proofs when an audience does not accept the factual accuracy or authority of the Bible? An evangelist can dangle the promise of heaven and threat of hell and have no effect at all on listeners—if, indeed, he can even *get* listeners.

I recall seeing, not long ago, a fire-and-brimstone evangelist plying his trade at a Saturday afternoon festival in Portland, amid of swirl of food booths, a Russian dance performance, and a constellation of merchants and arts-and-crafts exhibitors. There were hundreds of people around that ardent evangelist. Not a single one paid him any attention.

Apostate. That's the word for a person who has abandoned the orthodox faith and now poses a threat to the church, and it's the epithet that those of a fundamentalist inclination tend to use for people like Jim Henderson. For his own part, Henderson describes himself with memorable phrases like "an ex-Christian trying to follow Jesus" and "an evangelical on a mission to rescue Jesus from religion and take him public."[14]

Henderson takes subversive delight in looking for insight and allies not just in the ranks of his fellow Jesus followers but also among the proponents of a worldview that tradition-minded evangelicals often regard as dangerous. Why would a good Christian consort with *atheists*, of all people? Consider the over-the-top condemnation of atheism that an Illinois legislator hurled at an atheist activist who had the temerity to show up for a hearing and testify against what he felt was an unconstitutional state grant to a church. "This is the Land of Lincoln," Representative Monique Davis railed, "where people believe in God, where people believe in protecting their children. . . . It's dangerous for our children to even know that [atheism] exists!"[15]

What could a Christian possibly learn from the vanguard of godless degeneracy? A lot, it turns out. As more and more Jesus followers like Henderson are discovering, taking a look at yourself and your religion through the eyes of the unconvinced can be a revelatory experience.

From Henderson's partnership with the "Friendly Atheist" Mehta came numerous church visits, after which they published their observations on the Internet (leading, eventually, to Henderson's ChurchRater.com website, a clearinghouse of reviews on churches across the entire country). And there came new insights that Henderson could apply to the church consulting business he was running. Imagine it: an atheist giving blinded Christians the gift of seeing—of seeing themselves and their churches through the eyes of outsiders.

In the subsequent book and DVD, *The Outsider Interviews*, coauthored with Todd Hunter and Craig Spinks, Henderson captured what evangelical Christians sound like and look like to the legions of the not persuaded.[16]

They point out that nothing kills a "conversation" like going in, as well-meaning faith-sharers often do, with an "I'm right/you're wrong" model and mind-set. As someone who is in the influence game myself, I have likewise been struck by this off-putting flaw in conventional evangelism. As I once said when invited to speak to a group of missionaries-in-training, why would anyone want to enter a "conversation" when it was established from the start that one party was in the light and the other in the dark? If you want to have influence, I suggested, you have to be willing to *be* influenced. (I have often fantasized about turning the tables the next time a gospel-tract disseminator approaches me on the street. What if I tried to convert *him* to whatever theology is bouncing around in my mind at the given moment?)

In a similar vein, well-meaning condescension, à la speaking of the unconverted as "lost," is a poor advertisement for Jesus and a surefire turnoff for would-be listeners, Henderson stresses. So are outsized certitude and superiority. "Nothing sets off an atheist more than hearing a Christian say, 'I know Jesus is God and that I'm going to heaven when I die,'" Henderson says. "They also notice that we often say it loudly and arrogantly, which only serves to reinforce their negative opinion of our certainty."[17]

Do not, Henderson urges would-be evangelists, treat atheists, agnostics, non-evangelical Christians, or followers of other faiths as "projects," as he himself did in his younger days. He advises faith promoters to constantly check in with themselves, and God, and ask: Does my continued contact and eventual friendship with my conversation partners rest on their eventual conversion? Am I willing to stay in relationship with a person even if it is clearly not leading to her or his becoming a Christian?

The evangelism missteps identified by Henderson, combined with a fair bit of negative overreaction, explain why evangelism is regarded by many with extreme distaste. "The word *evangelism* still sends shivers down the spines of many people," writes N. T. Wright, a New Testament scholar and retired Anglican bishop from England whose writings enjoy a high degree of respect among new-century evangelicals in this country. "Some people have been scared off by frightening or bullying harangues or tactless and offensive behavior or embarrassing and naïve presentations of the gospel," he says in his book *Surprised by Hope*. "Others have never suffered such indignities but heard or read about them and are glad to have a good excuse to pour scorn on all evangelism—as though, because some people do it badly, nobody should ever do it at all."[18]

While taking pains not to be too harsh in his criticism of fellow Christians, Wright puts his finger on a key reason why much of what passes for evangelism today strikes the unconverted twenty-first-century hearer as irrelevant at best and annoying at worst: "Much evangelism," he writes, ". . . has consisted of taking the traditional framework of a heaven-and-hell expectation and persuading people that it's time they consider the heaven option and grab it while they have the chance."[19]

Again, that problem with the questions. To an individual suffering from economic hardship or personal trials, to a society sagging under the weight of numerous complicated problems, the solution offered by conventional evangelism seems of little help: *Jesus died for your sins—accept him and have eternal life!* The message has greater richness and applicability to contemporary life than meets the untrained eye and ear. But to those without the background knowledge of Christianity, without the vocabulary of the evangelical subculture, an encounter with this proclamation seems akin to finding oneself bleeding from a cut, in dire need of bandages, and having a "Jesus is Lord!" bumper sticker handed to you.

Then there's the matter of "truth in advertising." Truth-telling is foundational to Christian ethics, of course, enshrined in the Ten Commandments: "Thou shalt not bear false witness." Even the most herculean rationalizing cannot square that commandment with the not-atypical evangelism sales tactics described during a revealing episode of the Ira Glass radio show, *This American Life*, in 2009 (an episode that featured the more-candid-than-thou Henderson as a guest).

In his lead-in, the ultra-wry Glass framed the segment with a truly eyebrow-raising description: "Tricking people for the Lord Almighty." Picture this scene described by Glass's first guest in the segment, onetime Campus Crusade for Christ evangelizer David Ellis Dickerson: Students from a Campus Crusade group mingle with other college-age revelers on the beach during spring break. The Campus Crusade students—the women perky and attractive, clad in bikinis—pass out fliers inviting people to a luau happening that night. The fliers dangle the promise of music, food, drinks, and good times. No mention of the fact that the students they lure in are going to get a pitch—a sales pitch for Jesus. "You have this biblical imperative," explained Dickerson, who was raised in the evangelical subculture, "to spread the word to people who don't want to hear it." Dickerson would dread the onset of the unpleasant "aha" moment for the students they had lured in—first, when the recruits discovered the drinks were nonalcoholic; next, when they took in the first of the "Jesus has changed my life" faith testimonials that were sandwiched in between the goofy skits and air-guitar contests. [20]

Dickerson then described the faux data collection that his Campus Crusade fellows and he were instructed to perform on their college campus. They would approach people and ask them to take part in a "religious attitudes" survey. "We would ask them a series of questions," Dickerson recalled. "'Do you believe in God?' That kind of thing. It would eventually lead to 'Hey, do you belong to a church? Would you like to join ours?'"

"We got put in pairs," Dickerson continued. "My friend and I started at one end of the campus. While walking down I had all these ideas in my head. What if someone asked who was sponsoring the survey or what statistical model we were using? We had been in college long enough to know there's a survey and then there's a *survey*. We knew that if we hit up a statistics major we'd be in trouble! One woman comes by and my friend says, 'She looks busy or angry; let's avoid her.' This other guy comes by, and we thought, 'Oh, he doesn't look right either.' We kept talking each other out of confronting people. Finally, we looked at each other and said, 'We just can't do this, can we?'" [21]

Henderson also reached the point where he couldn't "do" evangelism anymore. Following Dickerson on the program, he told Glass, "The founder of our movement, Jesus, did not model this behavior. He never had to lower himself to a bait-and-switch. This has been an adoption by the church of American consumerism. It's really largely based on sales. Quite frankly, I *want* people to follow Jesus. I believe Jesus is God and all that stuff. But I'm completely done with the whole evangelism-as-sales-model deal."

When Henderson described his new model for "doable evangelism"— getting to know people, praying for people, listening to people, connecting with people, forming relationships with people, and letting the ecclesiastical chips fall where they may—Glass voiced puzzlement. "Where's the part where they come to Jesus? What you're replacing bait-and-switch with—it's all bait, and no switch at all!" Glass observed with a laugh. "You're just assuming that at some point something will happen and maybe it will be good. 'The bait was pretty good. Let's go with that!'"

"I kind of like that," Henderson responded brightly, as if a light had been turned on in his mind. "All bait and no switch. I might use that! Our goal is to get Christians engaged. We're not concerned about results."

Not concerned about results? It might strike some as a formula not for doable evangelism, as Henderson calls it, but for *pointless* evangelism. Yet when I think about Henderson's bait, and this crucial absence of a switch, I am reminded of just how great a role paradox and irony can play in the dynamics of Christian faith. By not concerning himself with notches on his evangelism belt, with statistics showing this-many-thousand "faith commitments" for Jesus, as some evangelistic organizations do, Henderson eludes some of the most problematic traps that snare many a well-intentioned evangelist and give Christianity a bad name. By giving up results-based evangelism, the new evangelicals typified by Jim Henderson achieve something else, something rather important when you think about it. Freed from results, from statistics, from evangelistic bottom lines, they can just be good, and let that do all the talking. They can let *that* be the result.

As often suggested by evangelical innovator Kevin Palau and others leading this new church movement, a skeptical public is willing to give religion an open-minded look only to the extent that its practitioners have more to offer than brittle doctrinal propositions about Jesus' divinity and the way to get to heaven. Show us something real, the public seems to be saying. Show us something special that actually transforms lives and communities in practical, positive ways, in the here and now. Show us you're willing to serve as the exemplars of decency and compassion, even if you pay a price. Without necessarily using Shane Claiborne's words, they seem to echo his sentiment: Do fascinating things.

These new-century "evangelists" exhibit little interest in a Jesus who buys you a ticket off this troubled planet and passage through heaven's golden gates, little interest in a Jesus of cultural conformity and status quo preservation. Instead, they speak of aspects of their savior that are "scandalous" and "intoxicating."[22] Evangelical spirituality writer Tony Kriz, who has done ministry work from Albania to ultra-secular Reed College, speaks of a faith that is anything but safe and comfortable. Kriz writes in his book *Neighbors and Wise Men* that faith, for him, is less like a middle-aged couple on a leisurely Sunday drive in the country and "more like a car driving seventy miles per hour on a windy, cliff-top gravel road."[23]

These new evangelicals have no time for the "proofs" of conservative Christianity that expend so much energy asserting who Jesus is that they forget what he taught, and did. "Much has been made of the factual 'evidence that demands a verdict' that Jesus is Lord," writes Paul Louis Metzger, founder of the New Wine, New Wineskins Institute and a leading articulator of the new ethos. "But today, 'Jesus is Lord' is a verdict that demands evidence in our lives. Otherwise, our faith is fiction."[24]

Metzger's brilliant flipping of that oft-heard evangelistic punch line— "evidence that demands a verdict"—into his "verdict that demands evidence" seem to perfectly encapsulate what these new Christians are up to. If Christians are privy to something profoundly important, if they are *in* on the cosmic truth, what evidence will their own lives present? What if Christians behaved in such a way that a skeptical public, over time, came to associate their faith movement with such radical attributes as consistent and inconvenient honesty, earnestness, compassion, selflessness, service to others? To put it in the simplest terms, in the terms I hear more and more from the Jesus followers I encounter, what if Christians came to be known as the people who were radically *helpful*?

Henderson calls the trait "otherliness." Some of it might strike you as a simple exercise in good manners, but it goes deeper: Be unusually interested in others, Henderson teaches. "Stay in the room with difference," he says. Refuse to compare "my best," Henderson instructs, "with your worst." (Imagine how the public debates would improve for the better if that were the norm rather than the current practice of derision and demonization.) Ignore conservative/liberal labels, he says, and identify with groups reviled and marginalized by American culture. Practice the spiritual art of serving, even in small ways, even in ways that no one will ever see. "Join others," Henderson urges, "in making [your] communities and world a better place."[25]

Evangelicals of an older-school mind-set will no doubt find all this lacking. There is clearly some bait here. But where's the switch, they might ask—the switch that happens when a person stands up and accepts Jesus as her lord and savior? Where's the *conversion*?

One reason this can be challenging to evangelicals of a more traditional ilk is that the expression of Christianity modeled by Henderson, the friendly provocateur from Seattle, cannot be considered unique to evangelical Christians. Indeed, anyone with a generous spirit and a deep concern for her or his fellow humans can be all or most of what Henderson urges those "recovering evangelists" to be. Moderate religionists have been citing for centuries the wisdom of Saint Francis of Assisi, who taught Christians to "preach the gospel always; use words if necessary"—as if to imply that believers' best "preaching" comes through their actions. Other religions, from Judaism to Islam to Buddhism, teach compassion and kindness. A current within atheism emphasizes the ability of non-believers to be "good without God." Do not underestimate what a stumbling block the wider, shared nature of this ethos can pose for a kind of Christianity that has always emphasized its uniqueness—its superiority over other religions, philosophies, and worldviews, and the ultimate emptiness/inferiority/folly of any life that has not been "saved" by the acceptance of Christ as one's personal savior.

Does Henderson's model even qualify as "evangelical"? In the sense that being an evangelical is about "following Jesus and making him known in the world," as Sojourners blogger Ernesto Tinajero aptly defines it,[26] then the answer has to be "yes." For the evangelical faith to remain viable in a changed age, perhaps this lower-key engagement with non-Christians is what evangelicalism will have to look like, will have to mean, for it to have any effect. Old-guard evangelicals alarmed by what might appear an excessively weak-kneed engagement with non-Christians, or with an unacceptably radical break from tradition, can find comfort perhaps in recalling that in an earlier iteration, in the nineteenth century, evangelicalism was strongly oriented toward deeds, toward action to improve the lives of the individual and society. It is not as though all this represents some alarming abrogation of the Bible. As one young church leader told me at the Christian medical clinic I visited, "Scripture says we'll be known by our love—not how many gospel tracts we pass out."

Those with a marketing frame of mind, and who thus appreciate the importance of defining and emphasizing what makes a given "product" different and better than anything else out there, will quickly spot another flaw in this form of all-bait, no-switch "evangelism." Isn't this approach too humble? Too quiet about Christianity's differentiated brand proposition? Too reluctant to shout out that Jesus died for your sins and you're bound for hell if you don't become a Christian? Yes. And that's the beauty of it.

If evangelicals are called to fulfill the Great Commission, to make Jesus known in the world, it's only sensible to ask, "What *will* make him known?" This is what the new evangelicals have begun to figure out. To the extent that the marketing model has any applicability, keep in mind that marketers have long understood that connecting with people depends on understanding their needs, wants, and preferences, and that any smart communication speaks to an audience on its own terms. Informing the unconverted masses that Jesus died for their sins, that they can enjoy eternal life and escape the eternal punishments of hell by becoming Christian, by being washed in the blood of Christ, promises all the effectiveness of a campaign to sell lawn mowers to people who are looking for a way to wash their dishes. And to the extent that it seems to shout, "I'm right, you're wrong," old-school evangelism promises to do worse than simply fail to connect. It can alienate.

The needless tragedy in all this is that Jesus *can* be an answer, if the evangelist can figure out the question. It's instructive to hear the testimonials of non-converts who have been positively influenced by their friendships and conversations with evangelicals. You'll hear of them getting over stereotypes and developing a new appreciation for their Christian fellow citizens. These are conversations that revolve not around heaven and hell but around how we can become better people, and how we can make this earthly life a little less hellish for those who suffer.

Matt Casper, the atheist coauthor with Henderson of *Jim and Casper Go to Church*, says his engagement with Christians was initially motivated by his wanting to disabuse them of their certitude and the idea that atheists all have tails and horns. But something unintended happened in the process. "I used to be a dick, and now I'm not," Casper told me bluntly when I talked with him about his partnership with Henderson. "My tolerance has expanded and my ignorance on matters of faith has gone away some. I've become less judgmental. I've seen Christians who really are trying to walk the talk. I'm not becoming a believer, but I am becoming a better person."[27]

Not as eloquent as the strains of "Amazing Grace," to be sure. It's hard to imagine a chorus swelling with the magical lyrics, "I once was a dick but now I'm not." But the age-old chords of conversion can be heard just the same—not a conversion to being washed in the blood of Christ, but a conversion to decency and a more generous understanding of this intriguing group of people called "Christians."

Conversion of a sort can also be heard in the "testimony" of former Portland mayor Sam Adams, a man who, because of his sexual orientation and liberal politics, would appear to have every justification to fear and loathe evangelical Christians—which Adams did to some extent before he got to know some, and before they got to know him. Speaking to an audience of next-generation Christians at the Q conference in 2011, the then-mayor "confessed" to once harboring a dim view of evangelical Christians, a view shaped by media stereotypes and his assumption that these Christians would want nothing to do with the gay mayor of one of the most progressive cities in the country. As he went on to explain, these notions were shattered in the most hopeful ways by the relationship that developed between city hall and the evangelical community during his term as mayor.

"[Portland] is a progressive, liberal city. I mean *very* liberal. I don't think we've elected a Republican here for a long time," Adams explained in the panel conversation. "It's been useful for me personally to [realize] that I'm part of a groupthink, that I've bought into media stereotypes—which are mostly not true. It's been very enriching for me personally and for the city as a whole. It's been humbling to see how much we actually do share in terms of our common concerns."[28]

I asked Hemant Mehta, the "Friendly Atheist" blogger and author, how his encounters with new-school evangelicals like Henderson have affected his views. He had an answer similar to Adams's—one of pleasant surprise over the decency of these people and their willingness to team up with any person, any group, keen on doing good. Mehta pointed out that the network of college campus atheist groups, the Secular Student Alliance, was encouraging its members to join forces with Christian groups for service projects. Mehta realized, too, that the Christians most often ridiculed by the strident "new atheist" authors like Sam Harris and Richard Dawkins were the Christians of the Religious Right, not the progressive and common good–oriented Christians whom Mehta had gotten to know. "It's not that we think the progressive Christians are right about God—they're still wrong—but their beliefs are relatively benign," Mehta told me. "They are not the type of dogmatic, delusional-thinking people that we're so used to associating with Christians."[29]

Strains of conversion—conversion from hope faded to hope restored—can likewise be heard in the testimonials of discouraged evangelicals whose own heads have been turned by the rising new currents. Randall Balmer, a religious studies professor and part-time minister, had this to say in an e-mail message that he sent to Kevin Palau after he heard about the Seasons of Service in Portland: "I confess that as I was walking upstairs to check my messages this morning (and getting dressed to conduct a funeral today), I was thinking that maybe it was time to throw in the towel on evangelicalism," wrote Balmer, who was raised in the evangelical church and still identifies as an evangelical. "I was feeling that the movement had been lost to the right-wing nuts and would never recover its roots in both the teachings of Jesus and in the noble precedent of nineteenth-century evangelicalism. And then I read the articles [about the Seasons of Service]. I don't want to sound melo-dramatic, but I can't tell you how much this lifted my spirits. . . . It's remarkable."[30]

Evangelical innovators of the Jim Henderson, Kevin Palau ilk still have some people to convince. Yes, Christian service with "no strings attached," as Palau describes his model, an all-bait, no-switch approach to representing the gospel—the Henderson mode—clearly can resonate with people who would normally feel inclined to run for the exits if they found out an evangel-ical Christian was about to make a pitch. But evangelicals of a more tradi-tional bent will clearly find this lacking. Aren't these postmodern Christians too worried about being *polite*—too "ashamed of Jesus," as it's sometimes phrased? Aren't a few ruffled feathers a price worth paying given the cosmic heaven-or-hell stakes of conventional evangelism? Really, are the soft pedal-ers doing non-evangelicals any favors by respecting their differing beliefs— differing beliefs that will buy those non-believers a ticket to eternal punish-ment? Are these new approaches to "evangelism" even worthy of the word?

And then there are the cynics on the other side of the equation, the people convinced that religion is inherently foolish and that any good that might come of it—large-scale Christian service, say, or a Christian campaign to bring relief to hurricane victims and poor people in need of medical care—is no advertisement whatsoever for the faith. As *God Is Not Great* author Chris-topher Hitchens grumpily asserted to me two years before his death, it's clearly not their noxious religion that accounts for Christians' good works, despite what they may say. What good, he asks, can come out of something inherently bad?[31]

The flame-throwing atheists and Christian exclusivists can carry on their unprofitable arguments until their faces turn blue. It is fascinating to realize how much they need one another to sustain their arguments, and books, and fund-raising appeals, and ax grinding.

Hitchens-style atheists need the most extreme evangelicals and funda-mentalists to be perceived as the real Christians, as the only Christians, if their ridicule is going to carry any ring of truth. I am struck by the scorn that many in the movement of "new atheists" tend to heap on religious moderates and progressives.[32] The reasons cited—that reasonable, non-fundamentalist religious people lack any courage of conviction, that they give a veneer of respectability to something that's all bad and only bad—are not, I suspect, the real reasons. More likely, the new atheists' out-of-proportion scorn for moderate and progressive Christians has more to do with the inconvenience this other kind of Christian poses for the black-and-white anti-religion argument. How can you go on railing about the evils of religion when there are appealing religionists all around, engaging in obnoxious acts of love and compassion?

By the same token, it's clear that the evangelicals who have bought their movement a bad reputation with their defensiveness and combativeness owe a debt of gratitude to the flame-throwing atheists. For it is the hard-hearted, closed-minded, blanket attacks on Christianity that have provided the fodder needed for the endlessly cited message one hears from right-wing Christian groups like the Family Research Council—that faith is under attack in America and that Christianity will soon be all but banned from public life unless Christians flock to the polls, vote for certain conservative politicians, and "reclaim America for Christ."

Let these argument wagers, with their fundamentalist religion and fundamentalist atheism, have each other. What the present challenges and emerging new times require are those people inclined toward what Jim Henderson calls "otherliness"—those who want to do something helpful and decent and are willing to do it with anyone who is ready to lend a hand.

By the time you come out on the other side of this examination of evangelism, this ongoing project to make Christ known in the world, you start to sense a certain irony in this "all-bait, no-switch" model of the ex-evangelists. Whatever a Jim Henderson might claim about not concerning himself with results, with conversion notches to add to his evangelist belt, a switch of a certain kind does indeed take place when this friendship model is carried through. No, it is not necessarily the kind of switch whereby an agnostic is lured to a fun-in-the-sun party that turns out to be a gospel presentation. And no, it's not a switch in the conversion sense whereby an atheist repents of his evil ways and proclaims Jesus as Lord.

It's the switch that gradually happens in the hearts and minds of the unconverted and unconvinced as they get a better idea about Christians and Christianity and a better notion of what becomes possible when they join forces with these people to accomplish good. It's the switch that happens as the process plays out countless times, in coffeehouses and living rooms and interfaith community-service ventures, and as people of goodwill spill out into the streets and neighborhoods to do something kind for people who really need it.

Is this "evangelism" adequate? That, of course, depends on what you are trying to accomplish. If the game is old-school evangelism, and the desired result is people parading to the megachurch altars (and voting booths) and declaring themselves Christian, the model is greatly lacking. If, on the other hand, you're a religious person moved by the biblical imperative that Christians "will be known by their love," or if you're a non-religious seeker of goodwill and common ground, this is a form of "evangelism" that you can celebrate.

As N. T. Wright asks, doesn't it seem "laughable" that Christians would proclaim the audacious news "that Jesus is Lord, that the powers of evil, corruption, and death itself have been defeated, and that God's new world has begun"? Indeed, it is laughable, Wright concludes—unless, that is, these things are already happening. "If a church is . . . actively involved in seeking justice in the world," he writes, "if it's cheerfully celebrating God's good creation, and if, in addition, its own internal life gives every sign that new creation is indeed happening, generating a new type of community, then suddenly the announcement makes a lot of sense."[33]

Call it goodwill-mongering, evangelism by attraction, promotion by non-promotion, or simply letting one's life speak for itself, but I am convinced that this is what will best represent the faith among the many Americans who do not share the evangelical faith, and who probably never will. Henderson and his fellow travelers are right in urging would-be evangelists simply to get to know people and become their friends, predetermined outcomes be damned. This reimagined form of witness trumpets good news all around— for Christians who, as Henderson puts it, want to be "normal," for those concerned with the public credibility of Christianity and the easing of conflict between Christians and non-Christians, and for all of the not-yet and never-will-be converts who don't want to be pitied or demonized but are more than open to some good news and some good people.

These new-century Jesus representatives seem to be arriving at just the right formula (or non-formula, actually) for making their faith real and known in these weary times. To reprise the insightful words of the theologian Paul Louis Metzger, *this* is the evidence demanded by the "verdict" of Christian apologetics, by that puzzling proclamation that "Jesus is Lord." *This* is how to make Jesus known in this changed and changing world.

This is the bait. No switch required.

Chapter Four

Unchristian Nation

At the center of the decades-long culture war, there burns a loaded assertion, a pivotal article of civic and religious belief that does yeoman's work in sorting out who's on which side. Someone's assent or objection to this partic-ular truth claim will tell you a lot about where that person stands on matters concerning God, Jesus, America, and the role of Christianity in our politics and public life.

Declare "Yes, that's right!" to this proposition, and chances are you veer right in your politics and theology and expect a special, elevated place for the Christian narrative in everything from public-venue prayers and school kids' history books to the thought process for choosing people for elected office. Say "No," and chances are you're a progressive and part of a more liberal Christian tradition, or another religion, or no religion at all.

The proposition: That the United States of America is "a Christian na-tion."

To hear from some of Jesus' feistiest champions in the ongoing national arguments, the hearts of the Founding Fathers burned with evangelical zeal for the Christian God and his intention that the fledgling nation would stand tall and bright, a shining city on a hill. Christianity, in this view, infuses the Constitution, our principles, our way of life. It is the source of the virtue undergirding America's unique success as a nation. Howsoever things go with the quality of our Christian piety and practice, so goes the health of the nation.

Contrast that with the statement by then-senator Barack Obama that America, "whatever we once were, is no longer a Christian nation. We are also a Jewish nation, a Muslim nation, a Buddhist nation, and a Hindu nation, and a nation of nonbelievers."[1] To hear it from some conservatives, the sentiment voiced by the man who would become president was a slap in the face, an appalling surrender of the country's proud identity and heritage. Fox News commentator Sean Hannity was one of several high-profile conservatives who took umbrage when Obama reprised the comment in his first year as president while speaking at a press conference in Turkey. The comments were offensive, Hannity charged, indicative of the president being "out of touch with the principles that have made this country great."[2] Yet, to many millions of Americans, Obama was saying nothing provocative at all, merely acknowledging a statistical and demographic reality.

Of course, saying we're no longer a Christian nation begins to loom larger than mere fact citing when the statement's implications are played out in the public square. And this we see in the now-common resistance against explicitly Christian (i.e., "in the name of Jesus") prayers in the halls of government or public school settings; in civil-liberties drives to remove crosses from public venues; and in campaigns that, to tradition-revering defenders of the faith, look more and more like an attempt to scrub the Christian religion right out of our public life, as if "Christ" were a dirty word.

The argument rages on, two sides shouting past one another, in dire need of someone with a level head and calming presence to step in, call a time-out, and point out to the word warriors that they would probably get a lot further in resolving the matter, if they actually cared to do that, by simply explaining what they mean by "Christian nation."

A nation whose constitution is replete with references to Christ and a requirement that all office holders profess his name? The no's have it. (In fact, that constitution mentions Jesus and Christianity exactly zero times.)

A nation that has always has had far more Christians populating it than followers of any other religious tradition? Chalk one up for "yes."

A nation that operates a state church and requires all citizens to support it with their tax dollars? Another one for the no's.

A nation with higher rates of religious participation than nearly any other in the Western, industrialized world, with most of that worship happening in Protestant and Catholic churches? One more for the "yes" column.

This exercise could go on for some time. Yet there is a more useful question lost in the shouting about whether we are a Christian nation and what a given response—yes or no?—implies about how things ought to go in our shared public life. It's a question that, if asked on a more regular basis, might turn things inside out and upside down and actually help foster a more constructive conversation about the kind of country we are going to have, and the role Christianity is going to play in it.

Who would have guessed that one of the leading framers of this reformulated big question would be the product, in a very real sense, of . . .

. . . Jerry Falwell?

It is a long way from Thomas Road Baptist Church in Lynchburg, Virginia—the church that Jerry Falwell built—to the east side of Manhattan. Not that the mileage is insurmountable. But in cultural distance, it's safe to say that western Virginia and New York City are light years apart. Yet for one of the key innovators and leaders of the new evangelicalism, this was precisely the road to discovery and invention: Lynchburg to Manhattan, with some zigzags in between.

Little needs to be said about the late Falwell and his impact on publicly expressed evangelicalism over the most recent chapter of the country's religious and political history. A founder of the Moral Majority in the late 1970s, a leader and tone setter for the broader Christian Right movement, Falwell was a consistent and adamant voice for evangelicals to influence the culture through politics—hard-line *conservative* politics played with a take-no-prisoners confidence and ferocity.

When you meet Gabe Lyons, it will not occur to you that this is a man who grew up in the fundamentalist bubble of Falwell's Thomas Road Church and received his higher education at Falwell's Liberty University. Tall and lanky, with longish bangs and casual, hip clothes, Lyons looks more like an indie-rock guitarist than a straitlaced, red-state church guy. In addition to the Bible, his reading tastes veer in some subversive directions; *Adbusters* is a magazine he cites as a favorite.

If you have a set idea of what an evangelical Christian with Lyons's background ought to think and say, you'll have that shattered in short order, too. "Having the quick answer to everything doesn't exhibit the humility that Christ had," Lyons once explained to me while discussing the curious name he divined for the annual conference he convenes for new-generation evangelical leaders, called simply Q—*Q* as in *questions*.[3]

When Lyons was a boy in the church, there was essentially *one* question that concerned him—consumed him, actually. Were he and the people in his life bound for heaven or for hell?

Lyons is sitting with me in a Manhattan café a block or two away from the rented townhouse where his family and he are living and where, on the bottom floor, he and his small staff operate the nonprofit that oversees Q and Lyons's other church-leadership endeavors. "I made the decision to accept Jesus when I was five," Lyons says, "and I made it again in sixth grade— because of my fear of hell. I was super-evangelistic. Hell was all I cared about. I called my friends at night and asked if they knew—if they knew for sure!—that they were not going to hell."[4]

His family and church context was, to put it mildly, conservative, both in the political and theological sense. "For us," Lyons quips with a grin, "the Southern Baptists were liberal."[5] This environment certainly rubs off on a person. Yet, in Lyons's case, some of it *wore* off as he began moving in different circles as a young man. The evolution of Gabe Lyons was never more apparent than at the 2011 gathering of Q, where Lyons shared the stage and had a civil dialogue with Feisal Abdul Rauf, leader of the so-called Ground Zero Mosque Project in New York and a figure very much in conservative and Christian Right firing lines at the time. Jerry Falwell, we can bet, would not have approved—of this or of numerous other things Lyons has said and done. Yet you will not hear Lyons disowning this spiritual father of sorts. Lyons explains that he has retained important lessons from Falwell, the man who personally offered him his scholarship to Liberty and who displayed a genius for promotion and entrepreneurship, for reaching, recruiting, and rallying people, that made a huge and lasting impression on protégé Gabe Lyons.

"I was officially in the bubble for twenty-two years," Lyons reflects. At Thomas Road, "I'd hear Jerry 150 times a year, hear him say again and again that Christians have to get involved in the culture. His techniques were different than mine are now, but the basic idea is the same: Christians need to engage. It was ingrained in me that Christians ought to be influencing morality in the world."[6]

While he was at Liberty studying elementary education, business, and marketing, Lyons honed his people skills as a socially extroverted student leader while growing his sales skills by peddling satellite-television systems at night in and around Lynchburg. Out of college, Lyons lived in San Diego briefly, then Atlanta for a longer period, while working as a promoter and marketer for the Christian motivational speaker John Maxwell. Maxwell's self-help recordings had been among the many Lyons listened to in his car while driving to sales calls in his college days. All the accumulated knowledge and motivation from his tape listening paid off. Lyons quickly advanced to vice president and a handsome salary in Maxwell's company and helped them launch a new conference—not Q, which would come later, but an event called Catalyst, geared to the under-forty Christian crowd.

The year 2001 is pivotal in American history for an event that needs no explaining. But it was a different event that same year—a personal one—that knocked the fast-advancing Gabe Lyons off his smooth stride and jarred Lyons, then in his late twenties, into some serious contemplation about his future, and about the Christian faith that still stood strongly at its center. Lyons and his wife, Rebekah, had their first child. Cade was born with Down syndrome.

For the former state championship–winning high school quarterback with the fast-track career and the sky's-the-limit future, the impact was profound. His son was clearly not going to fulfill a certain kind of dream that fathers often have for their sons: Cade was not going to be a star athlete or student; he was not going to be a smashing success in business or a profession. "He got me thinking about what's important in life," Lyons said as he thought back, ten years later, on his first son's birth. In the two years between Cade's arrival and the birth of the Lyonses' second son, Pierce, Lyons poured himself into reflecting, reading, and receiving the counsel and mentoring of a pastor to whom he was close. "God," he says, "was doing something in me. Something was being birthed."[7]

That pastor, though, was hardly the only midwife in that birthing process. Lyons, ever further removed from the evangelical bubble, was finding himself in more and more interactions with non-Christians. He was hearing these people's perspectives on Christians—and finding them, in many cases, to be quite negative. It was dismaying to learn how many people found evangelical Christians annoying. Instead of being known as a blessing to their society, as idealistic Christians might hope, they were seen by critics as hostile toward people of other persuasions and superior about their own tribe. They were seen as harsh political partisans, as closed-minded deniers of science. Lyons found himself feeling, at times, embarrassed by what he was hearing about the behavior of the people with whom he shared his passion for Christ. The top-of-mind associations conjured by that word *Christian* seemed to bear little resemblance to the principles of love and compassion that many expected to be the guiding lights of the society's most vigorous and public Jesus followers.

Defensiveness is one way to react to negative appraisals of one's faith and cultural group. Lyons chose another. He listened, put himself in the shoes of the critics, and considered whether aspects of their critique might be valid. Ever the marketer, he contemplated the dire ramifications that Christians' negative image would have for their ability to get a sympathetic listening in their strivings to attract people to Jesus.

Particularly influential in Lyons's remaking were the writings of Charles Colson, the man of Watergate infamy who found Jesus in prison and went on to become a prolific author and leading Christian voice on matters of faith and culture. Although no theological liberal, Colson emphasized an aspect of the Christian life that Lyons had seldom encountered at Thomas Road Baptist Church and Liberty University—Christians' imperative not just to save individual souls and pave the way for sweet rides in the afterlife, not just to go to battle in the political sphere, but also to strive as Christians to shape this earthly mess into something more beautiful, here and now—to *redeem* culture.

"That changed things for me," Lyons explains. "I'd grown up thinking souls were all that mattered. Colson awakened in me the idea that our mission was bigger than that. There was a way things *ought* to be here in this life, too. True Christians catch a vision for how all things can be, how all things can be closer to that perfect state."[8] This ideal state, this way things ought to be, was not something for which Christians should just pray and wait, Lyons realized, but something they were compelled to work for, bring forth, create.

Coming out on the other side of his season of reflection and rebirth, Lyons made an audacious decision. When he told his friend David Kinnaman he was quitting his lucrative job to start a nonprofit with a quixotic-sounding mission, Kinnaman, then vice president of the Barna Group public opinion research firm, had his doubts, to put it lightly. "Are you crazy?" he asked.[9]

In the account appearing within the book that the pair would eventually coauthor, Lyons explained to Kinnaman that he had found his life's purpose: "I want to help a new generation of leaders understand the perceptions and images that young people have of Christianity—what people really think of us," Lyons explained. "People have a lot of opinions about our faith, and every time I strike up a conversation with a friend or neighbor, it seems like those perceptions are incredibly negative. Let's face it—what people think becomes their reality. . . . Some of their thoughts about us might be accurate."[10]

Evangelical Christianity, in other words, had developed a bad reputation. And Lyons was convinced that it was at least partially deserved.

"The image young people have of the Christian faith is in real trouble," Lyons explained to his friend Kinnaman. "I don't understand . . . how that happened, or even whether it's something that can, or should, be fixed. But I want to help start conversations and lead people to start thinking about how to bridge this divide between us and them."[11]

As he made clear in his retelling of the conversation, Kinnaman was struck by Gabe's boldness in giving up an enviable vice president position and salary in favor of launching this new venture—*whatever* it was going to look like. Here was a still-green marketer trying to get his mind and arms around the colossal challenge of improving the public standing of a religion with hundreds of millions of followers and two millennia of history (and baggage). Here was a young Christian devoting himself to nothing less auda- cious than the rebranding of American Christianity. Maybe Gabe Lyons *was* crazy.

America is, in the eyes of the world, a pious nation. It is old news by now that we have rates of religiosity unmatched in other Western, industrialized countries. Impressively large percentages of the population profess belief in God, pray, attend church on a regular or semi-regular basis, attest to faith being an important aspect of their lives—and expect their elected leaders to likewise have strong faith lives. For several decades, Christian religion has been a conspicuous feature of our public life as a nation and culture, with outspoken Christians enjoying high-status success and talking openly and enthusiastically about their beliefs in high-profile spheres such as politics and big-time sports.

Of course, it's one thing to be "pious"—a word suggestive not just of devotion but also of a tendency toward showiness, sanctimony, and even hypocrisy—and quite another to be "religious," to be *truly* Christian (or Jewish, or Muslim, or Buddhist, as the case may be). How do Americans score on that harder test? Does the collective behavior of Americans add up to something we might accurately deem to be "Christian"?

If by "Christian" we mean more than affiliation and identity—if we mean lives lived in accord with the very challenging example and teachings of the Jesus of the New Testament—the United States of America clearly has a way to go.

Not to overstate the case or demonize the generally well-intentioned millions who populate this country. Americans give to charities at impressively high rates. We tend to reach out, with a helping hand as well as donations, when disaster strikes our fellow Americans and fellow humans. Americans are people who shovel snow from our neighbors' driveways, volunteer at soup kitchens and shelters, take care of each other's children and pets in a pinch, and shell out for more expensive energy-saving lightbulbs to reduce our carbon footprints—just because we feel it's the right thing to do. Americans are, in many ways, a *good* people.

Yet in other respects, one finds a wide and impossible-to-ignore gap between the nation's religious piety and our actual behavior. Any clear-eyed survey of the landscape around us, any assessment of the state of the common good, leaves one with grave doubts about whether we as a nation, and as a collection of individuals, live up to the high ideals of the culture's dominant religion. Can anyone say that we are, in this respect, a *Christian* nation?

Violence, for instance, is difficult to square with New Testament teachings about loving one's enemy, about turning the other cheek, about Jesus' followers seeking and bringing peace to their environments. Yet, for all our virtues, American society is, beyond any shadow of doubt, a violent society, inundated by weapons, murders, and other violent crime, by film and television entertainment dripping with blood and the glorification thereof.

In a tragic development that underscored the magnitude of violence in our society, a deeply troubled student went on a shooting spree at Virginia Tech in 2007, killing thirty-two people and then himself. Leery of renewed calls for tougher gun-control laws, defenders of gun rights were quick to point out that mass shootings, however horrific, are quite rare. Perhaps so—although maintaining that front became increasingly difficult in the years that followed, especially after the shooting tragedy at a Connecticut elementary school just days before Christmas in 2012, in which twenty-seven were killed, most of them children. But even if mass shootings are far from everyday occurrences, statistics show that Virginia Tech massacres do happen every day, albeit in a less dramatic form: gun violence kills close to thirty thousand people a year in America, or about eighty a day—more than double the number slain in Blacksburg, Virginia, during Seung-Hui Cho's rampage.[12] As I asked in one of my *USA Today* commentaries, is this rampant violence what one should expect of a country infused with the teachings and wisdom of Jesus, the "Prince of Peace"?

"The anger, the hatred, the bigotry that goes on in this country is getting to be outrageous." So stated Clarence Dupnik, sheriff of Pima County, Arizona, in the grim aftermath of shootings by a crazed gunman that left six dead and Congresswoman Gabrielle Giffords in critical condition. [13] Who can doubt the truth of the sheriff's statement given the political climate we have, one poisoned by vitriol and by rhetoric that seems stuck in perpetual attack mode? As surfaced in the coverage that dominated the media in the ensuing days, Giffords, a Democrat, had been one of about twenty members of Congress whose district showed up on a map that Sarah Palin published on her Facebook page. Giffords and the others were targeted—targeted in a disturbingly literal sense, by gun-sight icons—as vulnerable to Republican challenges in the 2010 congressional elections. [14] It would be grossly unfair to charge, as some overzealous progressives did, that shooter Jared Loughner was acting on behalf of Palin and her political allies. Yet there was something deeply disturbing about Palin's Facebook crosshairs map when seen in juxtaposition with the shooting—all the more so because of Palin's professed Christianity and the adoration with which many politically active evangelicals regarded her at the time.

There's the violence that plagues our streets and schools and the violent rhetoric that pollutes our public discourse. Then there's the violence projected by our government in the country's name and on our citizens' dime. Whatever one thinks of the necessity of the wars in Afghanistan and Iraq, can we say with straight faces that the military actions are those of a peaceful nation created in the image of Christ and steeped in his teachings? It seems particularly difficult to explain the interventionism in Iraq, a preemptive war launched on deceptive grounds that few theologians have been able to square with a Christian just-war doctrine that reserves military action for a special set of circumstances in which war is an unavoidable last resort. Add in the "enhanced interrogation" tactics used in the war against terrorism (better described as "torture"), add in the hundreds of billions of dollars spent on military and defense, add in the Obama administration's aggressive use of drone strikes to kill terrorist targets—the examples could go on and on—and you have a picture of a people who have a lot of killing done on our behalf. One can make a case that this violence is necessary, inevitable. Far harder is making the case that anything about this is deeply *Christian*.

The Bible is replete, of course, with imperatives for people and societies to do by right by those whom Jesus called "the least of these"—the poorest, the weakest, the most vulnerable—and to resist the human tendency to stockpile possessions far in excess of what we truly need. If heeding this call constitutes "Christian" behavior, is the United States a "Christian nation"?

Suffice it to say there is something deeply irreligious about the growing gap between our wealthiest and poorest citizens. The causes and consequences are complex, but it seems beyond question that we have cause for concern when recent decades have witnessed a growing concentration of wealth in the hands of the richest 1 or 2 percent of the population while growing multitudes struggle to meet the most basic needs for themselves and their families. One shudders to think what Jesus might say to a society that blithely accepts, even celebrates, an economic dynamic that produces a relative handful of citizens who own fleets of cars and maybe a private jet or two—necessary, of course, for the shuttling they must do between their four or five mansions—while some on the opposite end of the ladder double their worn-out cars as their places of residence.

Like care for the poor and vulnerable, hospitality to strangers is stressed in the Bible. Those who stand hard against immigrants can certainly make a case for the necessity of their policy preference. But when crackdowns on undocumented immigrants split apart families and cause other forms of human distress, when pious politicians reduce these people to dehumanizing labels like "aliens" and "illegals," the best you can say about the situation is that it's a necessary evil. There is nothing "Christian" about it.

In the interest of fairness, it must be acknowledged that social conservatives would offer their own set of yardsticks in this exercise of judging whether the collective behavior of Americans constitutes something one might call "Christian." As conservatives ask, can a country where abortion is commonplace truly be considered a Christian nation? Can a country that is home to, and tolerant of, rampant adultery, pornography, and alternative sexualities? Can a country where in many spheres of public life the name of Jesus is rarely, if ever, proclaimed?

As discussed throughout this book, it is heartening to see evangelical Christians—and, it must be added, Americans of more secular orientations, as well—asking hard and principled questions that go right to the heart of the kind of country and society we are going to be. But for now, we have what we have: a society of decent individuals who usually do the right thing in countless small ways—but a culture nonetheless marred by violence, greed, sexual abuses and misbehaviors, and politics that often bring out the worst in us. As a 2011 poll found, fewer than a quarter of Americans would give a high score—an A or a B—to the moral state of our union, with 37 percent assigning a D or F.[15] At least we can still recognize bad behavior when we see it. Americans may disagree about the manifestations of our social morality deficit—conservatives will emphasize abortion and sexual immorality; liberals, economic injustice—but we can surely agree that we ought to strive for something finer.

We have just reviewed aspects of the collective behavior of the nation. Focusing our attention on that sizeable subset known for their public passion for Jesus, what assessment can we make of *evangelicals'* contribution to the quality of our national life? Given that many social ills have grown worse during a time of heightened evangelical assertiveness and engagement in politics and the public arena, is it fair to blame them and their religion?

Not really, a broad perspective suggests. There is blame enough for any number of groups and global trends. However, it probably is fair to conclude, all factors considered, that Jesus' most publicly ardent followers have not had the uplifting impact on our national life, have not been the consistent force for decency and integrity, that idealists might expect from Jesus devotees getting busy in the public square. Whether through their policy prescriptions and voting behavior, their tone and tactics, or the examples they have set, the most visible evangelicals and most trend-setting evangelical movements have generally not infected their society with heart-changing virtue and goodness. In some cases, even, they have been more inclined than non-evangelicals to take hard lines and promote harsh measures, appearing, often, to be driven more by nationalism and party affiliation than by the teachings of their good book. Perhaps the fairest assessment would be that they've been human, all too human, and all too quick to set aside principle for the sake of pragmatism and power. "One of the greatest failures of Christians in this country," progressive evangelical leader Jim Wallis writes, "is when they don't think and act as Christians first. Instead, they think first as Americans, consumers, [and] partisans."[16]

The behavior of Christians, as Gabe Lyons correctly sensed, increasingly *mattered* if people outside the church were going to have a positive idea about Christianity. If evangelical Christians were just like everyone else—that is, flawed—but strutted their stuff with an unwarranted air of superiority, what idea would *that* create about the something special that supposedly formed the core of their lives? Gabe Lyons's inquiring mind wanted to know some things: What *were* the lives of evangelicals saying about the validity of their religion, about its ability to make a positive difference in the lives of individuals and societies? Since launching themselves more forcefully into the public square, what impression *had* Lyons's evangelical co-religionists made on those outside the church? With their behavior, how *had* they modeled the evangelical faith for the non-evangelical majority comprising moderate and liberal-leaning Christians and all manner of agnostics, atheists, minority religions, and none-of-the-aboves?

Lyons started where all serious marketing endeavors start. As he informed his friend David Kinnaman, the two were going to undertake a massive market-research project. They were going to study, in a more systematic and rigorous way than had previously been attempted, what Americans really thought of evangelical Christians and why.

What they found was cause for dismay. And extremely useful to know.

"Unchristian."

This was the arresting one-word summation, and the title of the ensuing book, that Lyons and Kinnaman divined from the data that they amassed in their survey of young non-evangelical Americans. What they heard from their survey subjects, though not surprising to the researchers, was unpleasant to contemplate: hypocritical, judgmental, overly political, pushy, anti-gay—these were the ideas their survey subjects had formed about Christians. "Christianity," Kinnaman and Lyons wrote for the book's blunt opening line, "has an image problem." The researchers discovered a remarkable swing in the ten-year period between the mid-1990s and 2004, when they launched the survey that informed *unChristian*. Kinnaman's Barna Group, in a 1996 study titled "Christianity Has a Strong Positive Image Despite Fewer Active Participants," had discovered a positive regard for the faith even among its non-participants.[17] But the young unchurched Americans surveyed for what would ultimately become *unChristian* had mostly negative or neutral impressions. Just 16 percent had a positive impression of Christianity, and just 10 percent expressed a favorable view of "born-again Christians." When the researchers floated the term "evangelical," the metrics plummeted even further. A miniscule 3 percent said they had a good impression of those bearing that descriptor.[18]

The authors quoted one survey subject who had this particularly grim observation: "Most people I meet assume that *Christian* means very conservative, entrenched in their thinking, anti-gay, anti-choice, angry, violent, illogical, empire builders; they want to convert everyone, and they generally cannot live peacefully with anyone who doesn't believe what they believe."[19]

Despite its unpleasant tidings, *unChristian* became a bestseller, its ideas circulating widely and persuasively in evangelical circles. In my own travels through evangelical America, I have found people citing it frequently—even those belonging to organizations and schools of thought that I had assumed were entrenched in their conservatism and impervious to the assessments and critiques of those outside the evangelical subculture. For example, when I traveled to the headquarters of Athletes in Action to research my book on evangelical Christianity in sports—AIA being a branch of the conservative international ministry Campus Crusade for Christ, as it was then called—I heard the organization's soon-to-be president citing the Kinnaman and Lyons book as he explained how and why his ministry was beginning to rethink its way of bringing the gospel forward in and through sports.

Lyons and his friend Kinnaman had captured a subculture's attention. And they had given concerned evangelicals the thorough diagnostics they needed to understand their religion's "image problem," not to mention the substance problems underneath it. To someone paying close attention to the findings and the arresting title of the book—"unChristian"—the root of the problem and the path toward correction were strikingly simple and clear: in a weird way, non-Christians were calling out their evangelical fellow citizens for behavior that added up to something very *un*-Christian. The prescription then revealed itself: If evangelicals were going to make a better account of themselves and their faith outside their subculture bubble, they did not need to hide or ditch their religion. They had to behave in a way that was *more* Christian—truer to the example and teachings of their savior and more in the spirit and mode of the first Christians, those who nurtured and grew the religion through its infancy.

In the years since the publication of *unChristian*, Lyons has positioned himself on the front edge of the change campaign under way in popular evangelicalism. The primary thrusts have included his follow-up book, *The Next Christians*, the church-group study guides he has developed, and the media and speaking appearances he makes. His real calling card, however, is the annual Q conference—a sort of TED Talks for postmodern evangelical leaders and leaders-to-be. The conference convenes some seven hundred church leaders and Christian "influencers" each spring for rapid-fire presentations on new ideas, projects, and possibilities in walks of life from science and technology to spirituality, politics, and pop culture.

More than anything, though, Lyons is using himself—his own life, career, message, and cultural stance—to show his evangelical fellows how a Christian can function credibly, and with positive impact, in a postmodern, post-Christian context. Perhaps the most striking thing about that stance is its simple nondefensiveness. Lyons, like so many like-minded new evangelicals, is strikingly at peace with the clear and not-going-away presence of fellow countrymen and countrywomen who do not share the evangelical faith and probably never will. He is conspicuously free of any anxiety about the reality that "Christian America" is over—and he can even see something positive about it.

"Christians can bemoan the end of Christian America," Lyons told me the first time I interviewed him, "or we can be optimistic about it. What's good is that it forces us to get back to the basics of serving people and loving our neighbors. Through history, Christianity has affected more people from that position than from a position of dominance."[20]

If you want to understand the difference between the old-guard evangelicals and the "next Christians," as Lyons calls them, you can learn a lot from Lyons's receptivity to people and forms of culture that do not bear the explicitly Christian brand.

I caught a glimpse of this the first time I attended Lyons's Q conference. During a break between the quick-hit presentations, I was surprised to notice that the background music filling the vintage opera hall in Chicago was not the Jesus music I was used to hearing at evangelical gatherings. Rather, it was the ethereal strains of Sigur Rós, a secular band from Iceland whose golden-voiced singer is gay. Beauty is beauty, whatever its source—as the Q generation clearly recognizes. As I also discovered, not all the speakers were evangelicals. Some were asked to speak simply because their expertise and message were important—to Christians and whoever else might need to know about the country's changing demographics, for instance, or the struggles of orphans in earthquake-ravaged Haiti.

What might also surprise the uninitiated is the absence of a cross, or anything directly symbolic of Christianity, in the branding on display in the Q conference program and stage design. On the program cover and throughout its pages one finds sophisticated and intriguing graphics evocative of geometry and technology. Projected in huge proportions on the screen behind the stage, there hangs that thought-stirring letter, *Q*. It looms like a question for each attendee—So, how *are* you going to make your faith credible and positive in post-Christian America?—while also suggesting where the young (and not-so-young) Jesus followers can look for cues. To biblical scholars, *Q* is shorthand for *quelle*, the German word for "source," and it refers to a theoretical document believed to have formed the basis for what would become the New Testament gospels of Matthew and Luke. Whether it's Lyons's intention or not, the message seems to be this: Go back to the source—go back to the beginning—to rediscover how Christianity can be vital and attractive again, now and in the future.

That "source" shade of meaning echoes Lyons's message about how our increasingly post-Christian culture compels evangelicals "back to the basics," back to a situation more closely resembling that in which the early Christian church operated. As any young evangelical today will enthusiastically inform you, the early Christians, struggling as they were to gain a foothold in pluralistic and often-adverse settings, spread their religion by becoming known as models of decency, by "branding" themselves as the ones who looked out for the poor, who adopted discarded orphans, and who strove to create loving and compassionate community with one another.

Timothy Keller, a New York City pastor who is looked up to by many young evangelicals, made the following observation about emulating the early church. Speaking with Lyons in filmed dialogue streamed on the Q website, Keller said, "You serve. You don't worry about politics. You attract people to the gospel by beauty of your individual and communal lives."[21] Those early Christians came to be known for two traits you might not expect to go together. They were seen as strange, as Keller put it—and trustworthy.

"Restorers." Such is the one-word summation Lyons conjures to describe essentially the same idea: that Christians can be at their best as viable agents of the Bible in post-Christian America by restoring quality and goodness, by striving to create something closer to the ideal state of affairs—a.k.a. the Garden of Eden, as it existed, in the Bible telling, before the Fall, before human beings' encounter with struggle, disappointment, degradation.

"The next Christians," Lyons writes, "believe that Christ's death and resurrection were not only meant to save people *from* something. He wanted to save Christians *to* something. God longs to restore his image in them and let them loose, freeing them to pursue his original dreams for the entire world. Here, now, today, tomorrow. They no longer feel bound to wait for heaven or spend all their time telling people what they should believe. Instead, they are participating with God in his restoration project for the whole world."[22]

These restorers, as Lyons dubs them, possess a few signal characteristics. Not offended by the broken lives and tarnished social institutions they see, they instead are "provoked," he writes—galvanized into action to make the

given situation better. Too often, in Lyons's view, evangelicals' response to a
drug-addicted person in their lives or community, or to pockets of their cities
plagued by gun violence or sex-industry activity, has been one of taking
offense, voicing stern disapproval, and withdrawing. Provoked Christians, by
contrast, are drawn to that which is degraded and are compelled to address it.
"These Christians don't run from areas that might typically offend a separatist Christian—they run to them," Lyons writes. "They seek out brokenness
and offer hope."[23]

"Separatist Christians," as Lyons calls them, are quick to call foul when it
comes to violent trash in the movie theaters or art that, at first glance, might
seem to denigrate religion. So pronounced is this tendency to withdraw and
condemn that the performing arts and fine arts have been all but ceded to
liberals and secularists. Lyons hails an up-and-coming generation of new
evangelicals who, by contrast, are more inclined to create than criticize and
who are busy producing all manner of "cultural goods"—music, magazines,
films, art, clothes. Don't expect to find crosses or Christian fish symbols
plastered on these creations, or lyrics laced with repetitive Jesus references.
These works are not designed to proselytize and rack up measurable conversions in the mode of conventional twentieth-century evangelism. The "next
Christians," Lyons says, "believe that part of service to God is bringing signs
that point to his Kingdom and tangibly express his love to those in need, even
when the measurable result of conversion can never be tallied."[24]

In *The Next Christians*, Lyons describes several other characteristics of
the new evangelicals: Christians who approach their work lives as "callings"
dedicated to advancing good in the world rather than as mere means-to-an-
end employment; Christians who engage with secular culture but remain
grounded in their faith; Christians who eschew the hyperindividualism advancing in America and instead embrace community; Christians who resist
the temptation to be, first and foremost, relevant and instead commit to being
"countercultural." With respect to that final characteristic, Lyons elaborates:
"They don't concern themselves with popularity, what they can achieve for
themselves, or whether the masses are following. Instead, they boldly
lead."[25] The next Christians, as Lyons sums it up in his book, are forming a
counterculture—a counterculture dedicated to the common good.

As he and I conclude our interview in the Manhattan café where we've
met, Lyons frames his quest in the simplest of terms. "I want to see the
credibility of the Christian faith restored in public life," he stresses. "If peo-

ple saw us doing good in the world, it could change their idea about what Christians are all about."

As I walk with Lyons to the Q office, he stops and chats amiably with a casual-acquaintance neighbor whose path we've crossed. When we move on a minute or two later, Lyons points out to me that the neighbor is, like so many others in this Upper East Side neighborhood, gay. "I wonder what he would think if he knew what kind of work I do," Lyons says with a grin.

Seeing Lyons operate in New York, thinking about the path he trod from Virginia to Atlanta to Manhattan—from the evangelical bubbles of Thomas Road Baptist Church and Liberty University to the mecca of urban, secular sophistication—I find myself recalling lyrics from a song about New York made famous by Frank Sinatra: "If I can make it there, I'll make it any-where."

So it is with the reoriented evangelical Christianity that Lyons and the like minded and like hearted are bringing to life. It's as if Lyons, with his own decision about where to plant his family and himself, is demonstrating in upper-case, large-font terms the way forward for the new evangelicalism. It's as if he's saying: Gravitate to the places that might seem the *least* likely environment for evangelical Christianity. Find ways to make your passion for Jesus tangible and helpful in situations and places where the same old, same old will make you and your faith a laughingstock. For these, increas-ingly, are the setting and modes in which Christianity will be operating in large swaths of the United States, particularly its urban centers.

Can Gabe Lyons and his faith movement make it in New York, and all that New York represents?

Realize that Lyons has his work cut out for him, in multiple respects. As Timothy Keller pointed out to Lyons in the above-mentioned dialogue, as much as younger evangelicals admire the early church, they must accept the fact that there is a significant difference between the challenge facing the Christians of the first few centuries and that facing evangelicals in America today. Today's new evangelicals, Keller pointed out, have considerable *bag-gage* to overcome. Or, to put it in terms that have often occurred to me, American evangelicals of the past few decades have surrounded the baby with a whole lot of unpleasant bathwater—and many people want to throw it all out, baby included.

Understand that Lyons has serious detractors among the ranks of more traditional evangelicals, who find his message too muted, too shy about the standard-fare truth claims of twentieth-century evangelicalism. Doesn't he

come on a bit too strong, they ask, in his assessments of what his evangelicals predecessors have done wrong? Does he really mean to suggest that
evangelicals of a more traditional orientation don't care about being and
doing good? Is he ashamed of Christ? How can his gay neighbor *not* be
informed that Lyons is an evangelical Christian and *not* have found himself
on the receiving end of a talking-to about the need to overcome his unbiblical
sexual attractions? Lyons's playbook, to these critics' eyes, looks awfully
similar to the social gospel of decades past—an experiment they judge a
miserable failure. From these quarters comes great consternation, too, about
the calm acceptance Lyons demonstrates about the end of Christian America.
One blog review trashed Lyons's *The Next Christians* as "dismissive arrogance" and excoriated him for "taking a rather large shovel and packing
down the dirt on the grave of Christianity in America, which he proclaims as
being dead." Challenging Lyons's subtitle, "The Good News about the End
of Christian America," the reviewer, a California minister, declared, "I don't
see anything good—at all—in the thought that 'Christian America' is
dead."[26]

And realize, too, that Lyons faces criticism from some inside the new
evangelicalism—criticisms that Q and all it represents are too white, too
male dominated, too high priced, too upwardly mobile, too hip, too much
about image, and too driven by marketing.

These observations have varying degrees of validity. The critique that
strikes me as particularly worthy of consideration is the one about the relative lack of diversity at Q. It's not as though women and people of color are
completely absent from the stage and crowd at the conferences I have attended, and it's not as though the Q organizers are not mindful of the value of
diverse speakers and attendees. But I believe Lyons and his compatriots
would do well to place greater emphasis on gender and racial inclusiveness.

As for image consciousness, I find the Q aesthetic—the edgy, thought-
provoking graphics and logos in the program book, the sleek stage design,
the constant presence of that evocative "Q" and all it conjures—to be one of
its most intriguing and appealing elements. One, this aesthetic bespeaks creativity, quality, and complexity and, in so doing, accurately conveys the ethos
of the conference and the larger movement it represents. Two, it serves as a
vivid and ever-present reminder to the mostly Christian attendees—and also
to the non-evangelicals who stumble upon videos of the talks on the Internet—that something new and different is afoot with these Q evangelicals,

that they are not the people who onlookers might have assumed evangelical Christians to be.

To the larger point, it's valid to be concerned about the potentially problematic mix of marketing and Jesus. Marketing, in its shallowest forms, can be crass, deceptive, and profit-obsessed—things no Christian would ever want associated with his or her religion. However, marketing at its best is greatly concerned with accuracy and authenticity, and to the extent that it depends on listening and responding to the concerns and perceptions of one's constituents—as all good marketing does—it's as natural and noncontroversial as the act of conversation and relationship building. In that sense, it can be both savvy and sincere—which are two characteristics writ large on the career and personality of Gabe Lyons and those with whom he's in league. Moreover, given the great weight evangelicals place on making their faith public, on reaching those who have not heard their "good news," it would be foolish not to apply the tools of marketing, albeit with a great deal of care and discernment.

The years and decades ahead will reveal whether Gabe Lyons and his project can make it in New York—or Boston, Los Angeles, Chicago, Seattle, or any other place where evangelical Christianity has a status nowhere close to dominant. What's clear now is that Lyons and those around him are on to something, something that could make a positive difference for their religious movement *and* the country. Imagine how the struggles and conflicts around Christianity's role in our politics and public square would change, and likely for the better, if the evangelical "brand" came to be idealism, commitment, and decency mixed in with let's-get-it-done energy and know-how—all aimed at enlarging the common good.

Certainly, many of those outside the camp will object to the supernatural beliefs and claims of evangelicals and their convictions about the nature of God, Jesus' divinity, and so on—as they do now. But as the Lyons vision becomes real and tangible, and as more and more evangelicals can be seen living up to it, doubters and naysayers will be faced with something tougher to shoot down: the concrete reality, on the streets and in their faces, of Christians making things better, of Christians who continually surprise and confound with their inconvenient, self-sacrificial acts of generosity. You won't violate the constitution or incur the wrath of the American Civil Liberties Union, for the most part, by engaging in acts of mind-blowing decency.

"That's the real beauty of it," Shane Claiborne told me. "Secular progressives who have a problem with the notion of a 'Christian nation' probably wouldn't mind if our nation looked a little more like Christ."[27]

New York Times columnist Ross Douthat, a man with conservative leanings and a strong regard for traditional religion, astutely summed up the challenge in a piece appearing a few days before Christmas in 2010. "Christians are no longer what they once were—an overwhelming majority in a self-consciously Christian nation," Douthat wrote. "The question is whether they can become a creative and attractive minority in a different sort of culture, where they're competing not only with rival faiths but with a host of pseudo-Christian spiritualities, and where the idea of a single religious truth seems increasingly passé.

"Or to put it another way, Christians need to find a way to thrive in a society that looks less and less like any sort of Christendom—and more and more like the diverse and complicated Roman Empire where their religion had its beginning, two thousand years ago this week."[28]

Lyons refuses the terms of engagement dictated by the two warring sides of the culture war and the argument about whether the United States of America is, once and for all, a "Christian nation." His, he says, is a third way, and his path is one that runs both higher and deeper. His is a *different* question, and it brings an entirely different yardstick to the exercise of measuring the degree to which this is a Christian nation.

"Rather than being engaged in a divisive cultural war in the hopes of turning back time, [younger Christians] are engaged in pressing social concerns that benefit the common good—not just the Christian good," Lyons writes. "Reaching out to all doesn't threaten Christianity; rather, it creates the type of relationships, perspectives, and dialogues that reinvigorate and renew their commitment to faith. . . . By forging a third way of thinking, young Christians have defused a cultural bomb and made way for two bitterly opposed constituencies to dialogue and perhaps work together."[29]

What a welcome change from the ad-nauseam continuation of a bitter and increasingly pointless argument. When it comes down to it, who cares whether one side can marshal evidence supposedly proving that America is, or is not, a "Christian nation," whatever *that* means?

Better by far the questions—the Big Qs—that Gabe Lyons and his fellow sojourners are raising high for American evangelicalism: If America is a Christian nation, wouldn't it be better if we actually behaved like one? Especially our *Christians*?

Chapter Five

Confession Booth

Mission Preposterous.

So it must have appeared to the small band of Christians at ultra-liberal, more-secular-than-thou Reed College. The challenge: Find a way to mount a positive presence at the end-of-school-year celebration of all that is weird, wild, and druggie at Reed—the infamous campus festival known as Renn Fayre.

"We sat down one day," recalls Tony Kriz, one of the group's advisers at the time, still a young adult himself and fresh from an extended stint doing Campus Crusade for Christ missionary work in Eastern Europe, "and we asked ourselves, 'Can we imagine having a presence at Renn Fayre?' How could we as a Christian group participate in the weekend—participate in a way where we'd truly be part of what's going on, not as outsiders, not in combat form, but truly a part of it, while also being true to what we believe?"[1]

What came next is now legend among the multitudes of younger Christians who have read the mega-selling Christian spirituality book where this story was first told, Donald Miller's *Blue Like Jazz*. "We batted around a bunch of ideas," recalls Kriz, whose goatee and penchant for wearing a hand-knit beanie earned him the nickname "Tony the Beat Poet." "Finally, one of us—I don't remember who it was—threw out the idea that we should do a confession booth."[2]

Christians setting up a confession booth in the midst of the debauchery of Renn Fayre. Right.

In the *Blue Like Jazz* retelling, it was Miller who suggested the confession booth. And it was a joke. "But Tony thought it was brilliant," Miller writes. "He sat there on my couch with his mind in the clouds, and he was scaring the crap out of me because, for a second, then for a minute, I actually believed he wanted to do it." Miller told him then, in no uncertain terms, that they were not going to set up a confession booth at Renn Fayre.

"Oh, we are, Don. We certainly are," Kriz responded with a smile. "We *are* going to build a confession booth. Here's the catch. We are not actually going to accept confessions. We are going to confess to *them*."[3]

Those present looked at each other, stunned by the insanity and brilliance of what they just heard. "It felt," Kriz recalls, "like a God idea."[4]

Renn Fayre arrived, and the makeshift wooden confession booth went up. Then, late on the opening night of the festival, in the midst of fireworks, frenzied dancing, a mob of naked bodies all painted blue, the Christians' confession booth opened for business. And, after a while, a couple of curious Reedies actually ventured in.

Two students came in and sat across from Kriz. He greeted them and began speaking his piece. "The dialogue went something like: 'Hi. This is a confession booth. It's great to have you here,'" Kriz recalls. "'This is a place where confessions are heard. If it's okay, I'd like to begin. Christianity has been responsible for a lot of things I would like to ask your forgiveness for. Things that I don't think represent the heart of Jesus. There've been the Inquisition, the Crusades, racism, wars waged in the name of God and Jesus. And these are things that I think make God's heart sad, that people who claim to know him would do this stuff. And I'm one of them. I want to ask for your forgiveness. Would you please forgive at least me?'

"The students would be completely caught off guard. Their response would be something like, 'That's the most effing beautiful thing I've heard in my life.' Then, after a moment of silence, every time, the students would say, 'Here's a little bit of my story.' Their story would just unfold. Pain, abuse, addiction, whatever it was, they would pour their story out and we'd sit and talk for twenty, thirty minutes at a time. Seems like that chair was never empty. As soon as somebody got out, somebody else would walk up and wander inside."[5]

When he read about the confessions at Reed, Dan Merchant was moved. Merchant, a television and film producer in Portland and, like Kriz, an evangelical with no interest in Christian culture wars, felt inspired to build on the concept. Merchant decided to set up a confession booth of his own and film it for his movie in progress, *Lord, Save Us from Your Followers*. He, too, would take his turn confessing the sins of the evangelical church. And he would do it in a setting that would match, even trump, the Reed campus in any measure of places where you would least expect a confession booth with a Christian inside. He would do it at Portland's annual gay pride festival. And his confession would zero in on a certain kind of sin: evangelical mistreatment of gay people.

"Christians are famous for saying, 'We have the truth.' How annoying is it to hear *that* from someone?"[6] Merchant, in his office in a Portland suburb, is wearing his usual uniform—a T-shirt, jeans, a slick pair of sneakers—as he recalls for me the creative thought process that compelled him to set up his confessional at the gay pride festival. He remembers how his mind was blown by the confession booth scene in *Blue Like Jazz*—by the idea of Christians being strong not in their loud assertions but in their willingness to be meek and vulnerable, to acknowledge their faults. "Jesus wasn't strident and arrogant and obnoxious," Merchant continues. "Particularly, if you look at his interactions with people who weren't believers, he was so respectful, so gracious and understanding. The only times he is popping off is with the religious guys who are telling him that he is doing it wrong. That's fascinating to me. When I see those kinds of examples, things that echo Christ's example, like Miller and Kriz doing the confession booth, I think, wow, what a fascinating way to connect."[7]

Organizers of the gay pride festival thought he was crazy when he approached them and asked for permission to set up his booth and film the proceedings inside it, Merchant recalls. They told him most attendees would probably breeze by and not give it a second thought. At most, they might do a double take—and then continue making their beeline to the beer. The festival organizers warned Merchant that few, if any, of the revelers would actually stop and brave the inside of the booth. But if he wanted to waste his time, he could go right ahead.[8]

As you know if you have seen the Merchant film, a steady stream of gay festival-goers did enter the booth. And what they heard stunned them. Penitently, sounding a little nervous at times, Merchant acknowledged the way the American evangelical church, in its rhetoric and behavior, had sinned against the gay community. Christians, he confessed, had condemned and demonized gay people with a coldness, a harshness, unbecoming of Jesus followers. Christians, he acknowledged, had turned a blind eye to the AIDS crisis because its victims were largely gay. Christians, he admitted, had told mean-spirited gay jokes. And Merchant did the hardest thing of all. Right to the faces of his confession hearers, square in the sights of the cameras and the movie audiences that would witness the event in the months ahead, he admitted that had done these things, too. And he was sorry.

Once they got over their surprise—this Christian is apologizing to *us*?—the confession hearers invariably opened up. They told stories of being shunned by their families because of their orientation. They spoke of Christians' incessant criticism of gay people and how it had convinced them they wanted nothing to do with those people or their religion. Some shed tears. One man, mentioning that Merchant himself must be gay if he were engaged in an act like this, was shocked and deeply touched when his confessor corrected the record and pointed out that he was straight. [9]

To witness the effect of his confession on his hearers was "a beautiful thing," Merchant reflects. It was hard, too—especially when their tears flowed. The painful dynamic around the evangelical church and the gay community was no longer a mere abstraction. "Suddenly, these people are living, breathing human beings," Merchant says. "If you believe what I believe, that gay people are loved by God just as much as I'm loved by God and as much as you're loved by God, then we can't really be okay with the fact that these people have been so hurt by us." [10]

As one senses watching the scene in Merchant's film, there is something disarming and powerful about evangelical Christians turning the tables and, after decades of showing a public face of judgment, condemnation, and superiority, confessing their and their movement's sins to their fellow human beings. Hostilities melt away. New avenues suddenly appear for conversation, for people getting to know one another.

Is this an act of selling out the faith? The opposite, actually. Recall how Tony Kriz framed the thought process of the Reed College Christians as they groped for a way to mount a presence at Renn Fayre: They wanted to be positive, and they wanted to be true to their Christian beliefs. Humbly acknowledging one's faults and failures and asking for forgiveness—confessing one's sins—*is* a deeply Christian thing to do. It is, to use the words of Tony Kriz, "a God idea."

It is also a *good* idea. I believe that all sides in the culture wars could use a little mutual confessing. Both the evangelicals and those ensconced within the secular, progressive camp have misdeeds and indefensible behavior patterns to 'fess up to. And both sides, frankly, would benefit from hearing acknowledgment of fault—some "repentance," if you will—from the quote-unquote other side.

Thinking about the behavior of evangelical Christians in our nation's public life and observing the correctives of the new evangelicals, I would identify some of the following behavior patterns as worthy fodder for Christian confessions, as subjects for apologies I would most like to hear if *I* were the agnostic, left-wing Reedie slipping into the Tony Kriz/Donald Miller confession booth at Renn Fayre.

If you are worrying that this narrative will turn into yet another secular broadside against people of evangelical faith, be patient; a role reversal of sorts is coming in the closing chapter. More important, bear in mind the fact that evangelicals themselves are among the most passionate and candid voices in acknowledging the misdeeds described below. Theirs are the diagnoses and prescriptions—the confessions and apologies—that carry the most credibility.

1. MISPLAYING THE GOD CARD IN POLITICS

It might seem like long ago given the lineup changes we have witnessed in the top tiers of American politics, but it wasn't that far back—2004, to be exact—when many Republicans of the evangelical persuasion were claiming with utter confidence, complete sincerity, that George W. Bush was God's president, and "GOP" stood for "God's Own Party." Typifying the spirit of the 2004 presidential campaign and the faith-and-patriotism-drenched Republican National Convention, one alternate convention delegate declared to the press, "President Bush supports God, and God supports President Bush, absolutely."[11] The then-president, for his part, had been invoking religious themes to justify the war in Iraq, stating on numerous occasions that freedom—the objective in Iraq, as he framed it—was not America's gift to mankind but "God's gift to every man and woman in this world."[12]

Events left the president's supporters with no choice but to tamp down the hyperbole about Bush's special status with the divine. Things took a turn for the worse in Iraq, then in New Orleans with the Hurricane Katrina debacle, and the president's approval ratings plummeted. The rhetoric about God and Bush, dubious even when the president was riding high, began to look downright foolish. God was the engineer of a war that was seeing more and more American soldiers killed and maimed by crude roadside bombs in Iraq? God was *for* the rampant "collateral damage"—many tens of thousands of Iraqis killed, not to mention six hundred thousand Christians eventually being forced to flee[13]—that was happening in the aftermath of "Mission Accomplished"? God was guiding the man at the helm of the bumbling federal response to a Katrina disaster, a response that contributed to thousands of people being left homeless and hungry while a nation watched on television, growing ever more appalled?

Before we start hurling stones, it is worth remembering that all of us can get caught up in the excitement of our various moments. And, yes, much of the rhetoric was stagecraft, theater; it wasn't as though every Bush promoter actually believed that God had literally chosen Bush and was directing his every move and thought like a celestial puppet master. Even so, the talking points began to sound utterly laughable—embarrassing, frankly—and one heard less and less of them as Bush's second term wound down.

Unfortunately, new examples of self-serving partisan God talk seem always to be coming over the transom. A true classic was offered in 2011 by Congresswoman Michele Bachmann, then running for the GOP presidential nomination, who asserted that recent hurricanes and earthquakes were God's wake-up call to the American people to rein in government spending (a comment that her campaign later said was intended as a joke by the evangelical candidate).[14] Any number of additional examples can be gleaned from the public comments of conservative Christian television commentator Pat Robertson. Many conservatives no doubt see the God invocations of liberal evangelical leaders such as Jim Wallis of Sojourners as similarly self-serving and inappropriate.

As I wrote in *USA Today* in the midst of Bush's second-term struggles and the cessation of hype about his special status with God, a lesson could be found in the Bush God-talk phenomenon—a lesson that our political leaders and string pullers, and all of us on the receiving end of their messages, would do well to remember when we are tempted by dubious God references made in the attempt to win points in rough-and-tumble political competitions: whether our cause is liberal or conservative, Democratic or Republican, we need to be careful, need to be modest, in our claims of divine backing, lest unfolding events embarrass us and discredit our sloppy playing of the God card.

2. HAVING A PERSECUTION COMPLEX

If we are to believe the rhetoric of some of the most seen, most heard evangelicals who appear in the media, if we are to accept what is printed in the newsletters and e-mail appeals of stalwart Christian Right organizations like the Family Research Council, we might conclude that Christians are being thrown to the lions these days, at least in the metaphorical sense. Christ followers are being persecuted! Sinister liberal politicians and activists are trying to ban all vestiges of our cherished faith! There's a war on Christians!

No, there isn't.

It must be said that certain anti-religion loudmouths have made this move too easy with the volume and mean-spiritedness of their polemics against Christians and their faith. And, yes, inexorable social trends appear to be stacked higher and higher against conservative-values Christians. To their eyes, much appears to have changed for the worse in American society in recent decades, making it more difficult for them to lead the godly lives they intend: stricter limits on explicitly Christian expression in schools and other public settings; growing public acceptance of homosexuality and out-of-wedlock births; television and movies drenched with sex and profanity; the gradual advance of other religions and of secularism in America, to name but a few of the trends that upset Christian conservatives.

These concerns and objections are understandable. But send them through the rhetoric-production mill, and what comes out on the other side sounds like this hyperbolic, credulity-breaking pitch for a "War on Christians" conference that the group Vision American organized in 2006: "Christians are under a constant, relentless attack—from Hollywood, the news media, activist organizations, and the cultural elite."[15]

If the objective is to rile people up to the point where they are willing to attend a given event, donate to a particular organization, or vote for a certain politician—which it usually is—this bombast might make sense. But it comes at a serious cost—to the credibility of the crafters of these messages, to those scapegoated as the perpetrators and defenders of these supposed menaces, and to our ability as a society to work through our differences and achieve something approaching common understanding. So, too, does it trivialize the real persecution of Christians in the early history of the church, and the real abuse unleashed on Christians today in some corners of the world.

"Every time evangelicals indulge in hysterics about the persecution of American evangelicals and 'how liberals are waging a war against Christians,' they weaken their own case against the tyranny of the majority in the Middle East and insult those congregations huddling behind drawn curtains in Egypt and Libya," journalist Molly Worthen wrote in *Foreign Policy*.[16]

"Scholars of evangelicalism have long observed that cultivating a persecution complex—even one that is mostly a self-perpetuating fiction—is not a bad way to maintain authority and stoke followers' sense of divine purpose. The trouble," Worthen rightly concluded, "is that this mindset may make evangelicals look less like their oppressed brethren and more like the very despots they hate."[17]

While cultural trends may feel like persecution to some evangelical Christians, coolheaded assessments of the situation demolish any case for the existence of a large-scale persecution campaign in the United States. If such a dark campaign is afoot, it can only be judged an abject failure. Evangelical Christians hold many of the highest political offices in the land,[18] not to mention positions of influence in business, sports, and many other walks of life. One of our two dominant political parties is so in the thrall of evangelical Christians that its candidates have to play up their faith and "values" bona fides early, often, and always if they stand any chance whatsoever of winning nominations and elections. This hardly conjures a picture of Christians on the run, hiding in corners, or, as the perceptive writer Worthen frames it, "huddling behind drawn curtains."

To the extent that evangelicals Christians do suffer from an image problem, a response of feisty defensiveness and over-the-top "oppression" rhetoric is the opposite of a remedy. It can only make the problem worse.

3. NEGLECTING THE PLIGHT OF THE POOR

We could debate endlessly what Christianity is "really about." Proclaiming Jesus' divinity? Making it to heaven and avoiding hell? Standing for traditional sexual morality? Becoming a better person? Creating a just society? Arguments are made for all of these and many more. But what seems beyond question is the centrality of an overarching Christian ethic—an ethic explicated and illustrated over and over and over in Bible stories and verses—that compels Jesus' followers to care for the poor. Depending on one's counting technique, the Bible contains as many as two thousand, even three thousand, verses dealing with the imperative to aid the poor—far more than you will find on heaven or hell, adultery or homosexuality, or other issues that are frequently emphasized in public arguments about what it means to be Christian. The ethic is beautifully evoked in the gospel of Matthew, in the oft-cited line from Jesus that says, "Whatever you did for one of the least of these brothers of mine, you did for me"[19]—"the least," of course, meaning the poorest, those without clothing and shelter, the sick and the imprisoned.

If we examine the behavior and rhetoric most visible in our public square over recent decades, if we ask non-Christians what they have seen and heard from their evangelical fellow citizens, will we reach the conclusion that those who make the most of their Christian faith have lived up to this calling? Have they put themselves on the line for "the least"?

Not nearly as well as one might expect given the centrality of faith in their lives, and given the centrality of the care-for-the-poor teachings in the Bible. Certainly not in the sphere of politics and in the public debates about the kind of society America aspires to be. Certainly not if we are to judge by the emphases and priorities of the Christians we are most used to seeing and hearing in our national life.

Evidence of this obscuring of the care-for-the-poor imperative can be found in public opinion data generated by Harris Interactive in 2009. Although 80 percent of those surveyed claimed familiarity with the Bible, nearly half—46 percent—incorrectly said that the Bible had more to say on heaven, hell, adultery, pride, or jealousy than any other issues.[20]

Curiously, only 13 percent of those surveyed could correctly identify the source of the following principle: "You must defend those who are helpless and have no hope. Be fair and give justice to the poor and homeless." Fifty-four percent misattributed it to a variety of contemporary politicians and celebrities, including Barack Obama, Oprah Winfrey, and Bono. Let the record show that the actual source is the Bible—Proverbs 31:8–9.[21]

How revealing that so many people would associate this message about justice for the poor with famous liberal politicians and celebrities instead of the Bible, its real source. An article about the survey in the *Washington Post*'s "On Faith" forum used these words to sum up a major takeaway: "Christians Losing Their Way."[22]

To be fair, relative neglect of the poor is not a fault that can be laid solely or primarily at the feet of evangelical Christians. Liberal religionists and secularists cannot claim anything approaching perfect virtue on this score, either. So, too, must it be said that many evangelical Christians *do* act on behalf of the homeless and hungry in ways large and small. We are talking here about emphases, priorities, levels of commitment—the degree to which evangelicals Christians have gone "all in" on the imperative to care for the poorest and most vulnerable segments of the population.

"The problem isn't that Christians aren't doing their share to address the ills of poverty and injustice. The problem is that we too often see our efforts as supplementary to our Christianity." So write Lamar Vest and Richard Stearns of the American Bible Society and the Christian international relief organization World Vision, respectively. "Care for the poor and suffering," Stearns and Vest continue, "should be at the core of our Christian faith because it is at the core of God's desire—written large across the pages of the Bible."[23]

When complaints arise about divisive insertions of Christianity into public debates, many defenders of the faith shrug, as if to say this is a relatively minor concern at most, a situation that cannot be avoided. They invariably aver that non-Christians will always take offense when the gospel is proclaimed—that Jesus himself is inherently divisive, a separator of believers from unbelievers, of the righteous from the unrighteous. Yet imagine how the dynamics would change if applying the Bible to our public life centered on the welfare of the least fortunate among us, if Christians became known first and foremost for accentuating and living out the care-for-the-poor message of the Bible? To the extent that this ethic was framed as a challenge to our capitalist economic system, this could have a divisive dimension in politics. But at the grassroots level, in the domain of non-political everyday behavior, it is difficult to imagine this ethic running into significant pushback or prompting credible charges of Christian divisiveness. Can you really see the public complaining about those obnoxious Christians who are spending their time helping the poor and sick?

Were this biblical imperative to become the main thrust of Christianity in action in our public life, a world of good would be accomplished—for the poor, of course, but also for the important project of creating a more positive understanding of evangelicals and a less warlike public square.

As the megachurch leader and author Rick Warren observes, "The New Testament says the church is the body of Christ, but for the last one hundred years, the hands and feet have been amputated, and the church has just been a mouth. And mostly, it's been known for what it's against. . . . I'm so tired of Christians being known for what they're against."[24]

In the public understanding, what *will* Christians be known for? "By their fruit you will recognize them," says the gospel of Matthew.[25] By their fruit—by what they do, by the good they create or the harm they cause—will evangelicals be known. By Christians' fruit will the validity of the faith be evaluated in an increasingly skeptical "post-Christian" America.

Would that the fruit became, above all else, evangelicals' abiding care for those most in need. How regrettable that, to this point, it has not.

4. OFFERING SIMPLISTIC, ONE-SIZE-FITS-ALL SOLUTIONS TO COMPLEX PROBLEMS

Alarmed by rising levels of gang activity and declining educational achievement in a large swath of inner-east Portland, Ben Sand and Anthony Jordan did what devout Jesus followers so often do when a social problem hits them in the heart and leaves them feeling "convicted," as it's often put in the evangelical parlance. They got busy bringing Jesus to the rescue. Sand, a young white man who grew up in Spokane, Washington, and Jordan, an African American and former high school football star who had been a half-in gang member himself before finding Jesus, launched a Young Life program in the affected area of the city.

Young Life can be thought of as the high school analog to Campus Crusade for Christ—a program to "bring the good news of Jesus Christ into the lives of adolescents," to quote its mission language. Jordan and Sand indeed did bring the news, and bring it well. Or so it appeared. Hundreds of kids, mostly kids of color and mostly from disadvantaged circumstances, were committing themselves to Jesus. By 2005, Jordan and Sand were directing what had become one of the largest urban Young Life programs in the country.[26]

As pleased as they were by the number of kids coming to meetings, attending Young Life summer camp, and accepting Jesus, the Young Life leaders were disturbed by something that wasn't changing in the kids' lives. Their circumstances tended to remain as dire and dysfunctional as before—a pattern of absentee parents, pressure from gangs, poor conditions in their schools. And even though they had confessed Jesus as their lord and savior, many of the young participants continued to succumb to the same destructive behaviors that had motivated Jordan and Sand to start the Young Life program in the first place. They kept getting arrested, dropping out of high school, getting each other pregnant, and having babies out of wedlock. "One kid who had accepted Jesus two weeks before shot and killed another kid," Sand recalls. "We went from celebrating his conversion to helping the police track him down."[27]

One of the final straws—not as dramatic as the murder, but disheartening just the same—was watching one of the most promising young participants suddenly drop out of school and take a job at Burgerville. "Anthony and I are looking at each other, and we're both thinking, 'It's time to shut it down,'" Sand says. "We realized that while all of these young people needed Christ, Christ was not *all* they needed."[28]

Instead of giving up or continuing to bang their heads against proverbial walls, Jordan and Sand stepped back for perspective, re-examined their challenge and strategy, and came back with a new solution—still faith-based, to be sure, but with a more varied and sophisticated tool kit. Jordan and Sand founded the Portland Leadership Foundation, part of a network of leadership foundations around the country operating in urban cores. In addition to providing academic support and college scholarships to disadvantaged high school students, the Portland chapter now advises directors of the numerous nonprofits and schools already on the ground addressing aspects of the city's urban challenge—nonprofits often in dire need of expert input on how to refine their strategies and solidify their finances. In a sense, Jordan and Sand transformed themselves from evangelists to expert helpers.

As impressive as it is to see a case study like this, the first part of Sand's and Jordan's story—the installation of the Young Life chapter in a struggling city sector—is probably more illustrative of what evangelicals have become known for over the sweep of recent decades: simplistic, one-size-fits-all solutions to complex, multidimensional problems. At least to outsiders' eyes, society seems to be in the midst of an urgent large-scale, real-life problem-solving workshop, one requiring the best thinking from science, the social sciences, public policy, any discipline you can name, and all the Christians appear to have brought to the table are their prayers, their faith-and-family nostrums, their proclamations that Jesus is Lord. Do these really *help*?

The truth is, Jesus can be a large part of the answer if you think about it a certain way. But it requires more work and more thinking than merely dispensing Bibles and running a Young Life chapter, as Jordan and Sand realized. It requires some translating, some extrapolating, some serious analysis of what it means to apply a two-thousand-year-old religion to complex urban problems in the twenty-first century—some serious augmenting of religion with rigorous data, thought, creativity, and strategy.

"Unhelpful" is not something evangelicals would want on their calling cards, but unfortunately, that is precisely the assessment we see in commentaries like this from Frank Bruni of the *New York Times*. "To get us out of this mess," Bruni wrote, "we need a full range of extant remedies, a tireless search for new ones and the nimbleness and open-mindedness to evaluate progress dispassionately and adapt our strategy accordingly. . . . Seeking relief from the country's woes through a louder, more ardent appeal to God strikes us as too much hope invested in too magical a solution. It suspends disbelief and defies rigorous reason."[29]

Bruni's piece was focused on then-presidential candidate Rick Perry and the showy prayer rallies he had held in 2011—one, a prayer for rain in drought-stricken Texas; the other, a call to the nation to turn back to God for solutions and succor in the midst of our national woes (the latter rally seen by many skeptics as a political event more than a religious event, set in a huge football stadium and just days before the launch of the Texas governor's campaign for president).

Times columnist Bruni was probably being a bit too rough; those with a generous view of Christians can appreciate the value in people humbling themselves in prayer, as if to concede their ultimate smallness and powerlessness in a huge, huge universe. But at the same time, it's easy to see how doubting Thomases like Bruni cannot help but roll their eyes when their Christian fellow citizens start grasping at supernatural straws. And to see Perry's prayer for rain, for divine solutions to America's problems, in juxtaposition with his perceived anti-intellectual, anti-science stance on burning issues like evolution and climate change is to sense a kind of blind faith, benighted faith, as observed by Bruni and many skeptics of similar stripes.

The *Times* writer had the decency to acknowledge in the column that secularists and liberals were prone to their own ideologies, their own "faiths," but his conclusion zeroed in on the evangelicals again, and it captured the essence of the grudge that many non-evangelicals have been nursing for many years. "Faith and prayer just won't cut it," Bruni wrote. "In fact, they'll get in the way."

Not a place where well-intentioned religious people would want to be—getting in the way of solutions to society's pressing problems. One can hope that the course change exemplified by the erstwhile Young Life leaders in Portland heralds the nature of things to come, the day when evangelicals are known for incessantly showing up where human need is greatest, showing up, first and foremost, *to help*.

5. GIVING UNYIELDING, UNQUESTIONING SUPPORT TO ISRAEL (AS IF THE PALESTINIANS WERE SOMETHING LESS THAN HUMAN)

As the United Nations approached a key vote on Palestinian statehood, Pat Robertson's Christian Broadcasting Network newsreel issued an urgent headline: "Robertson Asks Christians to Pray for Israel."[30]

Praying for Israel seems, on its face, a perfectly decent thing for the religiously inclined to do, as would praying for the people of any country. But be clear: Robertson's was not a simple expression of concern for the well-being of the people of Israel, or of the Jewish people around the world who identify strongly with Israel, but a petition to God to intervene in a pending vote by the United Nations on a thorny issue of international politics. As the article explained, Robertson was calling on Jesus' followers to pray "that the U.N. will not vote to create a Palestinian state, that Israel will never be divided into two countries, [and] that the U.S. will remain a strong supporter of Israel."

For non-evangelical writers on religion in public life, it's a little cheap to pluck something from Robertson's ample body of work while mounting examples of evangelical misbehavior. Yet, in this case, Robertson's call to pray for Israel, coupled with his absence of compassionate regard for the plight of the Palestinians—the other human beings wrapped up in this Middle East drama—typifies a larger state of affairs: a disturbing pattern that finds American evangelicals throwing their unquestioning, unyielding support behind the Israeli government's policies and actions, claiming it is nothing less than their Christian obligation to do so. Along with this comes what is at best a neglect of the humanitarian consequences borne by the Palestinian people and at worst a palpable enmity toward the Palestinians, as if they were somehow less than fully human.

True, there is something worthy of applause in this staunch evangelical support of Israel that we see today. It is substantially better than the anti-Semitism that stains Christendom's history. Nevertheless, much like that headline from the Christian Broadcasting Network, the equation—the urgent call to prayer for Israel and *only* Israel, apparently—is conspicuously one-sided, halfhearted.

"The evangelical tradition," evangelical theologian Paul Louis Metzger writes disapprovingly, ". . . has often favored the State of Israel over the

Palestinians and has not generally attended to the Palestinian people's concerns—Christian and Muslim Palestinians alike."[31]

One hears a more emphatic denunciation of the behavior pattern from Metzger's evangelical compatriot David Gushee, a professor at Mercer University who is part of a group called the New Evangelical Partnership for the Common Good. In an open letter to Christian Zionists, coauthored with Glen Stassen, a professor at Fuller Theological Seminary, Gushee writes an indictment that could peel paint: "The prevailing version of American Christian Zionism—that is, your belief system—underwrites theft of Palestinian land and oppression of Palestinian people, helps create the conditions for an explosion of violence, and pushes U.S. policy in a destructive direction that violates our nation's commitment to universal human rights. In all of these, American Christian Zionism as it currently stands is sinful and produces sin."[32]

Evangelical supporters of Israel do not have to believe that Palestinians are angels for them to have a heart for their suffering. They do not have to drop their legitimate concerns for the security of Israel and its people. Challengers of the orthodoxy, like Metzger and Gushee, are not asking all that much of their evangelical brothers and sisters when it comes to Israel and Palestine. Just this: Remember that nowhere in the New Testament does Jesus implore his followers to love only a favored few. Remember that the Palestinians are people—are "God's children"—too. Remember *them* in your prayers as well.

6. ACTING AS THOUGH ONLY THEY HAVE VALUES

Every fall, politically oriented Christian conservatives beat a well-worn path to the nation's capital for an annual event sponsored by a veritable "Who's Who" of Christian Right institutions—the American Family Association, the Family Research Council, Liberty University, and others. Politicians seeking to curry the favor of the organizers and attendees flock there as well, parading to the dais to deliver red-meat speech after red-meat speech denouncing the secularists and liberals and calling for the restoration of a godly America. The conference title has a nice ring to it: The Values Voter Summit. And that self-bestowed term, "values voter," circulates far and wide as a convenient label for the cadre of politically conservative evangelical Christians who get so much attention from the media and Republican politicians.

Problem: Who decided that you have "values" if, and only if, you're a conservative Jesus-confessing opponent of gay rights, abortion, and government regulation?

As I proclaimed in a *USA Today* column, *I* am a values voter. *I* "vote my values." And you are a values voter, too. We all vote our values, different though they might be.

There is something superior, something arrogant, about Republican evangelicals suggesting that only those Americans who share their staunch opposition to abortion and same-sex relationships possess something deserving of the term *values*. According to the rhetoric of Christian social conservatives, progressives are the "anything goes" lot. Secularists, liberal Christians, and followers of other faiths—they're the ones tearing America down with their moral weakness and their supposed hostility to the conservative Christian worldview and, worse yet, to God.

Inaccurate and unfair, as poor a representation of Jesus as you can imagine, this haughty contempt for "the other" extends well beyond the Washington-area hotel ballrooms where the "values voters" gather each year. For three or four decades, evangelicals (or, more precisely, a subset of their movement) have filled their churches and airwaves with rhetoric that elevates their own virtue and demeans those with different beliefs, different political persuasions.

In place of the ethic of Lincoln, in place of an approach to politics that would summon our "better angels," these Christians have projected "an exclusionary and intolerant faith," Seattle columnist Joel Connelly writes, "with a thinly veiled message: Our kind are superior because we're saved."[33]

Writing during the summer of 2011, when GOP presidential contenders were wooing Iowa evangelicals and the rhetoric was getting white-hot, Connelly continued: "What's missing is humility, one of the Seven Heavenly Virtues, and the unheroic attributes of modesty, openness, and charitable treatment of opposing views. . . . The result is a salting and deepening of national divisions. . . . Totally overlooked are thoughts like the opening words from the Prayer of Saint Francis: 'Lord, make me an instrument of your peace. Where there is hatred, let me sow love.' Instead, we are daily reminded of Dietrich Bonhoeffer's admonition: 'Cheap grace is the grace we bestow on ourselves.'"[34]

No doubt, shabby treatment of those on the other side of the argument is not a "sin" borne only by the nation's politically conservative evangelicals. It is emblematic of a larger problem that has hamstrung the country's ability to muster enough political agreement to devise and implement solutions to the national problems, a phenomenon that pundit David Brooks has rightly identified as "solipsism"—a word suggesting self-absorption or "extreme preoccupation with one's feelings and desires," as the dictionary puts it. With that self-absorption comes an utter failure to acknowledge the legitimate and inevitable existence of other schools of thought and the reality that none of us is going to have our way each and every time—the truth that we share this country and share the power, and that our political enemies might have something useful to offer. "The political culture," Brooks writes, "encourages politicians and activists to imagine that the country's problems would be solved if other people's interests and values magically disappeared."[35]

They will not disappear. Whether the "other people" are the Unitarians, the atheists, or the bleeding-heart-liberal Jesus followers, they exist. They have hopes and aspirations. They have numbers. The same applies to the problem of overly certain secularists who carry on as though human progress can proceed if and only if religion and its benighted adherents are consigned to history's dustbin. If history teaches us anything, the religionists and their faiths have staying power. It is highly unrealistic, not to mention just plain wrong, to expect that those with whom we disagree will cower or surrender, that their ideas will go *poof* and fade into oblivion. We ought to expect something better from believers in a savior who had the audacity to insist that his followers do nothing short of "love" their fellow human beings.

7. FOCUSING ON HEAVEN AT THE EXPENSE OF ADDRESSING THE VARIOUS HELLS ON EARTH

Running through American evangelicalism is a current of thought and belief that tells you this old world isn't worth much. This mind-set rests on a fatalistic regard for the fate of the planet and its people, coupled with a big bet on the sweet hereafter, an eternity of bliss and blessing for those who believe the right way. With this comes the conviction that staving off wholesale destruction is a distraction from soul saving or, worse, an act of faithlessness, of getting in God's way. At the extreme end of this train of thought come figures such as Todd Strandberg, founder of the Rapture Ready website, who opposes environmental protection on the following grounds: "The Bible predicts that during the tribulation hour, the world will come to near complete ruin," Strandberg writes. "I am strongly against Christians embracing the environmental movement."[36]

Work for a better future? *What* future?

For liberal religionists and non-believers, this stance has to be one of the least appealing aspects of the evangelicalism they encounter. To them, it smacks of a situation in which people in a boat are rowing frantically away from a waterfall, fighting a hard current, while another group in the same boat sit idly as the vessel drifts closer to the precipice, helping not a bit and waiting for the divine hand to pluck them (and only them) from disaster.

Fatalism might be an understandable response to the bloody travails of the twentieth century. There's nothing quite like world wars and holocausts when it comes to sapping the hope and optimism vitally necessary to creating a better future. And to the extent that proclaimers of this belief set have dedicated themselves to sharing this promised afterlife with as many non-believers as possible—a major point of evangelism—they cannot be accused of unalloyed selfishness.

Yet there is something disturbing about evangelical Christians abdicating responsibility to join in the work of staving off disaster and improving conditions in the here, now, and future—an assessment holding wider and wider sway even within evangelical circles.

The problem with end-times and heavenly preoccupations is the disempowering effect they have on one's ability to do anything constructive in this place, in this time. In his influential *Surprised by Hope*, the British author and theologian N. T. Wright calls on Christians not to focus so much on life after death that they forget what ought to be crucially important to Jesus' followers—life *before* death.[37]

Better by far is the commitment of so many up-and-coming evangelicals who, by fighting poverty, by organizing for the abolition of nuclear weapons, by trying to conserve an environment in which people can flourish for the long term, are channeling their passions instead into enhancing life in *this* time, and *this* place.

This imagined soul baring could go on for a while. Depending on his or her experiences and ideas, the non-evangelical confession-hearer might want an apology for many evangelicals' uncritical support for "enhanced interrogation" and other aggressive, violent tactics undertaken in the quest for national security. She or he might want some 'fessing up about the church's dehumanizing of women who have made the difficult decision to have abortions. Maybe the hearer would like acknowledgment of the willful mischaracterization of Islam and mistreatment of Muslims in this country, as though the cherished principle of religious freedom applies to everybody but followers of Islam. Maybe the hearer would like an apology for the way evangelicals of a more fundamentalist stripe have dismissed science and insisted on the promotion of creationism in public schools and other public venues. Maybe the issue is the way women have often been treated as second-class citizens in the evangelical church. Insert your pet grievance here.

The point—the phenomenon that's striking and impressive—is that for each of these misdeeds we hear acknowledgment and contrition from within the ranks of evangelical America. We see the "foul" being called by the people with the most persuasive vantage point of all on these matters: evangelicals themselves. And their basis for doing so is the one that speaks loudest to those whose behavior is at issue: the teachings and example of their savior.

Consider these confessions the beginning of an informal grassroots truth-and-reconciliation process, one that promises balm for the culture's old wounds and the opening we need if the country is ever going to get past its unproductive enmities.

Those of a secular, progressive persuasion, no matter how justified they might be in their negative views of Christians, would be wise to hear these confessions and consider their meaning. Isn't this the sound of invitation from potential new friends and allies? How could one not be moved by words of apology like these from Shane Claiborne?

"To all my nonbelieving, sort-of-believing, and used-to-be-believing friends: I feel like I should begin with a confession. I am sorry that so often the biggest obstacle to God has been Christians. Christians who have had so much to say with our mouths and so little to show with our lives. I am sorry that so often we have forgotten the Christ of our Christianity.

"Forgive us. Forgive us for the embarrassing things we have done in the name of God."[38]

I can only speak for myself. But to Shane Claiborne, Dan Merchant, Tony Kriz, and the legions of other evangelicals brave enough and humble enough to acknowledge the sins of the evangelical church, I respond with the words of the Reedie who slipped into that Renn Fayre confession booth and lent an ear to Tony the Beat Poet: These confessions are some of the most beautiful words I've heard for quite some time.

Apology accepted.

Chapter Six

Breaking Formation

Lisa Sharon Harper bled blue from the time she was young. The African American daughter of a Democratic activist, canvasser, and election judge, Harper grew up steeping in big-"D" Democrat politics and the simple philosophy articulated by her mother the time Harper asked why they had "Jimmy Carter for President" signs on their front lawn rather than Gerald Ford signs. "Democrats are like Robin Hood," her mother replied. "They take back money from the rich and give it to the poor."[1]

"It was good enough for me," Harper writes in an account of her faith and politics journey in the book *Left, Right, & Christ*. "I loved Robin Hood, so I would be a Democrat, too."

Until, that is, another force entered her life: evangelical Christianity.

Harper was attending a Christian youth camp in southern New Jersey in 1983, a year marking the early stages of Ronald Reagan's presidential reelection drive and a time of growing evangelical impact on media and politics, when she became a born-again Christian. Her life was infused with new purpose, new promise—and new political sympathies. As a devout friend in her Christian youth group informed her shortly after her conversion experience, "I would have to become a Republican if I was going to call myself a Christian."[2] This Harper also accepted, becoming a true believer in Reaganomics and proclaiming the wisdom of trickle-down theory to her decidedly unimpressed mother.

So it has been across the wider political and cultural landscape for decades now, a phenomenon catalyzed by the emergence of causes and crusades like Jerry Falwell's Moral Majority in the late 1970s and nurtured by a succession of Republican politicians who courted the "values-voter" evangelicals and folded them into the Republican Party as a GOP constituency. So strong has this allegiance become that, to many casual observers of the faith-and-politics dynamics in our country, the term *evangelical* seems as much a descriptor of a voting bloc and political stance as a Christian religious movement. Indeed, according to this view, to be a born-again Christian, as Lisa Sharon Harper was taught, *is* to be Republican.

A second "born-again" experience awaited Harper, however. She got an inkling of what was to come when she met her first evangelical Democrats at a church in New York in 1990. "I was fascinated," Harper recalls. "I almost wanted to reach out and touch them to make sure they weren't some kind of mirage." The next year, while attending a social justice–oriented church in Los Angeles, she saw something equally revelatory: Republican and Democratic evangelicals side by side in the pews, worshiping the same Jesus.[3]

"I realized," Harper writes, that "I don't have to betray the cries of my ancestors and the current plight of my people to be a follower of Jesus. In fact, by closing my eyes to the impact of conservative policies on my own family, I would fail to see that Jesus walked with my family and my ancestors. . . . It is okay for me to be a Democrat."[4]

She had a deeper realization, too, of a truth illustrated by the political mix at the urban church she had begun attending: Christianity should not be owned, controlled, and counted on as a permanent source of votes and support by a political party. "Indiscriminate allegiance to any political party is idolatry," she realized, "and to practice idolatry is to become an enemy of God."[5]

In a reversal of the political dynamic that the young Lisa Sharon Harper experienced when she accepted Jesus and the GOP into her heart, the first decade or two of the new century will quite possibly go down as the time of rethinking and de-linking the tight relationship between evangelicalism and Republic politics. Evangelical America appears to be in the early stages of becoming what a Christian movement ought to be—beholden to no political party, corralled by no one ideology, never easy to predict and pigeonhole, and never motivated, first and foremost, by winning elections and amassing political power. In the memorable words of one evangelical writer, "We're fed up with being the Republicans' lapdogs, but don't think we're joining the Democratic kennel."[6]

It's hard to imagine a more potent symbol of the changing religious-political zeitgeist, of the way politically expressed Christianity is breaking formation and veering out of the lockstep march of the Christian Right and Republican Party, than the replica statue that was paraded down a Lower Manhattan street during an Occupy Wall Street demonstration in the fall of 2011. To observers who were used to equating the religious voice in politics with bedrock conservatism, the sight of the replica golden "calf"—in the shape of a Wall Street bull, to be exact—might have triggered a double take. Here, a millennia-old symbol of idolatry, the spiritually fatal transgression of worshiping a god other than God, and scrawled on its base a one-word indictment many thought long overdue: "Greed." Politically involved religious people challenging not abortion or gay rights, but *greed*? Yes, they were. And even though the religious leaders assembled at Occupy Wall Street were an ecumenical and interfaith collection, not evangelical per se, the demonstration spoke volumes about the loosening hold of the Christian Right, and of conservatism more generally, on politically expressed faith in the changing culture.

The season furnished other arresting examples of tables turning, and of scripture and religiously derived morality being invoked not by conservatives but by those aiming to confront them. Congressman Paul Ryan was on the uncomfortable receiving end of such an exercise as he was leaving an event called the Faith and Freedom Conference, where he, a Catholic conservative, had delivered a speech promoting his budget proposal—a proposal widely criticized for being too hard on the poor and too easy on the rich. On his way out, Ryan was chased down by a protestor waving a giant copy of the Bible and explaining that he wanted to present Ryan with scripture so that he might learn the Bible's teachings about caring for the vulnerable.[7] In a similar spirit, a group of Florida pastors organized a mobile billboard urging the Republican presidential contenders, then busy courting evangelicals in the customary fashion, to say and do more about looking out for the poor.[8]

To those who had forgotten the religious underpinnings of the civil rights movement, or who had grown wearily accustomed to conservatives having a corner on the religious-rhetoric market, it had to come as a surprise: clergy and church members, in explicitly religious terms, criticizing an economic, political, and social dynamic by which the wealthiest 1 percent of Americans had amassed an increasingly large share of the society's wealth, with more and more members of the 99 percent fighting over crumbs. It surprised not because scripture has nothing to say about gross inequality and greed—quite the opposite—but because we have gotten used to liberal concerns being articulated in technical, dispassionate, and secular terms, and to the religious voice singing only in praiseful rhapsody about the free-market system and its fruits. "Jesus stood with the 99 percent!" one protester asserted for a television news crew at the march of the golden bull on Wall Street, as if to set the record straight. "Jesus believed in everyone having their fair share."[9]

As author, activist, and academic Frances Fox Piven wrote at the time, the Occupy Wall Street movement had "redirected public attention to the issue of extreme inequality, which it has recast as, essentially, a moral problem. Only a short time ago, the 'morals' issue in politics meant the propriety of sexual preferences, reproductive behavior, or the personal behavior of presidents."[10]

As with "morals," as with "faith" and "values." This language, too, is now being marshaled not just by religious conservatives but also by those passionate about addressing systemic social ills. In the midst of the Wall Street march strode a woman named Jennifer Butler, whose career and increasingly hard-to-ignore public voice pose a prime example of an expanded "values" conversation, as well as a forceful challenge to the Christian Right's ownership of publicly expressed Christianity. Try to square the right-wing stereotype of politically engaged Christians with these words by Butler, an ordained Presbyterian minister and executive director of Faith in Public Life, a Washington-based strategy center that she launched in 2006 as a counter to the Christian Right. "People know deep down that greed has been idolized for too long in our nation, with disastrous economic and spiritual consequences," Butler wrote in a *Huffington Post* commentary reflecting on the Wall Street march. "Americans have wised up to the fact that bad actors on Wall Street—and their servants in Washington—have segregated a grossly unjust concentration of our nation's wealth in the hands of the people whose recklessness and greed caused our economic collapse. . . . We're outraged. We recognize a great sin and injustice in our midst."[11]

For those with progressive or defiantly independent leanings, for those with a gnawing sense that something had gone terribly wrong with the application of Christianity to the country's issues, the sight of the golden bull at Occupy Wall Street had to be a balm for sore eyes. And to hear the word *sin* turned back on the conservatives? Sweet music.

Since the rise of the Religious Right several decades ago, Christianity in politics, with rare exception, has gone one way, and one way only: to the right. When raised to address such matters as abortion, stem-cell research, the place and rights of gay people, the "Christian voice" has often been assertive, black and white, quick to condemn, and well amplified by media organizations hungry for the most dramatic sound bytes. If this voice sounded judgmental, even harsh, so be it. "Moral clarity" has been the order of the day in conservative Christian America, and bringing this clarity to our politics has been the mission of the politically engaged evangelicals who have been shaking up elections and energizing the Republican Party since the rise of Reagan.

But for all the talk of "reclaiming America for Christ," as it's often been cast, for all the rhetorical certainty about what it meant to bring Jesus into politics, anyone with one eye on the news and the other on the Bible—on the full sweep of the good book—was bound to notice that something was missing. Didn't Jesus also teach about the evils of greed? Doesn't the Bible also speak, over and over and over, about doing right by those with the least?

The answer is rising from a growing chorus of Christians, evangelicals very much included: Yes, it does.

As demonstrated by the rise of organizations like the aforementioned Faith in Public Life, and by the increasing visibility and influence of the progressive evangelical group Sojourners, the Christian Right's monopoly of faith-based political expression faces challenges from religionists outside the walls of conservative Christian culture. But perhaps more significant, it faces such challenges from inside as well, as an up-and-coming generation of younger evangelicals raised in the church and serious about Jesus rethinks what it means to advance the ideals of the Bible in a twenty-first-century public square. The dynamic plays out in many ways—in the range and nature of issues addressed, in the rhetoric and the tone with which it is transmitted, and in the statistics capturing party affiliation and voting patterns.

First, the numbers: Typical of many studies tracking demographics, religious affiliation, and voting patterns, CIRCLE (the Center for Information and Research on Civic Learning and Engagement) released a study in 2010 tracking the decreasing reliability of younger evangelical Christians as ballot-box supporters of Republican politicians. For more than twenty years, the study noted, evangelical Christians, making up roughly 25 percent of the American population, had been key allies of the Republican Party and near unanimous in their support of conservative positions. "Now, though, one group threatens to complicate the picture: *young* evangelicals," the study authors wrote.

"While the cohort may once have been a consistent support base for Republican candidates, recent polls indicate that their votes may be up for grabs." [12]

It comes as no surprise that the candidacy of Barack Obama acted as a magnet that pulled many younger evangelicals out of the tight political alignment of evangelicals and the GOP. In the 2008 election, Obama captured 30 percent of the votes of evangelicals between the ages of eighteen and twenty-nine. That was eight percentage points higher than over-thirty evangelical support for the eventual president, the CIRCLE study noted. But more striking still, it was double the young evangelical support that materialized for Democratic nominee John Kerry in the 2004 election. [13]

Lest one write this off as an aberration owing to the special dynamics of the 2008 election—Obama's charisma and youthful appeal, an uplifting (albeit fuzzy) hope-and-change message, Obama's greater comfort talking about faith than the Democratic nominees before him—consider that there were already signs of fraying before Obama glided onto the scene. As tracked in a series of surveys conducted by the Pew Forum on Religion & Public Life, young evangelicals had been peeling away from the GOP since 2001. Whereas 55 percent of evangelicals in the eighteen-to-twenty-nine age group identified themselves as Republicans in that year, only 48 percent counted themselves as Republican in 2006. By 2007, the figure had dipped to 40 percent. (It was not as though the younger evangelicals were being driven into the arms of the Democratic Party, however. Over that same period, young evangelicals identifying as Democrats increased by a mere three percentage points, from 16 percent to 19 percent.) [14]

Still more insight can be gleaned from subsequent polling by Robert P. Jones and his Public Religion Research Institute, which in 2011 released a fascinating study probing Americans' evolving attitudes on abortion and same-sex marriage, two of the signature issues in the long-running culture wars. Not surprisingly, Jones's research found Americans' support for gay marriage rising significantly between 1999 and 2011, from 35 percent to 53 percent. But here's where it gets interesting, and perhaps frustrating to dyed-in-the-wool Democrat partisans who might have hoped that defection from the conservative positions on gay marriage would be accompanied by migration away from the conservative stance on other social issues as well: the percentage of Americans supporting legal abortion remained essentially fixed—57 percent in 1999, 56 percent in 2011. [15]

In a report summary, Jones underscored a "de-coupling" of the two core issues of the so-called values agenda—a de-coupling particularly conspicuous among millennials, the generation coming of age post-2001. On the issue of abortion, Jones wrote, millennials mirror their parents' views, a steady majority believing abortion to be wrong (albeit with 60 percent, similar to their parents' cohort, saying abortion should be legal in all or most cases). On the other hand, as Jones said, "They are much more supportive than their parents of allowing gay and lesbian couples to marry. This suggests that we may see these issues moving on separate tracks in the future."[16] In sum: No significant movement from generation to generation on the morality and legality of abortion, but a major shift on legal marriage for same-sex couples. (The Jones data covers the population as a whole; as will be explored in subsequent chapters, this same "de-coupling" of the culture war issues emerges from analyses of what is happening inside the evangelical category, as well.)

Bundled up in the same illuminating PRRI study came a finding that might seem puzzling at first glance, suggestive of moral confusion, but that makes a world of sense when we pull the wool from our eyes and knock decades of culture-war rhetoric out of our heads. A strong majority of Americans, as it turns out, are both "pro-choice" *and* "pro-life." The pattern was especially pronounced among millennials, three-quarters of whom indicated that "pro-choice" defined their views, with another strong majority, 65 percent, saying "pro-life" also fit them. "The binary 'pro-choice'/'pro-life' labels," Jones summed up, "do not reflect the complexity of Americans' views on abortion."[17]

How fitting that a research firm founded and operated by Robert P. Jones would reveal the false choice posed by a culture war and these two overly reductive terms, *choice* and *life*—fitting, given Jones's own story and the false choice he himself rejects as a political progressive *and* a person of faith. As Jones recounts in his 2008 book *Progressive & Religious*, when he was a professor at Missouri State University, one of his brightest, most engaged students came to him, confused and dismayed, when she learned that Jones had agreed to serve as the faculty adviser to the Students for John Kerry group. How, she asked, could Jones be a Christian *and* an organizer for a Democratic politician?[18] It was as though her professor's very existence served as a necessary corrective to the student's oversimplified view.

Seen through optimistic lenses, this refusal to accept false choices—between being pro-life and pro-choice, between being a Christian and accepting gay people, between being Christian and a political progressive or independent—can be read as a sign of a dawning new era and a collective act of coming to our senses. To reject simplistic choices is hardly a sign of moral weakness, as old-guard partisans and ideologues on both sides would suggest, but evidence of an overdue recognition that complex times and complicated issues require similarly complex frames of mind.

Of course, for religious people used to swimming in theologically liberal waters, and for secularists who pride themselves on the virtues of a free-thinking rational mind, the rejection of black-and-white propositions would seem to come fairly easily. (Emphasis here on "seem," as is explored in other sections of this book.) But can a mosaic of grays be appreciated by evangelicals, the subset of believers for whom Jesus and his divinity are nonnegotiable, for whom religious commitments and theological positions are not matters of preference and subjectivity, but of clear-cut right and wrong? Can the culture's chief delineators of left/right, good/bad, and Jesus/or else resist drawing hard lines in the sand and, instead, play well with others in the box of finely grained textures? Consider the answer suggested by the words and deeds of one Jonathan Merritt and one Jim Daly.

To news consumers, it probably seemed like the same old, same old if they happened upon a certain *Washington Post* article published in the early stages of the race for the Republican nomination. "Republicans," read the headline, "hope to spark political revival among evangelicals for 2012 race." Featured in the article was a longtime icon of the Christian Right, Ralph Reed, a high-profile figure during the 1990s and the first decade of the new century when he led the Christian Coalition. Here was Reed again, back for more in the new decade as the president of a group called the Faith & Freedom Coalition, back in the press explaining how he was determined to mobilize evangelicals in the mission to unseat Barack Obama in 2012.

Sound familiar? Not far into the article, however, a keen-eyed reader could quickly sense that this was not 1984 or 2004 all over again, that something different was afoot at that once-predictable intersection between Republican politics and evangelical Christianity. Yes, there were those four familiar words that have been firing up Christian Republicans and making liberal heads explode for years: "Focus on the Family." But the person appearing in the piece as the leader and chief spokesperson for the Colorado-based faith-and-values organization was not the one you might have expected, not the divisive firebrand and onetime GOP kingmaker James Dobson. Appearing instead was the man who has succeeded Dobson, the new face of Focus on the Family.

Worshiping the "idol of political power," Focus president Jim Daly admitted in the *Post* article, was "one of the errors that we've made, to be forthright and honest. . . . Christian leadership has become about the victory, and that's led to us becoming the predator and the world our prey. That's not . . . a Christian doctrine. I'm very concerned about the politicization of the faith. . . . I think being owned by a party is dangerous."[19] Stunning words from the head of a faith-and-family organization once seen as synonymous with Republican politics.

Also appearing in that revealing *Post* article, also stepping out of formation, was an equally fascinating figure from a decidedly younger demographic. From his comments, it was clear that Jonathan Merritt, an evangelical activist and author in his late twenties, the son of a prominent Atlanta-area megachurch pastor and onetime president of the Southern Baptist Convention, was not going to jump back in line just because Ralph Reed told him he should.

"Among the older generation," Merritt told the *Post*, "there was a comfortable conflation [of] faith and partisanship. To be a Christian meant to be a Republican. What you're finding is not a new evangelical left, but you're finding a rise of political orphans."[20]

Young evangelicals like Merritt, Reed predicted in somewhat condescending tones, would come to their senses, would quit their flirtation with political free agency, when they grew a little older. "The Grand Canyon that runs through the electorate demographically is ultimately not a profession of faith," Reed said. "It's behavioral. Once they are married, once they have children and once they are going to church weekly, it's game, set, match."[21]

Having heard this argument for years, I asked Merritt whether Reed might be right that this political shift among younger evangelicals was really an aberration, that aging and family life would usher them back into the Republican fold. "I think [Reed] is totally underestimating this shift," Merritt replied, adding that Reed's strategy, and the very nature of his new Faith & Freedom Coalition, likely blinded him to the real change taking place, and certainly compelled him to do what he could to resist it. "His success or failure," Merritt told me, "rides on people believing things aren't really changing."[22]

As discussed previously, the demographic data make it appear unlikely that younger evangelicals' non-Republican, nonpartisan, independent stripes will be washed off by the passage of time and experiences of later adulthood. The data—data showing that young Christians' ideas and attitudes are markedly different from those held by their elders *when they themselves were young*—in combination with the altered context in which evangelical Christianity now operates, suggest that these different markers are indelible, like the tattoos you'll find on many of these younger Jesus followers.

Merritt, the author of the 2012 book *A Faith of Our Own: Following Jesus beyond the Culture Wars*, is someone whose observations and insights cannot be ignored even if his years and résumé fail to match those of old-guard figures like Ralph Reed. As a well-educated writer and researcher, Merritt is versed in the data and trend lines, and as a seminary graduate, he is no stranger to theology. But he has more to go on than that. As one who grew up in evangelical church culture in the South and who frequently speaks to church audiences that include people who doubt and resist the shifts to which Merritt is attuned, he is intimately familiar with how things look from inside the walls of old-school evangelical America. He was right there with them himself, until young adulthood. As you'll invariably find with evangelical Christians, Merritt has a conversion story. But in this case, it's not just a story of coming to Jesus, which Merritt did as a teenager, but also one of a second conversion of sorts, by which he came to a whole different understanding of what it means to bring the evangelical faith to bear in the public and political arenas—particularly, in Merritt's case, around the issue of caring for the long-term, life-sustaining viability of the environment.

Before his "green" conversion, Merritt had not worried much about sustaining the planet for the long-term future. In many circles in orthodox evangelicalism, "environmentalism" is regarded as a liberal poison worse than any pollutant spewed into our air and water, and the faithful wait in confident anticipation of an imminent rapture—the glorious sweeping up to heaven of Jesus' true believers, with everyone else "left behind," to quote the title of the hugely popular fiction series that imagines the trials and tribulations of the unbelievers who do not make the heavenly cut. If the world is on its last legs by divine decree, it's hard to find the motivation to put your shoulder to the task of improving the long-term prospects of the planet and its people.

Through his teenage years and his time as an undergraduate at Liberty University, "I hadn't been a friend of creation," Merritt confesses in his 2010 book *Green Like God*. "I never recycled, and energy conservation was inconsequential. . . . Prior to my classroom jolt, I remember tossing crumpled fast-food bags out of the windows of my speeding blue Pontiac thinking I was being bold and cute. When people in my car called me out for being destructive, I laughed."[23]

That classroom "jolt" to which he refers was not the result of a long pull on an energy drink but rather his experience in one of his classes, with a favorite professor, while he was studying at Southeastern Baptist Theological Seminary. Talking about the nature of divine revelation, Professor John Hammett suggested to the class that God spoke both through scripture *and* through nature. "So when we destroy creation, which is God's revelation, it's similar to tearing a page out of the Bible," Hammett instructed.[24]

"Wham! Whap! Bang! . . . I took one straight on the chin," Merritt remembers. Since then, he has been at the vanguard of evangelicals who are passionate about what has come to be known as *creation care*, and who regard protection of the planet as an urgent priority for those devoted to Jesus.

"Christians are charged with the task of evangelizing the world, the argument goes, so we can't let environmental issues distract us from our true mission," Merritt writes. "They say that we have to choose between evangelism and creation care, and therefore, we must pick evangelism."

"It is a false dichotomy," Merritt rightly concludes. "Both are possible."[25]

On an assortment of other issues, from human trafficking to treatment of homosexuals, from Wall Street excesses to protections for the poor, from nuclear weapons to poverty, more new-paradigm evangelicals are echoing Merritt's refrain. When presented with the proposition that following Jesus means marching with the GOP, they are correctly insisting on a different way: the freedom to follow Jesus wherever it takes them on (or off) the political spectrum.

Why is the "gospel of love" dividing America? Such is the loaded question posed by the subtitle of Dan Merchant's arresting film, *Lord, Save Us from Your Followers*. The 2009 release featured Merchant, a humorous, friendship-mongering, post-culture-wars evangelical, traveling around the country clad in a jumpsuit plastered with bumper stickers and having a filmed conversation with Americans about the divisive role of Christianity in our public life. The beauty of the film's provocative subtitle, as viewers eventually realize, is its deliberately false premise. As becomes clear when you watch the movie and ponder its lessons, the "gospel of love" has not been dividing America. But something surely has.

Probe the roiled emotions and dearly held grudges of ardent secularists, of diehard promoters of the idea that we must shove the "fundies" and right-wing Christians off to the sidelines of American public life, and you get a sense that it's not the teachings and example of Christianity's central figure that has repelled the supposed opponents of the faith. It is not Jesus who has set progressive, secular teeth on edge but rather a certain subset of Christians, and the often-over-the-top reaction to them, that has fueled the culture wars. It has been a certain set of political positions and emphases, and the often-harsh means by which some high-profile Christians have pushed them, that has made publicly expressed Christianity a "divider" more than a "uniter."

To understand why the political, public face of Christianity has often seemed at odds with what many non-evangelicals think the country's dominant religion is supposed to be about—kindness, compassion, love, *goodness*—it's important to realize the different ways in which Christianity is brought forward in the public square. The idealist wants to believe it will always be a deeply lived-out act of emulating a Jesus who modeled an extraordinarily different (and difficult) way of being in the world. But because Christians are also human beings, they often prove to be woefully imperfect followers and modelers of the Christ who stands at the center of their faith, just as all of us fail to live up to our highest ideals. And because they are human, Jesus' most vociferous representatives in contemporary America have often fallen prey to the always-present temptation to engage their faith as, first and foremost, an identity—an identity based on correct theological positions and allegiances. As in: *We are Christians, over and against non-Christians. We must promote and defend our faith, our tribe, in competition with the faiths and philosophies of others.*

It follows that asserting the tribe's distinctive and superior views and values—that *winning*—becomes the ultimate objective more than emulating the savior. Up rises the familiar rallying cry—"Reclaim America for Christ!"—and the battle is engaged.

If, like me, you have often puzzled over the tight association between Christianity and conservative politics—how the former could produce the latter—consider the very strong possibility that the evangelicals you know from politics and media portrayals are *not* basing their policies and tactics on the "good book," at least not to the degree that their rhetoric would suggest. Not that you won't find biblical justifications for the positions that conservative evangelicals often promote, or some kind of biblically tethered explanation for why they deemphasize and neglect certain other issues. But the picture makes much more sense in view of the very strong likelihood that right-wing politics do not flow out of Christianity but rather that the two forces coexist alongside one another in the hearts and minds of the people who belong to and support the Christian Right.

Could it be that on certain key issues, Jesus' most vocal representatives—people who will tell you that faith guides every aspect of their lives—have been basing their politics not on the Bible but on something else?

Data from Public Religion Research strongly suggests "yes" on the matter of torture, for instance. In 2008, when "enhanced interrogation" stood center stage in the headlines and political arguments, Jones's polling found that 57 percent of white evangelicals in the South believed torture could be justified, in contrast with the 48 percent of the general public found to support torture in an earlier poll by the Pew Research Center. But the real lesson lay in this data point: the evangelicals surveyed by PRRI were far more likely to be basing their pro-torture stance on life experience and common sense (44 percent) than Christian teaching (28 percent).[26] In other words, as I wrote in a column at that time, the segment of the population presumably the most serious about living the Christian life is disinclined to be guided by the Bible on one of the central moral questions of the day.[27] The silver lining was the slightly different result that emerged when the pollsters tweaked the question and challenged the survey takers to reapproach the issue with the Bible in mind, particularly its "do unto others as you would have them do unto you" precept. A slight majority then agreed that torture should never be used.[28]

The absence of large-scale evangelical witness against torture—extremely questionable in view of Jesus' love-your-enemy teachings—represents the larger problem of a selective morality that has eroded the credibility of evangelical conservatives. "The failure to oppose capital punishment and torture," writes religion professor Randall Balmer in a history of American evangelicalism, "leaves the Religious Right open to the charge that their agenda is driven by hard-right ideologues rather than by moral conviction."[29]

As PRRI's Robert P. Jones pointed out in a conversation with me about his torture findings, evangelicals' majority support for the practice likely stemmed from two eminently understandable impulses: fear and the related but unrealistic yearning for absolute safety from terrorists. Understandable, but also problematic. Where was the Bible in this equation? Similar patterns emerge from a close look at some of our other hot-button issues. A 2010 poll by the Pew Forum found just 12 percent of white evangelicals indicated that their religious beliefs had a major influence on their views about immigration policy. Similarly, just 13 percent said their faith was the biggest influence on their views about government aid to the poor.[30]

These data points and others stand as powerful evidence of the truth of a penetrating observation made by politics pundit (and Catholic) E. J. Dionne, who writes, "We all have to ask ourselves whether what we claim to be hearing as the voice of faith (or of God) may in fact be nothing more than the voice of our ideology or political party."[31] Or, as progressive Christian author Greg Garrett phrases it, "We tend to make political—and other—decisions not out of Christianity's highest values like compassion, generosity, and responsibility, but out of secular American values like self-reliance, self-interest, and acquisition."[32]

As much as doubters might want to cry "hypocrite" or "gotcha," the fairer, more generous label to affix here, if labels are necessary, is "human." As silly as it sounds, evangelical Christians are people too, prone to the same frailties and fears as everyone. To be fair, who among us does not allow fear to guide their actions and positions, whether it's fear of terrorists or fear of our country being overrun by "aliens," as undocumented immigrants are often harshly portrayed? Or, from a different perspective, whether it's fear of the "Jesus nuts" and the repressive mischief they'll supposedly concoct if they get their hands on too many levers of power?

But here's the rub: in a very real sense—in a sense that the new evangelicals sense and rightly call out—evangelical America has positioned itself as somehow above the human and imperfect plane where the "rest of us" operate as participants in the public square, as if somehow their avowed certainty about their savior, and their relationship to him, make their political ideas automatically superior, above questioning, and beyond reproach.

Credit the rising current of new evangelical thought for articulating the case for, and living out, two much-needed correctives: one, a more earnest (and humble) effort to apply Jesus seriously, idealistically, and consistently to their engagement with a given public issue, in their tactics and tone as well as the content of their policies and positions, even at a cost to ideology and competitive advantage; and two, a surrendering of the misguided notion that Christians are always right and are called, therefore, to "win" in politics by any means necessary.

"The political, economic, and social systems in our country don't exist to glorify God," Merritt writes. "They were built to turn a profit, grow an empire, consolidate power. Some Christian churches, leaders, and organizations have been co-opted by these systems with the promise of benefiting from the resources and power they produce."[33] Merritt's call to his fellow evangelicals: Don't be fooled. Don't be lured in. Don't lose sight of the Christian's higher calling. He writes, "Senator Alan Simpson spoke truth when he noted that if one travels the high road in Washington, one won't encounter much traffic." Even if it's lonely and disadvantageous, the high road is the road for Christians to travel, Merritt continues. "The scriptures exalt servitude, not strength. They instruct that the last shall be first. Living out the teachings of Jesus will not inspire one to rise to the top, but rather to stoop to the floor and wash the feet of others."[34]

Walking that high road brings a cost. But as more Jesus-professing Christians are realizing, it brings freedom, too—freedom from the impossible false choices of old: between being a Republican *or* a God-hating secularist, between being "pro-life" *or* "pro-choice." They sense that on matters of personal morality, it's one thing for Christians to have heartfelt convictions about right and wrong but quite another to use the power of the state to impose their faith-based convictions on other Americans of different beliefs. Walking the high road also brings freedom from the misguided notion that there is always an official "Christian position" on a given issue or policy prescription. And it brings freedom to follow one's idealism and Christian heart to the places on the political spectrum that the believer discerns as right and just, whatever the political or partisan implications.

There's an insight deeper still that the exemplars of the new evangelicalism are articulating through word and deed. Not only are they breaking themselves free of conservative ideology and the Republican Party, but they are also weaning themselves from previous generations' fixation on politics itself. It is not as though the rising generation of evangelicals has abandoned politics. But it does appear to be standing up, clearing its collective throat, and declaring, "It's not all about politics, stupid!" (Except for the "stupid" part; these folks tend to be nothing if not polite.) They have seen that political wins can often prove to be Pyrrhic victories at best, no longer lasting the next election cycle—a realization confirmed by national elections in 2012 that saw the Christian Right and its candidates experience a thorough trouncing. And even when these temporal triumphs are achieved, they are paid for with allegiance to the cynical, rough-and-tumble winning-at-politics rules that do serious injury to Jesus' good name. They are seeing alternative venues and courses of action that can have deeper, longer-lasting impact than electoral politics.

As with younger evangelicals, as with American evangelicalism as a whole as the tides gradually shift. The growing detachment from politics "puts a lie to the idea that these people [evangelicals] are going to take over America," says Michael Cromartie of the Evangelicals in Civic Life program at the Ethics and Public Policy Center. "They have a lessened expectation about what politics can do to change society."[35]

Take back America for Christ by winning the next election? If this "taking back" were even the point, and if Christ ever possessed America in the manner this rhetoric suggests—both dubious—the new evangelicals are learning that politics alone could never achieve such ends. They are learning that there are far, far better rows to hoe if Christians are to work for a true, lasting restoration of a culture and a country—that politics as usual are actually *counter*productive to the extent they raise people's backs about Christianity itself, making it immensely more difficult to do what evangelicals want so badly to do: share the gospel, cultivate new disciples, and make the Christian faith a positive, helpful presence in society.

Let's hope it goes down as a low-point apotheosis and the beginning of a turnaround. The raw, downside truth about the ugliness in today's politics was revealed when shouts of "Yes!" and "Yeah!" burst out from the crowd at a 2011 Republican candidates debate put on by CNN and the Tea Party Express in response to a question from moderator Wolf Blitzer to candidate Ron Paul probing what should be done about a hypothetical young man in urgent need of life-saving medical care who had eschewed buying insurance. Should society, Blitzer asked, just let him die? The enthusiastic shouts in the affirmative were disturbing, to say the least. (Paul and the other candidates on the stage did not endorse the callousness; however, they said nothing to disapprove of it, either. Paul, for his part, gave the naïve-sounding suggestion that friends, family, and churches would step in to save the man and that such a saving was not the job of the government.)[36]

A chorus of "Yeah!" to letting a young man die—is this what things have come to in a country that many Americans exalt as the greatest on earth, a country known for levels of religious commitment and piety virtually unmatched in the industrialized world? Is this what it all boils down to for a Republican Party that's been known as the true political home for Christians?

If you are a secularly inclined progressive with a sour taste in your mouth about the apparent juxtaposition of religion and hard-heartedness in Republican politics, scenes like these might make you seethe about those conservative evangelicals we hear so much about. And while this "Let him die" callousness was seen as more of a Tea Party than a Christian Right phenomenon, there is no denying what careful sociological research has now revealed: that the Tea Party and the Christian Right are closer to one and the same people than the Tea Party myth and rhetoric, and the initial public and media understanding, would suggest.[37]

But if you find this revolting, and if you're tempted to implicate political evangelicalism—both completely justifiable responses—know that a rising current of evangelical Christians share that revulsion with you and weep that their savior has become tangled up in all the dysfunction and nastiness that have consumed our country's politics. Know that a different and altogether kinder ethic infiltrates the minds and heart of a new wave of evangelicals who remember that Jesus submitted himself to an endgame culminating not in political victory but in his humiliating execution.

These new evangelicals are re-pledging their ultimate allegiance to the figure who rode into Jerusalem to meet his fate "not on a warhorse but on a donkey," as evangelical reformer Shane Claiborne put it to me, and to "a Christianity that looks like Jesus' vision rather than a Christianity that plays the political game well."[38]

For those who are keen on understanding the political lay of the land in America—where the lines of struggle and division *really* run—it's important to comprehend that a new day has arrived when many of Jesus' most ardent, vocal followers can be found on both sides of our political conflicts or inventing "both-and" and "none-of-the-above" ways of engaging. Although no doubt confounding to partisan mobilizers, the new avenues for evangelical engagement in politics lead in directions that offer great promise and possibility for "the rest of us," for non-evangelical seekers of solutions to our most vexing and persistent challenges, whether they are the abortion stalemate, poverty, growing economic hardship, or the degradation of the most basic resources—air, water, planet—needed to sustain life.

"People of faith at our best may be the ultimate independents," writes Sojourners leader Jim Wallis, "engaged in politics only because of those moral issues that command our attention and willing to challenge all political sides on behalf of them."[39] These "moral independents," Wallis correctly says, have what it takes to change politics rather than *be* changed *by* politics.

Progressives would be wise to court these Christian independents and forge political partnerships and alliances with them where interests merge, rather than giving the knee-jerk response often seen from liberal-leaning secularists when they see that highly charged word *evangelical*. To dismiss these people as religious fanatics, as zealots who have surrendered their ability to think rationally—as automatically and obviously Republican and conservative—not only insults these Christians but also mocks what is supposed to be a hallmark of the progressive, secular train of mind: the ability to see clearly and to think expansively, with subtlety and nuance.

Things are changing in that sandbox that we all share as participants in the public and political life of the country. Everyone draws a hard line somewhere. But under the renovation in process, the line of the evangelicals is not the one you would expect given what we have come to know about them and the public/political face of their faith. For the new evangelicals, the only hard line is the one they draw around Jesus, and the more you learn about what that means, the more you realize these are people you can work with on many of the issues nearest and dearest to the progressive heart.

Not that the new evangelicals are on their way to becoming a solid Democratic Party constituency in the manner their forebears have been for Republicans, or that you can expect to find a headline in 2020 about Iowa evangelicals being the key to the Democrats' presidential nomination contest.

But if you can "tolerate" working with people who believe deeply in Jesus and have taken his message about love and compassion deeply to heart—if you can handle going to social-transformation battle with people who are prone to breaking out in prayer and religious language—you may find in these Christians an abundant source of energy, commitment, and support. If reducing poverty is your thing, or protecting human habitat for the long term, or stopping the abuse and exploitation of human beings trapped in sex or sweatshop slavery, you may find in these ranks some of your best friends for the fight.

To keep them at arm's length because of their evangelical faith, to disqualify them solely because they claim Jesus as their summons, would be as unfair as it is unwise. There is simply too much to be done.

Chapter Seven

Through the Logs in Their Eyes

It's Homecoming at "God's Harvard."

Alumni have gathered for a sunny weekend of fun, football, and friendship on the campus of Wheaton College, an evangelical school just outside of Chicago widely recognized for the high quality of its academics and the seriousness of its Christian commitments. Here on the grounds where the twentieth century's greatest evangelist, Billy Graham, got his college education, the happy grads pause and smile for the camera in groups of three, four, five, and more. Then it's back to socializing and rushing off to the next of the various events packing Homecoming 2011 weekend—a long reel of meals, receptions, speeches, plaque presentations, and, fitting for a campus with a motto proclaiming "For Christ and his Kingdom," gatherings and services in the campus chapel.

A large blue banner hangs over the tidy brick building known as Westgate that serves as home to Wheaton's alumni association. "Welcome, Alumni!" it bids. For one new alumni group joining the festivities for the first time, however, the rousing welcome is marked by an invisible asterisk of sorts. As is this new group itself, which is not officially recognized by the college and which, truth be told, poses something of a problem for the administration. Four dozen strong, not counting the partners and children they've brought with them, they are at Homecoming to make a bold statement about sexual orientation—one they share and one that could have gotten them booted from the Wheaton campus had they been open about it in their student days. They're gay. And not the least bit apologetic about it.

"OneWheaton," the group calls itself. That name, along with a rainbow, the symbol of gay, lesbian, bisexual, and transgender pride and diversity, is emblazoned on the T-shirts they don for the homecoming football game. A photograph appearing in *Time* magazine—one of several media outlets covering OneWheaton's homecoming debut—captures the members in a rousing, sports team–style show of togetherness: they huddle, each with an arm stretching into the center, hands spilling over hands. [1]

If the moment had a soundtrack, this might be the point in the score when a mounting disharmony and tension finally break, the chords and notes merging into sweet resolution. It's as if these gay and lesbian alumni are announcing a dawning new day in which evangelicals' acceptance of their non-heterosexuality does not require them to ditch their faith in Jesus and when more and more leaders and followers in the evangelical community are reaching the decision that most religious liberals reached years, even decades, before: that it's time for a new conversation, a new understanding, when it comes to homosexuality and the church.

"You're a Christian kid. You're having attractions to the same sex. This is very, very scary, partly because for you to even consider that [same-sex relations] might not be sinful, you feel like you have to throw the entire Bible out the window." This is how OneWheaton member Lora Wiens, a 2007 graduate of Wheaton's psychology doctoral program and now a clinical psychologist, sums up the dilemma that vexed her when she was a student. "That's at least as scary as being gay, probably even scarier, because [the Bible] is a huge part of what you are building your life around." [2]

Like many gay people who are coming out of closets in evangelical America, the members of OneWheaton don't want to "throw the entire Bible out the window," as Lora Wiens puts it. The urge to help current students navigate their own versions of Wiens's struggle prompted the formation of Wheaton's gay alumni group the spring prior to its first Homecoming appearance. The group's first big move was to distribute letters on campus, without permission from the administration, assuring students that their attraction to people of the same sex did not doom them to the horrible options with which they were likely presented growing up in their evangelical churches—choices like secrecy, celibacy, "pray-away-the-gay" therapy, or, on the opposite end of the spectrum, abandoning the evangelical faith.

OneWheaton's letter, copies of which were handed out as students filed out of the mandatory chapel service and left for pickup at other campus locales, was also aimed at countering a chapel event that had taken place in the preceding days, in which gay people were described as broken and their same-sex relationships as "tragic." The speaker had described how he had chosen celibacy as the solution to his own same-sex-attraction dilemma.

"You are not tragic," the OneWheaton letter declared. "Your desire for companionship, intimacy, and love is not shameful. It is to be affirmed and celebrated just as you are to be affirmed and celebrated. In our post-Wheaton lives, we have traversed the contradictions we once thought irreconcilable. Our sexuality has become an integral part of our broader pursuit of justice, compassion, and love. We can no longer allow ourselves or our loved ones to be trapped in environments that perpetuate self-hatred, depression, and alienation. As people of integrity we must affirm the full humanity and dignity of every human being regardless of their sexual orientation or gender identity."[3]

Thus began a relationship between the new alumni group and the gay, lesbian, and questioning students at Wheaton. A newly launched Facebook page grew to several hundred members in the months that followed, its participants posting prayer requests and photos of their adopted children while helping students work through the issues posed by their emerging sexuality.[4]

Wholeness, reconciliation, new options for Christian students who were coming face-to-face with sexualities that did not accord what has long been considered normal, healthy, and "biblical"—this is what the new group was offering, and it felt like a breath of fresh air to those in the Wheaton community who had previously seen no way out, and to those who counted themselves among the gay students' friends and allies. "As a former conservative Christian who actually became much more progressive and open-minded about my faith during my time at Wheaton (despite the best efforts of its administration), I am thrilled by the efforts of my fellow alumni and proud to be a small part of this effort," one straight alumnus announced online.[5]

As the OneWheaton founders said in their unauthorized letter to the school's students, "We've seen the harm caused by the stance of Wheaton and some churches that the only two options when struggling with sexual orientation and gender identity are to 'change it' or lead a life of celibacy. We aim to illuminate other options for living healthy, whole and honest lives, full of love and integrity."

There they were at Homecoming just a few months later, the gay and lesbian alumni of God's Harvard, as if to announce to the administration, their fellow alumni, the students, and the broader evangelical church in America that they were who they were, they were not ashamed, they knew

God loved them, and they were not going away. Lives and communities were being integrated; an excruciating dilemma was closer to resolution.

And the dilemma facing evangelicals of a different mind-set was becoming that much thornier.

It's not easy holding the line against growing acceptance of gay people in American society these days. At what seems like lightning speed to defenders of traditional morality, homosexuals have progressed from clear outcast status, from closets and shadows, to something approaching full inclusion in American life. Gay characters are so commonplace in television and movies, invariably portrayed in nondeviant ways, that few people give the matter a second thought. More and more gay politicians are being elected to office. After the 2012 elections, in which voters in Maine, Maryland, and Washington passed pro–gay marriage ballot measures, same-sex marriage was legal in nine states and the District of Columbia.[6] Although less so in older demographic groups and in rural communities, more and more Americans are rubbing elbows with people who are gay, in their workplaces and neighborhoods and social circles, and are coming to see that their non-straight acquaintances, friends, and coworkers can be just as smart, wonderful, responsible, flawed, annoying, and disappointing as pretty much any straight person they know.

As attested by public opinion samples, we have reached the point where a strong majority of the American public believes homosexuality should be accepted (58 percent to be exact, according to a March 2011 poll by the Pew Research Center for the People and the Press).[7] With respect to the more challenging proposition—that the institution of marriage should be legally available to same-sex couples—2011 was the first year in which a majority of Americans said "yes," albeit by a narrow margin.[8]

It seems clear this is a social trend beyond the point of no return. Even people who were brought up to believe homosexuality to be deviant behavior understand that condemning gay people, calling them "faggots," and telling cruel jokes about them—acts that were far more commonplace and socially acceptable two or three decades ago—are sure to brand one a bigot or a troglodyte, as they should. Since the civil rights movement of the 1960s, one of the worst labels you can have pinned to you in most circles is "racist"; a similar dynamic now prevails with respect to acts and words that are anti-gay. In most workplaces, organizations, and social environments, it's not *being* homosexual that will get you in trouble, but *criticizing* homosexuals for their sexual identity. In mainstream walks of life, whether someone is gay is rapidly approaching the point of being a nonissue. Unless, however, you're observing all this from the perspective of the conservative evangelical subculture. The inexorable advance of gay rights *is* an issue, a grave worry even, if you're part of a prominent evangelical Christian institution like a conservative church, a Christian Right political group, a faith-and-family advocacy and resources organization, or an evangelical college. In evangelical circles as in few others, the advance of homosexuality is very difficult to accept with a shrug or an affirmation. For it's been from these forces that the advance of gay rights has met its stiffest resistance. And it's been some of the best-known figures from this segment of American culture who have raised the stakes around homosexuality to high, high levels, as if this were one of the two or three issues that would determine, once and for all, whether the United States of America would live on as a healthy, moral nation. And the basis for this opposition—what they believe God says about sexual morality in Holy Scripture—is not something that can be lightly changed or abandoned.

For these reasons, Philip Ryken, the still-new president of Wheaton, was facing one *hell* of a dilemma.

Consider the bind in which someone like the Wheaton College president finds himself when a gay alumni group proudly announces its presence and major national media outlets like *Time* magazine cover the story. Imagine what you would do if you, like Ryken, had come of age during a time when your church culture condemned homosexuality in the strongest possible terms—as an "abomination," to quote the frequently cited passage from the Old Testament book of Leviticus.[9] Imagine what you would do if you, like Ryken, were the person in charge of one of the most respected and visible evangelical colleges in the country and had the privilege and pressure that go with that elevated status. To accept the sexual orientation of homosexual students and alumni (not to mention faculty and staff members) would seem, to many outsiders, the compassionate, loving thing to do. To denounce the new gay alumni group and its supporters—ban them from Homecoming perhaps—would seem, in the eyes of the larger public and academic world, cruel, cold, and out of step with the tolerance of the times. Yet lightly accepting this group and what it signifies would be sure to set off a tsunami of criticism from traditionalists in the Wheaton community and broader world of the evangelical church, while violating your own understanding of the Bible's teachings.

For some smaller, less-known Christian colleges, the stakes are considerably lower. But if you're the president of the best-known, most academically rigorous of the evangelical small colleges, you have no choice but to worry about your reputation outside the walls of church subculture. You've already been dinged by the influential college-rating service Princeton Review for being the least gay-friendly of America's top colleges.[10] If you're not careful, you may find yourself and your college called out by the Southern Poverty Law Center, which by this point had applied the label "hate group" to several well-known evangelical organizations leading the resistance to gay rights. If you're Philip Ryken, what *do* you do?

Ryken, for his part, threaded the proverbial needle. On the same day that OneWheaton passed out its fliers and announced its presence, the Wheaton president responded with an e-mail message to the campus community that reminded readers of the Bible verses forbidding homosexuality and other forms of sexuality immorality. Among them, Romans 1:21–27 ("Men committed shameful acts with other men, and received in themselves the due penalty for their error"); 1 Corinthians 6:9–10 (". . . wrongdoers will not inherit the kingdom of God . . . neither the sexually immoral nor idolaters nor adulterers nor men who have sex with men"); and Genesis 2:24 ("That is why a man leaves his father and mother and is united to his wife, and they become one flesh").

But even in offering these standard-fare Bible references, Ryken was careful to contextualize, careful not to single out homosexuality as especially deserving of biblically based scorn. As he put it in the e-mail, "Scripture condemns . . . sexual immorality, such as the use of pornography (Matt. 5:27–28), premarital sex, adultery, homosexual behavior and all other sexual relations outside the bounds of marriage between a man and woman."[11]

More indicative of the changing conversation around same-sex relations, Ryken took pains to avoid condemning the people in the campus's gay community. Some might have found it condescending or perfunctory, tepid at best, but there it was nonetheless: support for Wheaton's "LGBTQ individuals," as Ryken referred to them, using the standard acronym for the lesbian, gay, bisexual, transgendered, and queer community.

"We see each member of the human family as created in the image of God himself, and thus each of immeasurable value. This includes our neighbors and alumni who identify as LGBTQ," Ryken's e-mail read. "We recognize that the needs of LGBTQ individuals present a particular challenge for institutions like Wheaton. Many have experienced insensitive or callous responses in this community, for which we repent and seek forgiveness. We repudiate and condemn violence and injustice directed toward LGBTQ people."

"We carry a burden for our students, faculty, staff and alumni who experience same-sex attraction because of the pain they so often experience, and pray that we can be a community that loves those who identify as LGBTQ," Ryken continued. "While we recognize that Wheaton's stance may be unsatisfying to some of our alumni, we remain resolved to respond with truth and grace."[12]

In reader comments posted beneath a Patheos.com article on the Wheaton drama, alumnus Mike Clawson, a straight ally of the OneWheaton group, expressed pleasant surprise. The president's message, Clawson said, was "more gracious and sympathetic than we had hoped for (especially by comparison to the response received by the previous president when a similar group of gay alumni was formed in the mid-1990s)." The "conciliatory" tone, Clawson continued, "does indicate a baby step forward for the administration and indicates the degree to which attitudes are in fact shifting in the evangelical world. After all, if the president of an institution like Wheaton, who has a huge conservative base of constituents he has to avoid offending, still feels compelled to write a letter that is sympathetic and relatively friendly towards a LGBTQ group, how much more are attitudes likely shifting among those younger evangelicals who have no Christian institutions to represent, or church jobs or ministry reputations to protect?"[13]

The attitudes of those younger evangelicals indeed are shifting, adding still another dimension to the dilemma facing the old guard, perhaps the most significant dimension of all. As two of the new evangelicals' leading chroniclers, David Kinnaman and Gabe Lyons, reported in their meticulously researched book *unChristian*, less than a third of younger Americans who attend church regularly consider "homosexual lifestyles" a major problem.[14] And as documented by a more recent poll by Public Religion Research, 44 percent of evangelicals in the eighteen-to-twenty-nine age group have taken perhaps the hardest step of all and come to support gay marriage. While still shy of majority status, young adult support for gay marriage in that PRRI poll more than doubled that of the white evangelical demographic as a whole.[15]

"We've probably lost." That's how Jim Daly, president of Focus on the Family, sized up the situation in comments to the conservative *World* magazine. While young Americans' moral objections to abortion remain strong, Daly noted that just the opposite is happening with respect to same-sex marriage. "We're losing on that one, especially among the twenty- and thirty-somethings," Daly observed. "I don't know if that's going to change with a little more age—demographers would say probably not. We've probably lost that. I don't want to be extremist here, but I think we need to start calculating where we are in the culture."[16]

Daly could have pointed to any number of additional metrics and voices from within and outside of evangelical America to back his point. Like this: "The gay issue has become the 'big one,' the negative image most likely to be intertwined with Christianity's reputation," Lyons and Kinnaman reported in *unChristian*. "It is also the dimension that most clearly demonstrates the unchristian faith to young people today, surfacing a spate of negative perceptions. . . . Outsiders say our hostility toward gays—not just opposition to homosexual politics and behaviors but disdain for gay individuals—has become virtually synonymous with the Christian faith."[17]

Hostility and disdain—not something anyone would want associated with her or his religion, to be sure. And *not* something with which younger evangelicals (and younger *ex*-evangelicals) would want to be associated, especially given the reality that many of them know gay people, are friends with gay people, and cringe each time it's assumed that they themselves are anti-gay bigots on account of their being Christians. Kinnaman, in his subsequent book, *You Lost Me*, named the perception of anti-gay hostility as a major reason why many young adult Americans raised in evangelical churches were abandoning the faith of their youth. "Most twentysomethings," Kinnaman wrote, "assume that the voices of lesbian, gay, bisexual, and transgender people should be heard in cultural conversations of any consequence."[18]

As Kinnaman explained on the Christian Broadcasting Network in an interview after the release of *You Lost Me*, younger evangelicals—those still in the church as well as those who had drifted away—want to be free to have gay people in their lives. "Young people feel as though the church makes them choose between their friends and their faith," Kinnaman said. "They feel as though they can't be friend with gays and lesbians, for instance, *and* still be true Christians. . . . We often give them the wrong impression. Instead of talking about the exclusive nature of Christ all the time, we have to help young people understand that Jesus had a heart for outsiders. We often don't look much like Jesus in our churches. We look more like the self-righteous people Jesus condemns. We have to find that heart of Jesus, *for* Jesus, to enable this generation to love diverse people and the diverse relationships they have."[19]

The seemingly unstoppable march of gay rights, the growing social scorn heaped on those opposing homosexuals and their full inclusion in our society, the insistence of younger Christians on a different conversation about same-sex relationships—for these reasons and more, one can readily understand why none other than the Focus on the Family president would cite the need for older evangelical leaders to "start calculating where we are in the culture."

Where they are, when you step back and examine the situation, is painted into a corner, and in the process of trying to find a way out.

In one sense, the political predicament in which old-school evangelicals find themselves with respect to the same-sex relationships issue is a case of a once-effective strategy that has entered the backfiring stage. Consider the perspective of Randall Balmer, a religious history scholar who grew up in the evangelical church, and a razor-sharp articulator of ways in which popular American evangelicalism has gone awry. Balmer writes that Christian Right leaders instrumentalized the gay issue in the 1990s as part of a culture-wars political strategy, much as they did the abortion issue the decade before.[20] (The political-strategy dynamics around abortion will be explored in greater depth in the following chapter.)

With the demise of the Soviet Union, Balmer writes, "The religious right desperately searched for a new enemy." The movement needed, in essence, people and ideas against which it could define itself, in a way that would galvanize donors and voters. Although evangelicals' convictions about the immorality of homosexuality were sincere, Balmer writes, Christian Right strategists, "along with leaders of the Republican Party, sensed a political opportunity."[21]

Here, in essence, was a chance for political strategists to take a form of social change alarming to many traditionalists and turn it into a wedge issue that could deliver votes for candidates favored by social conservatives. And here was a means by which evangelicals could differentiate themselves from more liberally inclined Americans in a way that was reassuring to many in a time of rapidly changing mores and cultural practices around sex in general—including sex in their own evangelical communities and homes. As demographic research has documented, members of evangelical churches, despite church teachings against divorce and extramarital sex of the hetero variety, turn out to have rates of divorce and pre- and extramarital sex rivaling those of the non-evangelical demographics.[22] Ah, but there was one sexual sin evangelicals ostensibly *were* resisting, and about which church members could feel pure and pious. To a cynic's ear, it's as if they declared, "Yes, we may have our faults. But—praise God—we are not homosexuals!"

In an interview for Marcia Pally's 2011 book *The New Evangelicals*, renegade evangelical pastor Greg Boyd described the thought process in these trenchant terms: "[We] may be divorced and remarried several times. We may be as greedy and unconcerned about the poor and as gluttonous as others in our culture; we may be as prone to gossip and slander and as blindly prejudiced as others. . . . But at least we're not *gay*."[23]

Recent political history is replete with the tactics spawned by this model and mind-set: anti–gay marriage measures at the state and federal level, fights against special legal protection for gay people subject to bullying or discrimination, fights against requirements that agencies treat gay couples equally as candidates to be adoptive parents, rhetoric that portrays gay people as deviant and their allies as morally suspect, anti-God, and anti-American.

To attribute evangelical opposition to homosexuality as only or principally a political calculation is neither accurate nor fair. Yet there can be no denying its effectiveness in politics. As a differentiating factor and troops-rallying motivator, the emphasis on homosexuality—its elevation as an issue of make-or-break importance and an evil of nearly unmatched proportions—certainly helped achieve ballot-box victories in contests ranging from school boards and city councils to the U.S. Senate and White House. Its political utility helps explain why a matter that receives nowhere near top billing in the Bible came to play such a featured role in the rhetoric and on the priority lists of Christian Right organizations. Of course, if gay America had not started asserting itself, and if much of straight society had not responded by welcoming gay people into mainstream life, none of this would have happened. Christian Right strategists and organizers would not have had this particular form of social change to exploit as a wedge issue. One could ask who thrust this issue upon whom. But this was the opportunity that presented itself to politics-minded evangelicals. And seize it they did.

The strategy worked.

Until it didn't.

By the beginning of the second decade of the new century, it has become increasingly obvious that anti-gay tactics and rhetoric are as likely to cause

PR headaches and reputation stains as they are to yield positive results. The weakness of some of the positions taken by leading Christian conservatives is being recognized, revealed, and, increasingly, called out. On the matter of laws protecting sexual minorities from bullying and discrimination, for instance, *Time* magazine's Amy Sullivan correctly criticizes diehards for acting as though measures of this sort are trampling Christians' religious freedom. "Social conservatives believe that efforts to protect gays from assault, discrimination, or bullying impinge on their religious freedom to express and act on their belief that homosexuality is an abomination," writes Sullivan, a self-identified Baptist. "That's stating it harshly, but it is the underlying belief. . . . Freedom of religious expression doesn't give someone the right to kick the crap out of a gay kid or to verbally torment her. It doesn't give someone the right to fire a gay employee instead of dealing with the potential discomfort of working with him."[24]

From my viewpoint, a no-going-back turning point showed itself around the time that President Barack Obama signed into law a bill requiring the military to scrap its infamous Don't Ask, Don't Tell policy for gays and lesbians. Now, one of the most respected institutions in American life, not to mention one of the most rugged and rigorous, was accepting out-of-the-closet sexual minorities.

In the same general time frame, the Southern Poverty Law Center—a civil rights organization dedicated to advocating for threatened minorities and exposing hate groups—issued a report listing anti-gay groups whose tactics and rhetoric it deemed especially repugnant. These organizations, "most of them religiously motivated," SPLC said in its news release, "have continued to pump out demonizing propaganda aimed at homosexuals and other sexual minorities. These groups' influence reaches far beyond what their size would suggest, because the 'facts' they disseminate about homosexuality are often amplified by certain politicians, other groups, and even news organizations."[25] Appearing on the list were the names of several well-known groups whose leaders are frequently seen in the media. Among them, the Family Research Council, the American Family Association, and the Traditional Values Coalition.[26] To these organizations the SPLC was now applying a label traditionally reserved for the likes of white supremacists, anti-Semitic extremists, and backwoods militias. These gay-bashing Christian Right organizations were, the SPLC said, "hate groups."

(In announcing its list, SPLC singled out for positive notice one especially large and influential conservative Christian organization that was once known for strong anti-gay rhetoric and teachings—Focus on the Family; SPLC credited Focus for moderating its tone and, as that would suggest, made it clear it was not classifying Focus as a hate group.)

Around the same time that the military was ordered to accept openly gay and lesbian soldiers and the SPLC issued its new hate-group list, a group called Exodus International announced a surprising decision, as if to verify that, yes indeed, a new day had arrived. Exodus had been playing a lead role in organizing an annual "Day of Truth" at American high schools, a counter-protest to the "Day of Silence" campaign aimed at supporting sexual-minority students and sounding the alarm about the bullying those young people often face. Henceforth, Exodus announced, it would play no part in the day of so-called truth, and it cited a more profound biblical truth in explaining why.

"All the recent attention to bullying helped us realize that we need to equip kids to live out biblical tolerance and grace," Exodus President Alan Chambers explained, "while treating their neighbors as they'd like to be treated, whether we agree with them or not."[27]

As I wrote in a *USA Today* column reflecting on this trifecta of sign-of-the-times developments, one could clearly sense that American culture had reached a point on gay rights similar to that moment in a football game, or an election, or a relationship, when you know it's over even though it's not officially *over*—and that this newly arrived moment was posing a decision point, a day of reckoning, for the socially conservative Christian groups that led the resistance to gay rights. Would they continue fighting to the last ditch, continue shouting the anti-gay rhetoric that was ringing false and mean to more and more Americans? Or would they ease back gracefully, change their tone and tactics, and turn their attention elsewhere?

For those choosing to fight on, the extent and nature of the cost is increasingly clear. Consider the predicament of the late Charles Colson.

Colson might not have had many liberal fans and supporters, but this Christian conservative's work in prison ministry, and his efforts to make America a more decent and moral place, was certainly good-hearted in intent and, quite often, in effect. Yet some of his actions and rhetoric on the matter of gay rights made Colson appear just the opposite to those not on his side. Colson, for instance, described the push for same-sex marriage as "the greatest threat to religious freedom in America"[28]—an assertion that demonizes gay people and their allies and sounds like hyperbolic nonsense to many outside the conservative Christian camp. To those not buying it, the claim seems to suggest that denying rights to gay people is somehow central to the form of religion everyone knows Colson is most concerned about: Christianity. To be fair, it's true that in a series of worst-case scenarios—if, for example, conservative churches were forced to perform same-sex weddings or hire gay pastors, or if they faced government reprisals for anti-homosexuality preaching—we would have before us a gross violation of their First Amendment religious freedom rights. And, yes, one could speculate that gay marriage would constitute one major step down that worrisome road. But the simple fact is, few, if any, prominent gay rights advocates are pushing to abrogate congregations' rights to hire the preachers they want to hire, believe what they want to believe, and preach what they want to preach about homosexuality. For a Christian leader to claim that his side's religious freedom is threatened if two women get a marriage license at a government office is not a winning argument in today's America, and it has the effect of discrediting both the maker of the claim and the religion that is invariably invoked in the process. Religious freedom does not mean you will get your way in every public policy debate.

As Colson learned, maintaining this message and stance brings a different set of consequences in the new environment than it once did. Around the same time that the dramas around Don't Ask, Don't Tell and the SPLC hate groups list were playing out, Colson was helping lead a campaign called the Manhattan Declaration, which was mounting a vigorous defense of conservative values, including the principle that marriage should be reserved for heterosexual couples. When the campaign corralled the new technology of the day and launched an iPhone app bearing the words of their manifesto, it wasn't long before Apple started receiving complaints. Such "hate" and "homophobia," protesters insisted, should not be tolerated. Apple pulled the app from the virtual shelves.[29]

Numerous other examples attest to the price conservative Christians pay when they stand hard against gays and lesbians and refuse to accept the larger society's changing mores and growing embrace of gay people: a Christian university student booted from a school counseling program for refusing, on religious grounds, to affirm homosexuality while serving gay clients[30]; Catholic Charities affiliates in Illinois losing state funding for refusing to abide by new rules requiring their consideration of same-sex couples as foster and adoptive parents[31]; evangelical student groups losing their university recognition and funding for refusing to accept sexual-minority members.

Different details, the same general story: if it's gays you refuse, it's status and acceptance you lose.

Say what you will about the fairness of these dynamics—does opposing same-sex marriage, for instance, automatically constitute "hate"?—brouha-has like the one around the Manhattan Declaration iPhone app well illustrate the price that gay rights fighters increasingly pay as they strive to withhold rights from a certain group of Americans based on their identity. And even if they claim to harbor no enmity against homosexual people themselves—only their sin—they stand on shaky ground there, too. As more and more Americans are asking, how can you claim to respect and love people in gay relationships and then tell them with a straight face that they are not worthy, for instance, of a marriage license? "It's impossible to tell people we love them," says evangelical professor, author, and activist Tony Campolo, "if we deny them the basic rights we enjoy."[32]

As a I wrote in the aforementioned *USA Today* column, conservative Christian leaders are going to have to be very careful about their rhetoric and tactics going forward—careful not to continue giving the impression that being Christian is in large measure about opposing gay rights, and careful not to let the public expression of their faith become primarily associated with something that looks, sounds, and feels like hate to growing segments of the population. Fighting to the end might sound gallant, but it's not a road to glory so much as a ticket to infamy—an infamy akin to that borne by the likes of Bull Connor, George Wallace, and other villains of civil rights history. This is not a well-chosen hill for Christians to die on.

Place yourself twenty, maybe thirty, years into the future, and imagine how students and readers of not-so-distant history might regard the anti-homosexual claims made by Christian Right standard bearers like Tony Perkins and Bryan Fischer.

Perkins, head of the Family Research Council, continues to indict the advance of gay rights as a major threat to heterosexual marriage and families, and as a threat to Christians' religious liberties. At the time of this writing, deal-sealing statistical evidence or concrete facts have yet to materialize to substantiate the scare claims about the "homosexual agenda," as it's frequently called. Certainly the institution of the American family has been buffeted by the high winds of rapid social change. But social scientists generally indict divorce, out-of-wedlock births, and the phenomenon of single parenthood (especially the economic disadvantages often attached to that situation) as the most direct threats to the institution of the American family and children's healthy development. No matter. The FRC continues spewing its alarmist claims, warning its followers and donors that the gay rights movement is hell-bent on abolishing age-of-consent laws and promoting pedophilia; that gay and lesbian soldiers are more prone to sexually assaulting fellow service members; and that anti-bullying programs in schools are thinly veiled attempts to indoctrinate impressionable schoolchildren[33]—that gays and lesbians, in sum, are out to destroy the family and the American way of life as we know them.

The face of the Mississippi-based AFA—Bryan Fischer, director of issues analysis—takes the hyperbole and the baseless demonizing to even lower lows. As the Southern Poverty Law Center reported, Fischer has enlightened us with nuggets like "[h]omosexuality gave us Adolf Hitler, and homosexuals in the military gave us the Brown Shirts, the Nazi war machine, and six million dead Jews" and "homosexuals, as a group, are the single greatest perpetrators of hate crimes on the planet, outside the Muslim religion."[34]

It's impossible to square such demonizing nonsense with the truth-telling required of Christians by their Ten Commandments, or with the love and compassion teachings of their savior. As one new-evangelical pastor observes, the incendiary rhetoric around abortion and gay rights has become "a big bass drum that is beaten so loudly nobody can hear the sweet strain of the gospel."[35] No wonder younger evangelicals attest to cringing when the time comes to reveal to fellow students at their universities, or coworkers at their new jobs, that they're Christians.

Of course, ruffling some people's feathers merits little concern if you're convinced you're representing the capital-T Truth, as conservative Christian organizations are quick to assert. The problem is that such a stance is increasingly difficult to maintain as society begins taking a more complex look at what the Bible says and doesn't say about sex, and as growing ranks of unchurched Americans ask why it even matters what the Bible says on this (or any other) social issue.

Boston University biblical scholar Jennifer Wright Knust demonstrates in her 2011 book, *Unprotected Texts*, that the Bible's lessons on sex and marriage are highly nuanced, heavily contextualized, and often contradictory. The writings of the apostle Paul and modern interpretations of the Sodom and Gomorrah story guide much of conservative Christian thinking on sexuality. But other parts of the Bible veer in dramatically different directions, Knust argues—appearing to legitimize polygamy or reveling in exotic desire at one turn while, at another, elevating celibacy as the proper Christian practice.[36] Knust says it is highly misleading for marriage traditionalists to portray their stance as *the* biblical stance. "When read as a whole," she writes, "the Bible provides neither clear nor consistent advice about sex and bodies."[37] (Knust's perspective is but one, and a decidedly liberal one at that. Readers interested in a traditionalist's take on the Bible and homosexuality will find an authoritative articulation of it in the writings of Robert Gagnon, among others.)

The situation becomes even more biblically interesting when one considers Knust's ideas in juxtaposition with Bible teachings on the sinfulness of judgment, sanctimony, and undue attention to other people's sins. Consider that Paul, in the oft-cited passage in which he declares homosexuality wrong, ticks off other common transgressions in the same literary breath—greed, malice, envy, murder, slander, insolence, rebellion against parents, ruthlessness, deceit, and pride—and goes on to warn that "in passing judgment on another you condemn yourself, because you that judge are doing the very same sort of sinful things."[38] Recall how Jesus stymied the crowd of would-be stone throwers itching to deal out some vigilante capital punishment on an accused adulteress by inviting whoever was sin-free to cast the first stone.[39] And take note of how Jesus, in the cherished Sermon on the Mount, admonished those who would fixate on the "speck" in another person's eye when they had a veritable "log" in their own.[40]

Can it really be said on solid biblical ground, or from the standpoint of decent human behavior, that it's the Christian's job to continue carrying on about homosexuality as though it's the whopper of all sins? And to continue opposing and condemning it at every turn? Imagine where *that* course would leave Christians and their faith movement twenty or thirty years down the line.

To their credit, new-school evangelicals and those influenced by them—some who are themselves gay and Christian—are devising routes of escape from the corner into which these culture-war dynamics have trapped one prominent aspect of evangelicalism in our time. Their voices and their sharp articulation of the need for change, through their words and actions both, are difficult for fellow believers to dismiss as mere anti-Christian hostility, for these critics are themselves evangelicals. And even if they, too, might be driven at times by calculation like Christian Right strategists who fashioned a political tool out of homosexuality, their proofs are found in the same Holy Scripture that sprung the rhetoric about homosexuality as "abomination."

For some change creators, the departure from traditional evangelical teaching and tone is so complete that they are not even in the same room as that painted-in corner, not even in the same *building* as groups like the Family Research Council. Consider people like the OneWheaton members: gay, discerning no need to repent and pray away the gay, animated by the conviction that God loves them and made them as they are, and intent on following Jesus. And consider the community of passionate allies and advocates typified by Jay Bakker, the son of the famous televangelists Jim and Tammy Faye Bakker, and the founder of Revolution Church in New York, who invokes Jesus in his preaching for radical inclusiveness and full rights for gays. Bakker, who is straight, declares flatly and unambiguously that homosexuality is not a sin.[41] God loves everyone, Bakker declares; Jesus saves all.

Others tread a more subtle line but seek peace in their own ways. Although not ready to deem homosexuality biblically approved and morally pure, they are strongly motivated to respect and love the gay people with whom they share space on their campuses and in their social circles, workplaces, neighborhoods, cities, and country. They withhold judgment and keep their mouths wisely shut about their friends' and fellows' sexual orientations. They have come to see homosexuality, God-blessed or not, as an issue of less than make-or-break importance. Being associated with the homophobic haters is about the worst fate they could imagine for themselves.

"Young Christians increasingly have family members who are gay, have people in their lives who really matter to them who are gay, and that changes how they approach these issues," Gabe Lyons explained to me. "This doesn't mean their convictions on the matter have changed, but in this new environment, people don't want to see their friends being discriminated against; they don't want them labeled as someone who should be feared and blamed."[42]

Others of a more traditionalist bent on matters of the heart and bedroom are responding to the changing climate with pragmatism and tolerance. Evangelical professor and writer David Gushee—a liberal on some issues but not on same-sex marriage—described for researcher Marcia Pally an approach that might be termed accommodationist: "Traditional marriage—one man, one woman—is sadly fading as the paradigmatic way we do relationships," Gushee says. "I'm doing what I can to strengthen it where I can, in the church. But we're losing that argument even within our churches. The homosexuality issue is just one piece of the change. We're going to have to get more refined in our thinking. There is a category called pastoral accommoda-

tion, where you don't change the structure of your beliefs but you accommo-
date realistically to the patterns around you, so you can actually be of some
use to the people who are coming your way."[43]

In explaining its withdrawal from the Day of Truth, Exodus International
marked a promising path forward for conservative Christian groups that have
staked so much on their resistance against homosexuality—a path that offers
them a way out the corner of the room reserved for those deemed fundamentalist bigots and bullies. Note that Exodus head Alan Chambers did not
announce a change in his organization's conviction that people can be saved
from homosexuality through faith in Christ. Note that Chambers and his
organization—"the world's largest ministry to individuals and families im-
pacted by homosexuality," as it describes itself—were not suddenly affirm-
ing homosexuality and demanding marriage equality.

What Exodus International did implement, though, was an adjustment in
tone and tack, and, as Chambers's explanation revealed, it was a change that
did *not* require him to throw away his Bible. The opposite, actually. Chambers, in his statement about teaching high school students to treat their neighbors as they themselves would like to be treated, was invoking a foundational
Christian principle, a principle long regarded as the basis for decent human
behavior. Why would Christians want to be seen behaving any other way?

Not to be Pollyanna, since the entrenched views of older and more traditional evangelicals will continue to exert resistance against gay-rights advances for some time; not only does prevailing sentiment in these ranks hold
homosexuality to be wrong, but it also regards it as an *important* wrong with
significant negative implications for the entire society—a wrong that needs
to be fought. The popular press still furnishes fresh reminders of the torment
that gay people, and gay teenagers in particular, often endure at the hands of
bullies—bullies who find cover in the anti-homosexual railings of some conservative Christian figures.[44]

The traditional-but-softer approach of figures like Wheaton president
Philip Ryken has its own problems. It's good that Ryken, in his e-mail to the
Wheaton campus, expressed concern about the pain experienced by the students, faculty, staff, and alumni who "experience same-sex attraction." But
fairly or not, critics will find something disingenuous about his compassionate talk when the same communication commits the very act—the presentation of Bible verses against homosexuality—that often causes gay people to
experience this pain.

On the flip side of this coin, the new evangelicals spoken of so admiringly in this book face their own set of traps and perils with the new courses they plot. They, too, face temptations to base their "convictions" about homosexuality on popularity and opportunism. What *will* they do about those passages in scripture that condemn homosexuality? Fine lines are being drawn, and tread.

Nevertheless, the change is real; the change is inexorable. Each day finds more young evangelicals entering adulthood and bringing their new perspectives with them into the public arenas, voting booths, debates, and conversations. As they enter, and as students of the old school bow out with the passage of time, the dynamics shift. Even if they deem homosexuality wrong, new currents of thought in popular evangelicalism conceive of it as one drop in a sea of sins and not demanding of the same moral indignation and intervention as, say, human trafficking or greed-fueled indifference to glaring poverty.

Each day seems to furnish small and sometimes big signs of a new evangelical conversation about homosexuality. Who would have imagined twenty years ago that gay Wheaton College alumni would form a group and show their rainbow colors proudly—and that the college president would respond not *just* by citing anti-homosexual Bible verses but also by waxing compassionate about the need for the Wheaton community to love and respect its LGBTQ members?

This is the sign of a tide that has clearly shifted. As is the appearance of a story on Pat Robertson's conservative Christian Broadcasting Network about an ex-homophobe now on a mission to reach out to sexual minorities with the message that the church and he are sorry for their mistreatment of gays and lesbians.[45] As is the admission by one of conservative Christianity's leading representatives, the Reverend Albert Mohler, that his Southern Baptist denomination must repent of its homophobia.[46] As is the emergence of ultra-masculine Christian sports figures like ex-football star Michael Irvin, who has revealed that his brother was gay and has pledged "100 percent support" for any gay pro athlete willing to come out of the closet.[47] As are the growth of gay student groups at Christian colleges[48] and the rising chorus of evangelical voices like that of Tim King, communications director for the progressive evangelical group Sojourners.

King was in graduate school and facing a dilemma—his lesbian Christian friend was coming out of the closet and losing many of her Christian friends in the process—when he found a different hill for his last stand. It was not a stand against his friend's sexuality, but a stand *for* her.

As King wrote in a moving article for the Sojourners website,

> I read every theological argument for and against homosexuality I could find. Every Bible verse and possible interpretation I learned. That's when I went to a Gay-Straight Alliance meeting on my campus. . . . I went into that meeting struggling in my head and my heart and hoping for an answer to my question, "Is it okay to be gay?"
>
> That night, I heard the stories of struggle, loneliness, shame, and rejection of others who were LGBTQ. I heard about the pain caused by Christians who actively persecuted the gay community. I listened to the deep hurt caused by well-intentioned people who created churches and institutions full of shame that ostracized anyone struggling or questioning their sexuality. I soon realized that my question was getting in the way.
>
> God worked in my heart. I realized that my primary job as a follower of Christ wasn't to try and answer the question, "Is it okay to be gay?" and then enforce my answer on others. My job was to love my neighbor as myself. . . . My responsibility was to speak out on issues of civil rights for the LGBT community and actively work to make the church a more welcoming place. I learned that "How do I love?" must come before, "Who is okay?"[49]

The culture wars have not ended. But they certainly are morphing. From the relative lack of anti-gay rhetoric heard in an otherwise harsh Republican presidential nominating process in 2011 and 2012, one can certainly deduce that the pollsters and strategists realize there is little political benefit yielded anymore in demonizing homosexuals and promising to turn them straight or stuff them back in closets. "The Gay Menace," as commentator Paul Waldman observes, "just doesn't have much political potency anymore."[50]

Why? A significant part of the answer can be found within evangelical America—the group that the exploiters and dividers could once count on for responding to this kind of red meat but that is now evolving away from this particular fixation.

Moved by their experiences with their gay siblings, friends, coworkers, and classmates—congregation members, even—they are finding it next to impossible to continue with the stereotyping and demonizing. They are thinking anew about what the Bible says and doesn't say about homosexuals, and in what contexts. Even some of the dyed-in-the-wool traditionalists are finding their ears ringing with the words of a savior who invited any and all who are sin-free to cast the first stone at the adulteress of the famous Bible tale and all she stands for. Cognizant of their own flaws, honest now about their own sins—the church's sins—more of Jesus' people are seeing those of a different sexual orientation in a new light. Past the logs in their eyes, they are seeing "the gay issue" in a different way.

So much so that the once unthinkable is coming into view: a day when gays and lesbians might be welcome at Homecoming at Wheaton College and all it represents. Officially.

Chapter Eight

Pro-Life . . . Seriously

She was, the legislator told her, the first evangelical Christian who had ever come to speak with him about something other than the pro-life or traditional marriage causes.

Stephanie Tama-Sweet, then a lobbyist for the fledgling Oregon Center for Christian Values, recalls that the conservative evangelical Republican did not point this out to compliment her, or to hail the moment as something positive and long overdue. More like, where did she get off invoking the Bible in her advocacy for the environment?

"I was meeting with him on an environmental bill," Tama-Sweet recalls, "that I had testified for in front of his committee. I had read from Genesis at the hearing and had talked about the Christian responsibility to be good stewards of the Earth. He sent me an e-mail arguing against my use of scripture. I set up a meeting with him to talk further about our beliefs, the bill, and why I, as a Christian, thought we should be involved in protecting the environment."[1]

Invoking the Bible on behalf of the environment? Tama-Sweet had some explaining to do. However, few, if any, find themselves surprised or in need of elaboration when they hear an evangelical political figure or activist invoking the Bible and speaking up for "life" in Salem or most any state's capital. And despite the vague, noncontroversial appeal of the word *life* in most contexts, no one is unclear in the least about the more specific and vastly more divisive meaning of the term when it's invoked in the political arena, as it so often is.

Abortion—it's the issue that has turned *life* into a four-letter word in many progressive quarters, the culture-wars flashpoint that has probably done more than any other to confine politically minded evangelicalism to the right wing of the body politic. By the same token, there is no division in American public life that new evangelicals of Tama-Sweet's ilk are better positioned to transcend and transform than the one between those long-stale-mated forces arguing about whether women should be allowed to terminate their pregnancies.

"Tremendous sadness, a lot of anger." That's how Tama-Sweet, in her early thirties and now a lobbyist for the American Heart Association, de-scribes her response to narrow, politically charged invocations of "life" in evangelicals' strivings to pass anti-abortion legislation and, often, castigate those who get in their way. When I sat down at a northeast Portland coffee-house with both her and her husband, Shoshon, many progressives around the country were agitated about developments in the Virginia Legislature, where Republicans had nearly passed into law a measure that would have required women to undergo invasive transvaginal ultrasounds before having abortions, regardless of whether the woman and her doctor deemed them necessary.[2] A slightly milder version of the legislation eventually passed, saving women the discomfort and affront of having ultrasound wands in-serted into their bodies, but still requiring them to undergo external transab-dominal ultrasounds.

"It makes me sad," Tama-Sweet explains, "because this kind of thing is so far from what Jesus wanted. And I feel angry because it's such a false representation of Christianity. Abortion *is* an incredibly important issue, but it's been politicized and used to create divisions—sometimes by people who don't even follow Christ but who want to use this issue and people's vulner-abilities to get their political agendas across."[3]

Tama-Sweet, a blonde woman who grew up in a Baptist family in Minne-sota and did her graduate studies at evangelical Biola University, is on mater-nity leave when we talk, having had her second child just weeks before. When her leave is up, she will resume lobbying for bills and policies that improve Oregonians' health. Her disgust with abortion politics, she explains, owes to the way that outsized obsessions with abortion drain energy and resources from other urgent issues that go begging for attention from acti-vists and strategists, party leaders and office holders, church leaders and churchgoers—issues that also affect "life," any way you cut it.

"It drives me nuts to see how politicians use the abortion issue, how effective it can be," Tama-Sweet says—effective at mobilizing Christian conservative voters, she explains, and effective at demonizing women who have abortions, the doctors who perform them, and the politicians and voters who work to keep abortion available. "I think it also ruins the political process and drives away many moderate Christians who might be more inclined to get involved in politics. There are so many other important issues people are not organizing around. When it comes to Christian values, abortion is *not* the only issue!"

As Tama-Sweet and her equally passionate husband affirm while we talk, American public life seems stuck on abortion. It's the issue we can't get past, the thing that keeps sucking the oxygen out of the room. Much the same could be said about the effect of the issue on evangelical Christianity itself. It, too, often seems stuck on abortion. Quite apart from the serious and worthy discussions one could have about abortion policy, ethics, and morals, including the religious dimensions of all these, abortion as a culture-wars flashpoint sticks to evangelical Christianity's public reputation in the most polarizing ways. Because of the passions and tribal identities it ignites, because of the top billing it has enjoyed in evangelical politics, abortion has become such a conspicuous feature of evangelical Christianity's "brand" that it seems at times to have obscured the cross itself.

Stephanie's husband, Shoshon, jumps into the conversation with equal verve as we continue talking. The strong association between Christianity and harsh anti-abortion rhetoric and politics, he offers, is the main reason many secular progressives "get hives" when they hear that word *evangelical*. Unlike his wife, the thirty-six-year-old Shoshon Tama-Sweet came to Jesus only as an adult and speaks from considerable experience when he talks about the way the issue plays out on the non-evangelical side of the tracks. He grew up in an environment where Christianity was disdained, he says, where people, "when they hear the word *Christian*, think of hateful, divisive people who want to control women's bodies. There's so much anger and misconception that you have to wade through before you can get to a conversation about Christianity. Abortion—it's destroyed the conversation about Jesus."

My own experience and research convince me that Shoshon Tama-Sweet is right. The several times I have been at pro-choice rallies, I have been struck—intimidated even—by the venom in the exchanges between legal-abortion supporters and the ever-present anti-abortion counter-demonstrators. These are not people who are going to have a productive conversation about *anything*. Of course, secular people are not the only ones "getting hives," as Shoshon Tama-Sweet phrases it. Abortion—its legal availability and prevalence—makes conservative Christians break out as well, evoking all manner of negative ideas and emotions about liberal, secular America, and the means by which abortion became legal: a decision not by the country's voted representatives but by the United States Supreme Court.

The abortion issue seems to make many in the new-evangelicals movement break out in hives of yet another variety. Among Christians of the Tama-Sweets' generation and inclination, the issue of abortion is the scarlet letter *A* that subjects them to unwanted stereotyping and gets in the way of their connecting with people and causes outside of evangelical subculture. It's not that they consider abortion unimportant, unworthy of attention or consideration. But they long to have a different conversation about it and, along with it, conversations about a host of other "life" issues as well.

Having noticed the absence of anti-abortion messages, talks, and exhibitions at the numerous conferences of new-paradigm evangelicals I've attended, I probed the issue with a pastor and conference organizer I know. The theme of justice prevails at these events, I noted, and impressively so— justice for starving children in Africa, justice for victims of modern-day slavery, justice for children languishing in unstable foster-care environments. But wouldn't a passionate abortion fighter have a legitimate beef about these gatherings? All this passion for justice, but not justice for embryos and fetuses?

The pastor's first response was to say that he would need to speak anonymously. The matter was highly charged, he said, a "lose-lose." "The abortion conversation is stalemated," the thirty-something pastor continued. If he had anti-abortion presentations or exhibits at his events for younger Christians, "I don't know if I could get ten people to come. The polarization around that issue is like World War I trench warfare. If you headline with abortion, all of a sudden it seems like there is nothing different about that conference. The anti-abortion thing dominates. If you fly that flag, you would make it feel like a political event for a reactionary special-interest group."

Not that younger evangelicals have all decided abortion is fine. Quite the contrary. As discussed in previous chapters, polling data indicate that they, like older evangelicals, tend to believe abortion to be morally wrong. What's different is that abortion shares the stage with other issues in their thoughts and prayers, and on their agendas. And more to the point, they are loath to wield the issue like a political weapon and continue grinding the axes of old.

"The deeper issue," the pastor continued, "is that people my age grew up with the anti-abortion stance being co-equal with Christianity. If you were a good Christian, this is what defined you. You grew up this way. This was the be-all and end-all that degenerated into [Christianity appearing to be] owned by this Moral Majority, conservative Republican movement." The idea took hold, he said, that women who have abortions, and people who support them, "are bad, evil people. And we Christians are the good guys!"

Evangelical, Christianity, abortion—words freighted with complicated, explosive baggage after years of culture war. Same for a pair of otherwise-innocuous terms that liberals and conservatives have been wielding and parrying in the ongoing culture battles.

Life and *choice*—how did it become so controversial to be in favor of one or the other? And why wouldn't sensible people support *both*?

There was a time when evangelical America considered abortion to be a "Catholic issue." Religious history professor Randall Balmer points out the absence of a strong evangelical stance against abortion around the time of the monumental *Roe v. Wade* Supreme Court decision in 1973 and the several years that immediately followed. In his book *The Making of Evangelicalism*, Balmer cites the passage by the Southern Baptist Convention of a resolution calling for the legal availability of abortion "under such conditions as rape, incest, clear evidence of severe fetal deformity, and . . . evidence of the likelihood of damage to the emotional, mental, and physical health of the mother."[4] W. A. Criswell, former president of the Southern Baptist Convention, said at the time, "I have always felt that it was only after a child was born and had a life separate from its mother that it became an individual person."[5]

Revealingly, it was political strategizing in the late 1970s, several years after the *Roe v. Wade* decision and during the formation of what became the Christian Right, that made abortion the red meat into which political evangelicalism would sink its teeth, Balmer says. Evangelical leaders, already coalescing around grievances including a challenge to the tax-exempt status of fundamentalist Bob Jones University for racial discrimination, held a conference call to consider other issues they might add to their agenda. As Balmer reports, drawing from a conversation he had in 1990 with Christian Right founding organizer Paul Weyrich, "A voice on the end of one of the lines said, 'How about abortion?' And that, according to Weyrich, was how abortion was cobbled into the agenda of the Religious Right."[6]

How revealing that political calculus—not theology, not doctrine—was, by this telling, such a powerful catalyst in elevating abortion to its status as Issue Number One for evangelical America. Cynicism is one obvious response to knowing this; so, too, might be grudging respect for the political shrewdness of the choice made by Weyrich and his fellow founders of the Christian Right. "Instrumentalizing" abortion, to use Balmer's phrase, proved highly potent, not just in spurring righteous indignation over the slaughter of unborn babies, as the often overheated rhetoric terms it, but also in evoking and channeling unresolved animosities over liberal advances of the 1960s and 1970s: the sexual revolution, enhanced rights for women, and the erosion of Christian prerogatives that were once taken for granted, such as officially sanctioned prayer in public schools and the ability of fundamentalist institutions like Bob Jones University to ban interracial dating if they felt so moved. Abortion has proved to be a politically useful wedge issue *par excellence.*

But whatever progressives might think about the evident insincerity of the process, the fact remains that the anti-abortion message resonated powerfully with those who became the foot soldiers of the Christian Right. And as the spate of anti-abortion legislation of recent years testifies, it continues to resonate powerfully. It did so, and does so, for a reason. However painful it might be for progressives to concede the point, abortion resonates in part because there is something disquieting, at the very least, about the termination of hundreds of thousands of pregnancies each year in this country. Call it what you want—a fetus, an unborn child, a clump of cells—it is ended by abortion. Despite the very legitimate arguments mounted by the defenders of safe, legal abortion—absolutely including the need for society to respect the rights of women to make decisions about their own reproductive organs—pro-choice America has not been able to persuade or placate the many millions of America who oppose abortion and clamor to severely restrict it, if not ban it altogether.

To the ears of unconvinced evangelicals, "choice" can sound like a flimsy justification for the termination of a pregnancy—a trivial concern at best when juxtaposed with something as powerful and compelling as the notion of life. Yet in a mirror-image way, "life" has proven to be a similarly inadequate and oversimplified concept in the ranks of progressive America, widely seen as a disingenuous pretext for a project that, to many women and their advocates, amounts to an insidious assault on womens' dignity and rights.

So it goes with abortion in American public life: two bumper-sticker arguments, both refusing to address the legitimate principles on the other side of the debate, locked together like two fists pressed hard against each other, neither conceding an inch. Not the healthiest use of time and energy for the bodies attached to those two balled-up hands. Destructive, even, when you remember that a few on one side—the supposedly Christian side—have even resorted to deadly violence.

As attested by the above-mentioned pastor who organizes conferences appealing to the younger, new-century evangelicals, abortion indeed is a stalemated issue. Consider the public-opinion trend lines of recent decades. Like those warring front lines in World War I, like those mud- and death-filled trenches we associate with that long-ago war, the lines remain in essentially the same place as when the abortion culture war started nearly forty years ago. Gallup, which has been polling public opinion on abortion since the 1970s, found 54 percent of Americans supporting the legal availability of abortion in some circumstances in 1975. The figure has hovered in the mid-50s range ever since, landing at 57 percent in 2009.[7] The two polar views—abortion should always be legal, or always *il*legal—likewise remained in more or less the same position in 2009 as in 1975. And the proportions are eerily similar. The 2009 Gallup poll (done jointly with *USA Today*) found 21 percent of Americans favoring legal abortion in all circumstances, and 18 percent opposing abortion in all circumstances. In 1975, both percentages were matched at roughly 20 percent.[8] (An interesting wrinkle here: The "always legal" figure had grown significantly from the mid-1970s to the mid-1990s, reaching the point in 1994 where "always legal" outpaced "never legal" by a 33 percent to 13 percent margin. But, heartening to anti-abortion forces, those percentages have returned to roughly equal proportions.)

Other opinion sampling has found a slight majority of Americans holding to the view that abortion is morally wrong, which anti-abortion activists are quick to cite. Yet believing something wrong is not the same as insisting on its illegality; all sorts of acts and ways of living are widely considered immoral—selfishness, for example, or sex with another person's spouse—yet no one is working to criminalize these. As this would suggest, the data show that many who believe abortion is wrong also believe it should be legally available, albeit with limits.

Among those who love to wage or watch a battle, attention fixes on the passionate warriors of the abortion fight and their crusades for the opponents' unconditional surrender: no abortion under any circumstances, or no restrictions whatsoever on a woman's ability to access abortion. What is lost in the drama is the fact that these forces, even when you combine them, are a minority; well over half the population rejects the simplistic, either-or proposition framed by culture wars and takes a more nuanced approach to abortion. It should, in the majority view, be legal in some instances and not in others. The culture war that gets the headlines is, when you think about it, a war that most Americans are sitting out. To the majority in the broad and nuanced middle, abortion is neither the evil of all evils nor a casual act akin to brushing off a fly.

And as it turns out, the complex, textured nature of the abortion debate is poorly described by the binary suggested by the culture-war argument between the "pro-life" and "pro-choice" vanguards. In 2011, the Public Religion Research Institute released results of a survey that shed valuable new light on the public opinion around abortion. Some 70 percent of the people polled in the survey said "pro-choice" described them well. Nearly two-thirds, meanwhile, said "pro-life" described them.[9]

The math, clearly, does not work out. How can you have more than 100 percent of something? To those with a taste for the trench life, this was suggestive of the public's moral confusion about abortion. But to Robert P. Jones, who oversaw the survey, the math-defying result was evidence of the public's good sense in not falling for false choices and simplistic bumper-sticker arguments. As Jones and his PRRI colleagues wrote in their report, "Despite the polarizing rhetoric in the public debate, when given the opportunity, a significant number of Americans identify simultaneously as both 'pro-life' and 'pro-choice.'"[10]

Around the same time, another poll found the public weary of the old abortion debate and longing for a different, broader discussion. Polled by the Democratic polling firm Lake Research Partners, this sample of Americans was critical of Congress for an outsized focus on abortion and too little attention to reproductive health and access to birth control.[11] Seventy-nine percent of those surveyed agreed with the following statement, 49 percent of them agreeing strongly: "We may have different opinions about abortion, so rather than continuing to argue about this one issue, our elected officials should focus on the broader context like providing greater access to birth control, teaching comprehensive sex education, and improving maternal health and childbirth outcomes. These are issues that will allow us to come together."

There's plenty in that statement to make Christian conservatives uncomfortable, particularly the parts about sex education, which some conservatives associate with promoting sex, and the notion that conservatives should give up the fight to make abortion illegal. However, it's hard to imagine much opposition to working for improvements in "maternal health and childbirth outcomes." As the pollsters' statement posits, there indeed are goals that can unite most well-intentioned people.

There is a phrase worth remembering from the PRRI report that found Americans trending toward "both-and" instead of "either-or" on the matter of life and choice: "*When given the opportunity,*" the report said, Americans are both pro-life and pro-choice. And why wouldn't they be? It's time the framework gave them that opportunity. It's time to release the abortion issue from an unhelpful and misguided culture-war context and understanding. Set my people free!

In Atlanta in 2010, billboards began popping up with a most alarming message. The signs blared their warning in upper-case letters juxtaposed with the face of a concerned-looking African American toddler. Black children, the message read, were an "endangered species." These arresting billboards were the most visible thrusts of a campaign described by its organizers as a protest against our country's "ugliest form of racism," against an elite conspiracy to perpetrate eugenics and black genocide. Encountering these messages quickly, without context, any progressive would likely have saluted the campaign for bringing overdue public attention to our country's persistent racial injustices—until, that is, he or she noticed the campaign's website address: toomanyaborted.com. Its creator: Georgia Right to Life, which had joined a new front in the anti-abortion movement attempting to link abortion to a sinister plot to destroy black America.

As I wrote in a *USA Today* commentary on the campaign and its ramifications,[12] some positives and possibilities could be pulled out of the wreckage of hype, manipulation, and incendiary insinuations about the supposedly evil intent of abortion supporters. Give credit to the abortion-is-genocide vanguard, I wrote, for demolishing the usual left-right boundaries in their mixing of cries against racial injustice (typically a liberal cause) with anti-abortion politics (usually a cause of social conservatives). By bringing new national attention to disproportionately high rates of abortion among African Americans, they had succeeded in shining a much-needed spotlight on distress in black communities.

Abortion rates among African Americans indeed are too high to shrug off. That's true whether it's the causes that concern you most—poverty, a lack of educational and economic opportunity, a lack of access to contraception, a lack of sexual responsibility, all of which lead to abortion—or whether it's the effect you find galling—abortion itself. According to 2011 statistics from the Centers for Disease Control and Prevention, blacks have about 40 percent of the country's abortions, despite making up just 13 percent of the population.[13] Over the first decade of the twenty-first century, more than a third of black pregnancies ended in abortion, far higher than the white rate.[14] Add up all the major causes of death among blacks—heart disease, diabetes, cancer, violence, etc.—and they do not match the number of abortions.[15] This was the kernel of truth in the inflammatory, disingenuous claims about a racist conspiracy, "womb lynchings," and "genocide." (What the alarmist rhetoric ignored was the more reassuring statistic that black birth rates, despite abortion, have been higher than the country's overall rate: 16.5 births per 1,000 black women in 2006, compared with 14.2 overall.[16])

As I argued in that *USA Today* commentary, the relatively high rates of abortion among African Americans *ought* to be of great concern to progressives even if they're not inclined to wring their hands over abortions or criticize those who have them. What circumstances, we should ask, would lead to so many women getting pregnant against their intentions and, upon finding themselves pregnant, deciding that they were not in a position to go through with it?

Although not intentionally, the abortion-as-genocide campaign had revealed, to my eyes, a gradually emerging field of possibility that has been generating more enthusiasm in recent years within both religious and secular circles. Whether we see abortion as the problem or the manifestation of a whole host of other social malignancies, the door of opportunity appeared to be opening wider toward healing progress on the issue that is surely the most persistent argument-starter in the ongoing culture wars surrounding faith and politics.

As I went on to argue in that piece, abortion reduction is a cause that ought to appeal to all but the most devoted grudge-holders and ax-grinders in the decades-long abortion wars. *Of course* turning abortion into a crime, and turning some women and doctors into criminals, would yield a reduction in the incidence of abortion. But unless accompanied by a dramatic reduction in unwanted pregnancies, it would also lead us back to the bad old days of illegal and dangerous abortions and a thicket of other unintended consequences. In a country where a majority of the population does not share the religious affiliations and beliefs that fuel the anti-abortion fires, there are paths forward that are more unifying, more respectful of the competing principles and religious convictions in play, and, it is likely, more effective.

In a very real sense, the key to fewer abortions is fewer unwanted pregnancies—or, to put it another way, cultivating of a set of conditions in which the pregnancies that do occur are pregnancies that the responsible parties want to bring to term. Reverse-engineer it, and you surface numerous tactics and outcomes that are tolerable, if not downright appealing, to both sides. Holistic abortion-reduction efforts would pump strength into many causes dear to liberal and progressive hearts: better access to birth-control information and contraception; fewer rapes; better health care for mothers and children; better schools and economic prospects such that prospective mothers and fathers feel more confident about bringing a child into the world; and the acceptance by men of more responsibility for the reproductive consequences of sex. Achieve progress on all these, and you have an outcome that Christian conservatives would presumably want, too: a society in which more unborn babies are actually *born*.

With respect to black abortion rates, if there is a genocidal conspiracy afoot, the perpetrators are not Planned Parenthood, as the abortion-is-genocide campaign charged. Nor are they the doctors who perform abortions and the women who make the often-wrenching decisions to have them. Rather, they are the forces and factors conspiring to cause unwanted pregnancies. The hard work of taking on all these invisible conspirators will not bring the same visceral gratification as lobbing word grenades at those on the other side of the argument. But this is where practical progress is waiting to be made if Americans are brave enough to go beyond arguing about abortion and actually do something about it.

While working on the column about abortion and "genocide," I broached the abortion-reduction argument with Catherine Davis of Georgia Right to Life, the spokesperson for the toomanyaborted.com campaign. She was having none of it. It was a "smokescreen," Davis told me, aimed at deflecting attention away from what she saw as the essence of the problem: the legal availability of abortion and the presence of Planned Parenthood clinics in predominantly black neighborhoods.[17]

Sadly, because of politics and distrust, abortion reduction does not appear to have generated significant momentum yet. Despite plenty of lip service about the benefits of holistic measures to curb abortion, the pro-life/pro-choice culture war appeared to grow even fiercer in the months and years immediately following the appearance of those "endangered species" bill-boards in Atlanta and other cities, with battles breaking out in numerous state legislatures over laws requiring ultrasounds for women seeking abortion, bestowing "personhood" on embryos, and the like.

Are abortion-reduction rhetoric and strategies really just a smokescreen? It's no surprise that after decades of rhetorical warfare and millions of abortions, a Christian social conservative like Catherine Davis would have trouble trusting the intentions of liberals who refuse to lay high abortion rates at the feet of individual women and doctors and the availability of legal abortion but instead point to a complex of social problems that liberals care about and declare, "Solve these, and you'll get what you want!"

To liberal ears, dismissing an attack on the root causes of abortion as a mere smokescreen is frustratingly predictable, too. It seems to furnish evidence of what many legal-abortion supporters have been saying all along: that when it comes to abortion, social conservatives are more interested in punishing and demonizing their liberal enemies, and maintaining the sharp edge on their ever-ready political wedge, than achieving practical progress.

Arousing even more liberal suspicion and distrust are the constant and seemingly disingenuous invocations of "life" by anti-abortion crusaders. As one culture war–weary evangelical pastor admitted to me, the pro-life message is "just noise" to the unconvinced when its proclaimers are failing to stand up for human life in *all* its forms (and, we might add, when they continue to spout a message of "keep government out of our lives" on seemingly every other issue). So, too, does anti-abortion railing fail to persuade beyond the ranks of the converted when it comes without evidence of genuine compassion for the women actually affected by anti-abortion measures.

"When you push for the rights of someone (i.e., an embryo) with which the public has no real relationship at the possible expense of the actual people they see every day (i.e., the mother), it's a tough case to argue," writes author and church founder Christian Piatt. "Had the [anti-abortion] movement begun with a grassroots effort to serve those women in a loving, nurturing way, I think it may have been different. Had the group promoting this legislation spent a decade or more caring for distressed mothers, providing them with medical care, parenting skills, adoption alternatives, and other help that recognizes . . . them as more than the carrier of a group's political agenda in her womb, things might have turned out different."[18]

The Christian social conservatives we associate with anti-abortion crusading, it seems, have little to say when the "life" being threatened is the collateral damage wrought by American bombs dropped on an enemy country, citizens poisoned by mercury pollution, or children born into circumstances of poverty and discrimination that stack the deck against any realistic chance of a happy, productive life. There is, in sum, a massive sincerity deficit.

An evangelical friend of mine framed it in even blunter terms in a conversation we had about the dynamic: until pious white megachurch members start adopting black orphans, he pleaded, would they please stop with the endless railing against abortion?

Distrust, antipathy, unconvincing half-arguments, perceived hypocrisy and insincerity, an immovable object versus an irresistible force—such is the bleak state of affairs that has developed over the forty years since the United States Supreme Court made abortion a legal right. Maybe this is how it will always be. But what would happen if evangelical Christians *did* channel their passions to fighting the degradation of life outside the womb? How might the game change and the stalemate break if evangelical Christian church members *did* start adopting abandoned children? What if evangelical America *did* take this whole pro-life thing seriously?

Don't tell Stephanie and Shoshon Tama-Sweet that their careers are not dedicated to "life." As a lobbyist in Oregon's state capitol, Stephanie helped push for the passage in 2009 of landmark legislation that expanded health care coverage by eighty thousand children and fifty thousand low-income adults; priorto this, Oregon bore the dubious distinction of having one of the highest rates of uninsured children in the country.[19] She has also worked for law and policy that help lower-income people access better housing and nutrition.

"As a Christian," Tama-Sweet said in an interview with the evangelical magazine *Christianity Today*, "I was drawn to the [health care] issue because of the clear value Jesus placed on the physical, mental, and spiritual well-being of people. My favorite verse is John 10:10 ('The thief comes only to steal and kill and destroy; I have come that they may have life, and have it to the full'). I have also personally experienced the stress of not having health insurance and know that the cost can be extremely high—too high for many people—to pay out-of-pocket. Lack of insurance can be a major cause of stress for families, often forcing people to seek emergency medical help, which is costly and drives up the price of health insurance for everyone in the system. I believe my work is furthering the work of Christ in the community because I'm helping to bring about structural change that influences real peoples' lives and helps them live the life that God intended for them, to help set up a more beloved community."[20]

When I asked her about the evident insincerity of the Christian Right's pro-life message, Tama-Sweet brought up the writings of progressive evangelical Ron Sider, founder of the group Evangelicals for Social Action, and spoke passionately about the need for Christians to be consistent about "life."

"If you're going to have integrity," she explained, "you have to pay attention to the whole lifespan, from conception to death. This minute focus on fetuses takes discussion away from the wholeness of life. It obliterates the issue of how we treat human beings outside the womb who are being abused, who are being sex-trafficked. What are we going to do about all these children who *are* born? Where is church for *those* kids?"[21]

Anti-abortion crusaders sometimes portray themselves as modern-day abolitionists. The analogy misses the mark, however, by seeming to suggest that women who have abortions, and the doctors who perform them, are the slavers of our time. If you want to know who the real modern-day Christian abolitionists are, look at the growing movement of evangelicals who are fighting the slavery that actually exists in our time, on a scale that might surprise you. Millions of people around the world, many of them children, live in a state of bondage, trapped and trafficked as forced laborers and prostitutes in a lucrative global trade. This country is hardly immune to the problem. Communities across the United States are both a source of trafficked people and a destination for victimized people smuggled out of Asia and elsewhere. Rising up to fight for these victims' dignity and freedom, for these invisible people's lives, is a movement of anti-trafficking activists typified by Shoshon Tama-Sweet.

Serving in a position once held by his wife, Shoshon Tama-Sweet was, at the time of our interview, executive director of the Oregon Center for Christian Voices (previously known as the Center for Christian Values). He was spending many of his working hours, and more than a few evenings as well, fighting to expose sex trafficking in Portland, raising awareness of the problem in and around the city and trying to convince state legislators to pass laws making operations more difficult for sex-slave traders and handlers and the adult-entertainment business establishments under whose roofs they often operate. Coupled with that was a drive to free the victims of the sex trade and start them on their educations and progress toward healthy lives.

Tama-Sweet has found the work exhausting and, at times, depressing. Yet he asks, "If Christians aren't willing to do this, who is going to do it? We have an entire belief structure that's built around loving our neighbors and setting the captives free. It's built into our theological DNA. It makes you realize you've got to do it."[22]

Unless, that is, it's a political wedge you're looking for. Fighting modern-day slavery appears to have scant utility in that regard—which is, of course, the beauty of it. As if to demonstrate the power of the anti-trafficking issue to transcend culture war trenches, the conservative Christian Broadcasting Network published in 2012 an article enthusiastically touting an event called Freedom Sunday, aimed at raising churches' awareness of the global trafficking problem. Yes, *that* Christian Broadcasting Network—the media organization under the leadership of Christian Right icon Pat Robertson. There it was in CBN's news broadcast and on its website, mixed in with the usual come-to-Jesus messages and the dire warnings about the Muslims and secular liberals: an interview with an official from Robertson's Regent University touting the institution's anti-trafficking educational efforts and its first annual symposium on trafficking.[23]

Of course, CBN's and Regent's efforts could be dismissed by skeptics as mere spin and bandwagon jumping. Even so, CBN's embrace of the issue speaks to the universal appeal of the anti-trafficking ethic, and to Tama-Sweet's suggestion that fighting slavery is in Christianity's "DNA." As does the fact that almost anywhere you roam on the circuit of younger evangelicals' conferences and nonprofit networks, you will find herculean efforts to liberate those forced into slave labor and prostitution.

This ethic of freeing slaves and standing up for the exploited and powerless is hardly the exclusive province of Christians, of course. Progressives would claim this as part of their DNA, too, seeming to put them in league with none other than Pat Robertson. Stopping human trafficking—the most useless wedge issue ever.

Likewise for orphan adoption. The turn of the decade witnessed a drive in evangelical America, spearheaded by none other than Focus on the Family, to persuade and inspire church members to take foster-care kids into their families as true adoptees. Focus, a parenting advice and support network better known in progressive circles for the harsh political stances and rhetoric of its ex-leader, James Dobson, launched its Wait No More adoption campaign in 2008 and proceeded to hold events in a dozen states the next few years, with nearly eight thousand people attending from two thousand churches. "The message to the church is that we need to be the family for these lonely kids," says Kelly Rosati, Focus vice president for community outreach and the mother of four children adopted through the foster care system.[24] At the time of my conversation with Rosati, more than 1,900 families had initiated the adoption process after attending one of the "Wait No More" events.[25]

During my visit to Focus on the Family, while I listened to Rosati detail the orphan-adoption operation, I recalled the words of my evangelical friend who admonished the evangelical church for not backing word with action on the life issue, who suggested the church needed to shut its mouth about abortion until its people started adopting orphans. And it occurred to me that, however unlikely it is that I'll become an advocate for criminalizing abortion, I am at least more willing to listen to anti-abortion advocates and respect their views if they show genuine compassion for disadvantaged children outside the womb—if, indeed, they put their money where their mouths are and take the huge step of adopting orphans. Like many progressives, I would also appreciate hearing more genuine regard for the circumstances, dignity, and rights of women. The most recent literature from Focus at least says some of the right stuff in that regard, stating as one of its pro-life principles, "May we not pass judgment on the woman facing an unexpected pregnancy, but surround her with support."[26]

It's fascinating and encouraging to see the ways in which the "pro-life" ethic and commitment are broadening under the influence of post-culture-war evangelicals, right along with the overall political and activist agendas of these Jesus followers. Consider the evangelical response to mercury pollution. This is a substance so toxic to pregnant women and their as-yet-unborn babies that there are medical warnings against their consumption of fish and shellfish in which mercury collects after its emission from coal-burning power plants. Isn't this a life issue? Isn't it also a life issue to address the lethally poor water quality in some parts of the world? Absolutely yes, answer people like Mitch Hescox, president of the Evangelical Environmental Network. As Hescox argued in testimony before Congress in 2012, "Anything that threatens and impedes life, especially . . . the unborn and young children, is contrary to our common beliefs and values and exacts a moral toll on the nation's character."[27] Or as Boise, Idaho, pastor Tri Robinson says of his evangelical congregation, "Abortion is a huge factor for us . . . but I also see the environment is killing people, especially young children."[28]

Climate-change deniers, Christian and otherwise, often denounce environmentalists for summoning more compassion for trees and spotted owls than real human beings. Perhaps the label fits some on the extreme fringes of eco-activism, and even mainstream environmentalists have done too little to make clear the humanitarian basis for their work. But for nearly everyone involved in or sympathetic to the environmental movement, concern for affected human beings—for life, you might say—is deeply embedded in their attitudes and action. More evangelical Christians today, in numbers surprisingly large, likewise see the connection between what's happening to the planet and the welfare of those who live on it. A 2011 University of Maryland poll found that roughly three-in-four evangelicals, when presented with the concept of faith-based stewardship, agree that addressing climate change is a moral imperative.[29] In a similar vein, a poll commissioned by Faith in Public Life and Oxfam America discovered that more than 60 percent of white evangelicals agree that climate change, by causing more droughts and crop failures, handicaps the ability of the world's poorest people to support their families.[30] Climate change—a family values issue? A life issue? Yes, and yes.

So it is with the rising chorus of evangelical voices objecting to punitive immigration laws and policies that separate families and leave undocumented workers subject to abuse and exploitation. Same for the way more evangelicals are realizing that nuclear weapons pose a dire threat to life and, through efforts such as the Two Futures Project, are working to reduce and eventually eliminate nuclear stockpiles. Same for the evangelicals who rally to end extreme poverty on the planet via enterprises like the :58 Campaign, named after a verse from the book of Isaiah in the Old Testament. Same for the evangelicals who push for U.S. government programs against AIDS and malaria in developing countries and fight mass rape in Congo—part of a wave of activists dubbed "the new internationalists" by *New York Times* columnist Nicholas Kristof.[31] Death-row prisoners, torture victims, innocents killed by war and genocide, struggling families whose access to health care extends no further than emergency-room visits—these people, too, are increasingly found in the constellations of life about which evangelical Christians care, and whose lives they feel compelled to protect and enhance.

Not only is the life agenda expanding, but the debate about its abortion component is also becoming more textured and rigorous as new-school evangelicals like the Tama-Sweets of Portland age toward center stage.

Typifying the new currents of evangelical thought on the abortion issue, Shoshon Tama-Sweet objects to the roles men have played, and have failed to play, by the old rules of the game. Why, he asks, are the onus and stigma placed primarily on the women who have abortions? They did not become pregnant by Immaculate Conception, after all. "There should be a guy in the picture somewhere," Tama-Sweet says. Politics being as they are, men are the people who are typically spewing the harsh anti-abortion rhetoric and passing punitive laws in state legislatures requiring that women undergo ultrasounds and the like if they exercise their legal right to have an abortion. Yet when it comes to assigning the blame and responsibility for unintended, unwanted pregnancies, "the guy," Tama-Sweet correctly points out, "just evaporates."[32]

Also typical of evolving evangelical thought on the issue, both Shoshon Tama-Sweet and his wife object to abortion being seen as an individual moral failure—the individual being the woman who seeks an abortion. "If a sixteen-year-old kid is getting an abortion," Shoshon Tama-Sweet says, "there's been a lot of *group* failure. The Bible has a lot to say about the morality of a community as whole. With abortion, there's a whole community failing—schools, churches, families, all failing and all having a collective responsibility."[33] Crackdown legislation may gratify abortion opponents. But listening to the Tama-Sweets, you quickly realize how little it does to address the reasons why people are finding themselves with unexpected, unwanted pregnancies and seeking to end them.

Of course, it's easy to imagine an anti-abortion culture warrior quickly becoming impatient with all this contextualizing and responsibility sharing. Isn't all this just another smokescreen, to use the term of the Georgia Right to Life spokeswoman? Isn't it just another attempt to misdirect attention away from the individual sin that is the real cause of each abortion, and the great societal sin of legally available abortion? After all, if Christians are spreading themselves thin addressing this wider array of life threats, who will be left to join in the protest marches outside Planned Parenthood clinics or on the steps of the U.S. Capitol? For evidence of the troops' dispersal, an old-school culture warrior need look no further than data collected at the 2012 Iowa caucuses, where 57 percent of Republican caucus-goers pegged themselves as evangelicals—yet just 13 percent called abortion the most important issue in the election. Same story at the New Hampshire Republican primary, where a paltry 6 percent of voters gave abortion top billing.[34]

If the new evangelicals' approach to abortion is disappointing to the evangelical old school, it is also likely to disappoint non-Christian progressives who might find themselves impressed by the new school's different conversation about gays, poverty, and the environment, and who half-expect to learn that they lean progressive on abortion. The fact is, they do not. Poll after poll finds that younger evangelicals are just like their elders in holding abortion to be morally wrong, and its prevalence a true social problem in need of solving. After decades of culture wars, where you never cede an inch lest your enemy take a mile, pro-choicers are loath to talk about abortion as something regrettable. From this standpoint, a voice of moral objection to abortion can still rankle, even if the Christian raising that voice is young, hip, and progressive on so many other issues. Moreover, to the extent that the credibility gap of the anti-abortion movement has handicapped its ability to build broader-based support, isn't it ominous to see signs of credibility being restored?

There is far more for a progressive to cheer than rue in this changing dynamic. What if "pro-life" actually became a serious moral and religious commitment across the spectrum of threat-to-life issues—if it breathed new fire into progressive campaigns to curb poverty, abuse of women, and degradation of the environment, for example? What if this slogan, this political wedge birthed by the Christian Right, generated something holistic, principled, and positive—even, in some ways, *progressive*—and did liberals the favor of calling them to account for their own failures to live up to their political and ethical creeds?

Consider what the Tama-Sweets, two young Christian parents from Portland, Oregon, two evangelical progressives committed to the fight to end sex trafficking and improve the health of less advantaged citizens, see for abortion-supporting progressives—secular as well as religious—in this shifting sand.

After our meeting, both Stephanie and Shoshon sent me e-mails in which they, at my invitation, turned their well-intentioned critiques away from the conservative positions that we had discussed in person and toward the progressive/secular camp and the problems with its stance on abortion.

Like conservatives, for progressives to be at their best they need to address "the other side of the argument," Stephanie said. "Progressives are, all too often, fearful to embrace issues that feel conservative, issues like foster care and the role of fathers. . . . Until we are ready to have the conversation in its fullness I don't think we will be able to make progress."[35] In other words, even if it seems prudish to talk about sexual responsibility or the problem of strip clubs that serve as covers for sex trafficking, even if it feels old-fashioned to insist on men being committed to the children born of their sexual freedoms—even if it feels *conservative* to speak of abortion as something regrettable and worth reducing—progressives must be willing to discuss these uncomfortable topics candidly if they are ever going to influence anyone beyond the already-converted.

Shoshon Tama-Sweet offers yet another arresting insight about the inadequacy of progressive pro-choice rhetoric as we have come to know it. "The framing," he told me, "suggests that abortion is about power, and about women retaining power over their own bodies. There needs to be some acknowledgment that all too often abortion is a sign of *powerlessness*, and that if our society has a group of women who exist in a structural class where their best option is to murder their own child—well, that can hardly be a sign of progress or of a healthy society. The abortion-as-empowerment argument lets progressive women off the hook of acknowledging how anti-mother and anti-child our society is. If a woman gets an abortion because she cannot afford a child, or cannot complete college and also have a child, or will be excluded from the eligible marriage pool because she has a child, or will be denied career advancement because she has a child, then our society is failing."[36]

Shoshon Tama-Sweet went on to enumerate some of the key elements of a truly pro-women, pro-children, pro-family—pro-life—abortion-reduction strategy: greater maternity-leave provisions and financial incentives for family formation, the inclusion of premarital and marital counseling in health insurance plans, tuition reduction or education debt forgiveness or grants for single mothers. It would add up, he says, "to a huge network of care making it more easy, accepted, and valued for women to have children and remain full participants in their own education, careers, relationships, and community life." The opposite of the pro-life picture now fixed in our heads, this agenda would empower women, not control them and their reproductive organs.

The new evangelical conversation about abortion includes some talk that is bound to make dyed-in-the-wool pro-choicers squirm. Do the Shoshon Tama-Sweets of the world really have to use terms like *murder* to describe what happens when a woman aborts a fetus? Perhaps it's consoling to know that these are not the people pushing for laws requiring women to have ultrasound wands shoved up their bodies if they seek to have an abortion—and also that this new conversation is probably even more inconvenient and uncomfortable for old-school anti-abortion fighters. Think about it: How confounding it must be to find your political wedge and rallying cry, your "pro-life" piety, backfiring in the form of progressive-sounding policies on everything from environmental stewardship to poverty amelioration to rights and dignity for single mothers.

Credit is owed to new evangelicals like the Tama-Sweets for eschewing the comforts of one camp or the other in the abortion argument—pro-life or pro-choice—and for refusing to abide by all the do's and don'ts required by such permanent allegiances. As painful as it may be for progressives to give it, credit is owed to these Christians for this, too: their pesky habit of reminding progressives—quietly and respectfully, perhaps, without headlining their conferences with it, but reminding them just the same—of the vulnerable form of life or potential life that *is* at stake in abortion politics, too often overlooked by progressives, and holding them to the progressive commitment to champion *all* the underprivileged and undervalued.

Indeed, imagine what things would look like if this pro-life thing were taken seriously, at face value, and carried out to its full extent. Suffice it to say that a divisive political rallying cry would be transformed into a broadly inclusive ethic rich in meaning, importance, and socially uplifting ramifications. Would that the coming years might witness a surge in resonance and growth for this idea and movement, with new-paradigm evangelicals living up to the commitments of their faith across the board and non-evangelicals right there with them, more fully implementing the ideals of their own beliefs and philosophies.

It's clear that Christians of the Tama-Sweets' persuasion are willing to make the first move. "A politically active, pro-child, pro-mom alliance of explicitly pro-life and pro-choice Christians would have a dramatic effect, not by moving the battle lines, but by having people walk away from the trenches toward a positive win that both camps can believe in," Shoshon Tama-Sweet concludes. "Or so I pray."

Chapter Nine

From Behind Church Walls

Where were *you* on September 11, 2001?

For most Americans, the day is seared in our memories. Many of us can recall with impressive specificity where we were when we heard the news or witnessed the unfolding disaster on television or in person—what we felt and thought, how we were affected, what we did to find out about loved ones in New York City or inform our families and friends if we ourselves were in Manhattan that day.

The memory is certainly a loaded one for Julie Clawson. At the time, Clawson was fresh out of a graduate school program and vying for an editorial position with a Christian publisher. As a final step in her candidacy, the aspiring young editor and writer had been invited to join the staff at a working retreat held at a country club in the suburbs west of Chicago. Other than a vague and understated report from a member of the wait staff—something about a plane crashing into the World Trade Center in New York (a small private one, Clawson figured)—the assembled heard and thought little about the day's news, and continued with their work. "When we broke for lunch, the head editors called the office and then quickly left," Clawson recalled in a reflection piece she wrote ten years after the events. "The rest of us stayed on, and even watched a *Bibleman* episode for possible review, fairly oblivious to the events of the day."[1]

Fittingly, the episode of *Bibleman* (a Christian video series for youths revolving around a scripture-quoting superhero) drove home the message that young Christians needed to limit contact with non-Christians because of the bad influence the encounters could have on the good young Christians' faith.

Only after the video viewing and other tasks and activities were completed, only after she got in her car and turned on the radio, did Clawson begin to learn the magnitude of the day's world-changing events.

"I rushed home to my tiny basement apartment that had no TV reception and tried futilely to get online, but the dial-up lines were all busy for hours. I recall going out to get the special evening edition of the newspaper and crashing the Wheaton College student lounge (with their TV and cable hook-up) just to get some idea of what was happening," Clawson wrote. "The next day I was scheduled to host my church's table at the Wheaton College ministry fair, which meant I spent the day surrounded by not only college students but also by representatives of every church and parachurch ministry in the Wheaton area. It was a surreal day as people attempted to process the shock and openly share the subsequent anger and hatred that had started to develop. That evening my church held a prayer meeting, and I recall praying that this act of terror would not lead to people lashing out against the innocent as a form of revenge. I was informed afterward that my prayer was inappropriate."[2]

The editorial position she had been so close to securing vaporized after that, the casualty of a hiring freeze and restructuring, she was told.

"It's strange to reflect back on the day the world changed," Clawson wrote. "And a bit eerie to recall that I spent the afternoon of September 11 watching the *Bibleman* episode about how good Christian students need to stop hanging out with their non-Christian peers because they can be a bad influence on their faith, and then spent the next day listening to evangelical leaders responding to their enemy in hate. I couldn't have known it at the time, but within those first two days after the attack, I caught a glimpse of how the events of September 11 would shape the church over the next ten years. The world has irrevocably changed. . . . Over this past decade, this new world has forced me to abandon a naïve faith that cared only for the state of my own soul, and embrace the fact that I am connected to others as a child of God."[3]

What Clawson finds eerie is also revealing. Apart from the particulars, her story captures the experience of many a new-century evangelical. Despite being raised on Christian-cleansed music, news media, television, and other form of popular culture—*Bibleman* and innumerable cultural works created in that same image—despite being schooled to respond to threats by retreating behind the walls of evangelical subculture, they are sensing the wider world around them and venturing forth to take their places in it.

To hear it from the rising generation of believers (not to mention some middle-aged and older evangelicals who embody the shift equally well), the creation of alternative Christian culture was the worst idea *ever*. As they see it, the walls built to protect innocent evangelicals imprisoned them instead, placing tight limits on what they are allowed to create and consume, learn and explore. Moved by a new rallying cry—*engage!*—new-century evangelicals are finding faith-stirring beauty in secular creative works and making their own contributions to that once-verboten place called mainstream culture, where pop songs don't mention Jesus over and over and where scientists follow trails of evidence to discoveries and knowledge unrestricted by locked-down and literal understandings of the Old Testament.

Over the walls they're coming, creating fascinating possibilities and challenges on both sides of the barrier.

Christian rock, Christian rap, Christian movies, Christian art, Christian news, Christian television, Christian novels, Christian colleges—these have been the hallmarks of evangelical subculture for decades. The impulse to create a cleansed and Christian version of seemingly everything has even brought forth a Christian pro-wrestling circuit and a Christian natural science museum that depicts a young-earth creationist view of the planet's early days, complete with exhibits showing human children playing while dinosaurs munch their plants nearby; this, despite a geological record revealing that dinosaurs died off some sixty-five million years ago, some sixty-two million years before the earliest forms of human beings arrived on the scene.

With a shift in perspective, one can understand why the shapers of twentieth-century American evangelicalism felt compelled to create a parallel culture of their own. For well over a century, the modern world has dealt one blow after another to tradition-cherishing Christians set on continuing what were once default understandings of how to read and apply the Bible, how to enter into relationships, marriage, and family creation, and how to produce and consume literature and other media. If you find yourself at a party where everyone is ridiculing you and your beliefs, it seems only sensible to leave the premises and throw your own bash.

One of the biggest and most pivotal blows was the public relations trouncing that Christian fundamentalists and, by extension, the larger evangelical movement experienced in a landmark court case in 1925. The Scopes Monkey Trial, as it's usually referred to, was not landmark in the sense that it was legally momentous—it was not—but "landmark" in that it marks, in most accountings of American religious history, a turning-point moment in the relationship between conservative evangelicalism and the larger culture.

Students of American religious history know the story well: A high school science teacher in Tennessee, John Thomas Scopes, was tried and convicted for violating state law forbidding the teaching of evolution in the state's schools. The real show, however, was the courtroom dueling between the two high-profile lawyers in the case: William Jennings Bryan, the celebrity evangelical preacher and politician who presented the state's case, and Clarence Darrow, the razor-tongued lawyer who argued for the schoolteacher defendant. What stood trial in the court of public opinion were creationist ideas and those who propagated them, and Bryan and his side were knockout losers.

"Although Bryan and the prosecution won the trial in purely legal terms, the trial was nonetheless a devastating public relations defeat for fundamentalists, now treated by the American press with scorn and derision," Andrew Himes writes in his history of American fundamentalism, *The Sword of the Lord.* "The image of fundamentalists was a caricature of rural idiocy and anti-intellectualism, delivered with a southern drawl."[4]

Himes, the product of a stout fundamentalist family and the grandson of the prominent fundamentalist leader and publisher John R. Rice, evokes a larger, decades-long pattern with that description of the public relations outcome of the Scopes trial. One can detect that same pattern today in secular progressives' mocking reactions to evangelical standard bearers of our time, from political figures like Rick Perry and Michele Bachmann to end-of-the-world prophesiers who see their promised end dates come and go, and then are left to explain or slink away. For those with progressive and/or secular leanings, these folks are always good for a laugh or a dose of self-justifying anger. With the title of his 2011 book, Himes captures the common response of evangelicals and fundamentalists to the rough treatment they often receive in mainstream secular culture and media; *Sword of the Lord* is the name of the fundamentalist newspaper founded and operated by his grandfather to serve his co-religionists in a way that mainstream newspapers could not, and would not.

Given the profound transformations in the culture over the past century, one can question, in sympathy with the fundamentalists, whether it was they who separated from mainstream culture or the other way around. A Sunday evening spent watching original series on HBO will furnish a vivid lesson in why religious traditionalists would attest that it wasn't they who changed but culture—a culture that changed for the worse. Suffice it to say that the skin and blood you see on such programs as *True Blood* were not common fare in movies and television in more "innocent" times. Popular culture today is drenched with heresies, sex, obscenities, and violence that would have been unthinkable decades ago. Now, "nothing's shocking," to quote the title of an album by the rock band Jane's Addiction. But to some Americans, quite a bit of it *is* shocking. And if the culture is marching in that direction, they would much rather peel off, stay behind, and maintain their own culture.

Understandable though it may be, this response has serious problems.

One of the best articulators of the phenomenon from a new-evangelicals perspective is Julie Clawson, she of the discomfiting *Bibleman*-on-9/11 experience, she of not-dissimilar experiences around other blockbuster cultural productions. "I had read *The Da Vinci Code*," Clawson recalls, "before it got really popular (I was on an 'intellectual thriller' reading kick at the time). A year or so later I heard the pastor at the church I worked at talking about an upcoming Sunday school series he was leading about how evil the book was. He was shocked to hear that I had actually read the book, since he had not and had no plans to read it (even as he taught a class about it). I soon learned that his was the typical response of many evangelical Americans. When confronted with an idea that is outside the way they had been taught to see the world, they engaged fight-or-flight—denounce the work as evil or protect themselves from being exposed to its ideas."[5]

It was not just *The Da Vinci Code* and its heretical speculations about Christ having a wife and child that needed to be feared and resisted. It was literature for youths, too, very much including the J. K. Rowling fiction series much loved today by millions of children, adults who read it to their children, and young adults who read it *as* children. Over the past two decades, while moms and dads were curling up with their kids each night for another session with *Harry Potter and the Sorcerer's Stone* or *Harry Potter and the Chamber of Secrets*, a good-sized subset of Christian parents was standing firm in their conviction that their children needed to be protected from this evil. Never mind that Harry Potter and his fictional allies were engaged in a traditional good-versus-evil quest. The books and movies depicted magic, smacking of the occult to alarmed evangelical parents and culture warriors.

Critics of the anti–*Harry Potter* vanguard enjoyed a good, snickering laugh when a network of Christians started circulating on the Internet, in righteous vindication, an article that appeared to confirm their fears about the *Harry Potter* creator and her sinister, Satan-loving ways. There it was in black-and-white, under the headline, "*Harry Potter* Books Spark Rise in Satanism among Children."[6] The problem—the trap—for the Rowling-bashing Christians was that they were too insulated to realize that the source of this exposé was a humor publication and faux-news website specializing in spoofs, *The Onion*. It was, in other words, all made up—made up to satirize alarmed Christians, specifically, who then had the decency to fall for the prank and furnish still more laughs for those in the know.

In an article titled "The Christian Industrial Complex," the influential evangelical activist and writer Shane Claiborne recalls what it was like to be young and confined to evangelical subculture.

> When I became a Christian, I learned I didn't have to stop buying stuff—I just had to start buying Christian stuff. An entire world of retail spending possibilities lay before me: the Christian industrial complex. There were Christian T-shirts, bumper stickers, even Christian candy—"testa-mints"—peppermints wrapped in a Bible verse. We were taught "secular" was bad, and supplied with charts that countered popular mainstream bands with a Christian alternative. We burned our old tapes (which is what we listened to back in those days) and went to the Christian albums. We were often sadly disappointed. They just didn't sound like Metallica. As a friend of mine quipped: "All these Christian artists say, 'God gave me this song,' and then you listen to it and know why God gave it away." I later learned that Christian art doesn't have to be a mediocre counterfeit of the original. [7]

We could go on with other examples of Christians overreacting to secular art, of Christians manufacturing cleansed and "counterfeit" copies of Metallica and other rock bands, and similar measures. The point, however, is not to get in one more good cynical laugh but to demonstrate the ways in which retreat from culture doomed evangelicals to giving a poor account of themselves in spheres such as popular music and literature. The point, especially, is to cast light on why many evangelicals of more recent vintage feel compelled to liberate themselves and their faith from the confines of Christian subculture, and how they are leading the charge in the overdue enterprise of diagnosis and prescription.

The emerging new ethos was proclaimed in the 2008 book *Culture Making*[8] by evangelical writer Andy Crouch, who proposed a new relationship between Christians and culture. Instead of condemning culture or making poor copies of it, Crouch called on his Jesus-following fellows to *create* culture. He summoned them, in essence, to join in the ancient and never-ending human quest to use art, broadly defined, to make sense of our existence, exult in the beauty around us, express our pains and sorrows, and wonder out loud about the mystery and majesty of it all.

Honoring God remains at the center of the culture-making enterprise for the new evangelicals. But realize that what Crouch and his fellows urge is worlds apart from what has been the standard evangelical practice of recent decades. Instead of entering what seems like a competition to squeeze the most "God" and "Jesus" references into a pop song or the most explicit gospel message possible into a novel or film, "Christian" art is moving in more subtle, nuanced, and holistic directions; you don't have to be an evangelical to "get it" or enjoy it. You're not going to be subject to an unwelcome gospel pitch.

Whether they are creating or consuming, the cultural change agents are dispensing with the notion that the only good cultural works are those with *Christian* stamped on them.

As the twenty-something evangelical Brett McCracken wrote in a 2010 article, "My Christmas list is full of items you'd never find in a Christian bookstore: Jonathan Franzen's *Freedom*, the new Kanye West album, *Mad Men* on DVD, and a blonde ale aged in French oak chardonnay barrels. What's changed? I'm still a churchgoing Christian, unashamed of the 'evangelical' label. . . . I just think I've come to realize that 'good things' doesn't always have to mean 'Christian things,' and that there is a lot of art and culture and goodness out there that is just as truthful and soul-enriching as something with a Jesus fish on it."[9]

As someone who has always been deeply affected by the best of the "secular" rock and pop music I listen to—you could even say I am spiritually moved at times—and as a resident of a thriving downtown district that was little more than a collection of run-down, abandoned warehouses a quarter-century ago, I have often wondered how evangelicals account for the good things in culture that are not explicitly Christian, for the beauty, rebirth, renaissance, and excellence that come, seemingly, without God. If you're an evangelical Christian with a strong belief that good can only come from God, that secular is suspect, how do you account for the good creations of non-Christians? Condemn them? Claim them?

How about just being okay with them while acknowledging—even enjoying—what's good about them? How about learning from them, participating in them, and contributing to their ongoing creation? Such is the thought process of new-paradigm evangelicals. They recognize the folly of dismissing secular beauty and its makers; they make peace with secular excellence by understanding that their all-powerful and mysterious God can work in any context, through any person or process, just as they understand that something called "faith" can blast through more powerfully in a Bruce Springsteen anthem than in a mediocre "counterfeit" Christian analog found on a chart such as the one that Shane Claiborne used to consult as a teenager. (For prime examples of the spiritual punch that "secular" music can pack, listen to Springsteen's "The Promised Land," Nada Surf's "Always Love," or the Decemberists' "June Hymn," to name but a few of innumerable possible examples.)

I broached this topic with Dan Merchant, a filmmaker and writer who, in addition to being an evangelical Christian, attends non-Christian rock shows by the dozens. As a teenager growing up in the evangelical church, did Merchant ever have it suggested to him that he needed to stop listening to the Beatles and the other secular bands that captured his imagination?

"What about burning my cassettes and albums?" Merchant responded with boisterous laughter. "Would that be considered a 'suggestion' to stop listening to them?"[10]

From the vantage point of an aspiring evangelical musician or filmmaker, the prospect of a reliable, "captive" Christian market might seem attractive. Until you realize that the price of entry—the "Christian" seal of approval—essentially disqualifies your work from being known to the many would-be appreciators outside the Christian orbit.

One evangelical who has figured this out is Micheal Flaherty, co-founder of Walden Media, which has produced an all-star lineup of blockbuster movies appealing to Christians and non-Christians alike. Among them, *The Chronicles of Narnia* films, *Charlotte's Web*, and *Amazing Grace*, the last of which tells the story of British (and Christian) abolitionist William Wilberforce. Flaherty describes his mission as simply telling good stories on the screen, stories with uplifting universal themes that tap into eternal human quests and longings.

At the 2011 edition of the "Faith Angle" conference—an annual interaction between journalists and influential newsmakers and culture shapers convened by the Ethics and Public Policy Center—I asked Flaherty about younger evangelical culture creators who want no part of the "Christian" label. He got a big laugh from the media members in the room when he responded by mentioning how one would-be Christian rock band, The Fray, got rejected by Christian music labels "because they didn't have enough JPMs—'Jesuses' Per Minute—in their songs."[11]

Riffing on a C. S. Lewis quote, Flaherty elaborated in a more serious tone:

> We don't need more Christian novelists; we need more novelists who are Christians. I like a lot of [Christian pop] music. But I think it's self-defeating. This whole ghetto has been built up that really marginalizes us. . . . Look at one of the most successful musicals in the history of Broadway theater, *Les Miserables*. I mean, it doesn't get any more on-the-nose Christian than *Les Miserables*. You know, "My soul belongs to God, I know I made that promise long ago, gave me hope [when] hope [was] gone, strength to carry on." But no one calls that a "Christian" musical.
>
> You read U2's lyrics, you read interviews with Bono where he talks about grace, you go to a U2 concert and [you hear how] he puts a psalm to words, but no one's calling them a "Christian band." [Christians] should not retreat one inch from what they love and what inspires them, but I do think that it would be helpful for them just to go out there and just be known as great artists.

As for The Fray, "They sent their disk on to Sony," Flaherty noted, "and it went on to be number one on *Billboard*. So that was the best thing that ever happened to them, that they went out there in the mainstream."[12]

The experience of venturing out from behind the walls of evangelical subculture—the promise or the peril, depending on your point of view—found beautiful expression in a performance I witnessed by a dreadlocked spoken-word poetry artist named Garret Potter. The poem, titled "Holy Surprise," tells the story of how Potter, newly converted to evangelical Christianity, left his thoroughly Christianized home state of Texas for Portland, Oregon, when he learned of the Northwest city's unchurched ways and heathen reputation. Here was a prime mission field to plow! But when Potter migrated to Portland and started mixing it up with the locals, the change that happened was not the change that the erstwhile Texan had planned.

"Told that less than 3 percent of Portland went to church, I only assumed it was common sense to join the rescue," Potter riffed, rapid-fire, in his performance of the poem. He continued:

Of course I'd been warned about their vices and dark sides. Their reputation wasn't so good in traditional conservative evangelical Christian South. We were the world wrestling heavyweight Bible Belt champions, and Portland was the nemesis. . . . I came preaching the gospel like it was secret knowledge and passed out absolutes like they were life preservers. But now I only scatter questions, hoping they land in fertile ears. . . . I came proclaiming love, and they showed it to me in ways I had never known. I came condemning sin, and they showed me mine. . . . I'd been a fool to think of them as wrong, and I as right.

I came to Portland as a missionary, and Portland helped me become an observer, a listener, an appreciator, and a little more teachable learner. I came wearing my agendas like locals wear their old Ramones T-shirts, proud on the outside, and they accepted me still. Portland let me see its waterfalls and mountain peaks, its firs and ferns. . . . They taught me the word "sustainability," "compost," "permaculture," "free-piling," and "skill-sharing" . . . how to do it yourself or shop local.

With two question-mark arms raised heavenward I am asking different questions. I am seeking different places. I am knocking on the cover of every sacred historic text trying to expand on the context for a faith in the transcendent. And four and a half years of change later, here I am, still inside of Portland. . . . It is part of me now.[13]

A Christian with a more traditional mind-set might take serious issue with the poem and the story it conveys. What is there to celebrate in the story of a righteous, newly converted Texan moving to the great unchurched mecca to convert the tree-hugging heathens and hipsters only to *be* converted, *by* them? Doesn't this just strengthen the case for remaining walled off and separate?

As discussed in previous chapters, ideas about conversion and mutually beneficial interactions between Christians and non-Christians are undergoing fascinating changes in the midst of the transformation taking place in American evangelicalism. It's important to realize that Portland did not rob Garret Potter of his faith. Potter influenced Portland; Portland influenced Potter. As his poem attests, the Portland experience did indeed change his faith. But what it became is something Potter and his co-sojourners would likely deem more Christ-like.

To open oneself to new perspectives, to expose one's faith to new challenges—some of them uncomfortable—is the risk that new evangelicals take, the price they pay, when they scale the walls of insular church culture and venture forth into that wider pluralistic world, with more on their agenda than passing out Bible tracts, literally or figuratively. It's as if a sizable swath of evangelical America is awakening to the even *worse* price paid by sticking with the safe alternative. There are compelling things happening out there on the other side of the walls—as well as tragedies-in-the-making that are in dire need of good-hearted creative intervention.

Why, the new evangelicals are asking, should they disqualify themselves?

When it comes to evangelical Christians ceding important spheres of culture to the secularists, nothing stands out quite like the field of science. It takes no great leap of imagination and analysis to understand the basic how and why. In hundreds of reenactments of the essential storyline from that Scopes Monkey Trial of the 1920s, science has followed curiosity and evidence to new understandings, new breakthroughs, new products—and, to be candid, new potential for nightmare scenarios—while evangelical Christians, on the whole, have held their anti-evolution ground and adopted a more general stance of suspicion, even hostility, toward science.

When you're reading the news about the latest campaign to cleanse evolution from the school textbooks; about alarmed parents insisting that kids be taught that the "theory of evolution" is unproven, up for debate, "just a theory"; of activists demanding that school classes and their instructional materials present creationist explanations for the origin of the planet and its people, you can lay your money down on this near-certain bet—that the agents of these types of actions are conservative evangelical Christians.

Data from the Pew Forum on Religion & Public Life confirms the degree to which evangelical America and the rest of society have parted company on the issue of evolution. This is true even with respect to the divide between evangelicals and other Christians. In 2005, Pew found that 70 percent of evangelicals believed that living organisms have not changed since their creation, in contrast with the much smaller percentages found among Catholics and mainline Protestants (31 percent and 32 percent, respectively). [14]

What of scientists? A 2009 Pew poll found 97 percent of that group, not surprisingly, accepted that humans and other forms of life have evolved over time. [15]

Imagine a scenario in which an aspiring young scientist arrives at the laboratory where he has just secured a position, or travels to a university campus to interview for a tenure-track position in the biology department, and immediately reveals that he does not care what the fossil record suggests:

God created the Earth and its inhabitants in their present form just a few thousand years ago. He knows what he knows because the Bible tells him.

This hypothetical man can believe what he wants to believe. But with a stance like this, his science career is not going to shoot ahead on the fast track, to state the glaringly obvious. A far-fetched scenario? Yes, because things would rarely, if ever, get this far. Chances are, the would-be scientist would have decided long before, likely under the tutelage of his parents or pastor or both, to find a different line of work, realizing that science was no place for evangelical Christians with a fundamentalist inclination on matters concerning human and planetary origins.

Conservative evangelicals have also featured in an equally sharp divide that has developed in this country over the issue of anthropogenic (human-caused) climate change. One ought to be careful in this discussion to untangle politics from faith and science; when conservative evangelicals are smearing climate science from pulpits or the political campaign trail, the rhetoric is often fueled by anti-liberal political convictions more than rigorous engagement with the theological complexities or scientific evidence. And the dynamics are changing on this front as more evangelicals recognize the imperative to steward God's creation, as they conceive it. Nevertheless, a review of the ongoing climate-change argument up to this point generally finds evangelicals lining up on the anti-science side of this standoff, too. For instance, a 2011 survey found just 31 percent of white evangelicals believed that the Earth is getting warmer and human activity is the cause—as against 43 percent of white mainline Protestants, 50 percent of Catholics, and 52 percent of the religiously unaffiliated. [16]

To those concerned about the future of the church and its ability to retain its young, evangelicalism has a serious science problem that needs urgent intervention.

"Many people I talk to think it's impossible to embrace both mainstream science (especially evolutionary biology) and traditional Christian faith. Scientists tend to scoff at faith as being anti-intellectual, while Christians tend to reject scientific conclusions out of hand if they don't fit with their view of the world. This should not be!"[17] So states a young woman scientist interviewed for David Kinnaman's book *You Lost Me*. It isn't just the validity of the young scientist's criticism that worries those, like Kinnaman, who see trouble ahead for the evangelical church if it doesn't change on this score. Perhaps even more disturbing is the vantage point from which this ex-evangelical scientist levels her critique. She is part of a category Kinnaman labels "exiles"—young people who have left organized evangelicalism out of the conviction that they could not follow their consciences, hearts, and dreams if they remained active in an evangelical church. The young scientist concludes, "Christians, of all people, should pursue truth with a spirit of confidence, and the church should take a more active role in encouraging that pursuit."[18]

As Kinnaman acknowledges, not everyone in the Christian community would assent to that assertion—far from it, in fact. Nevertheless, it's clear that more cracks are appearing in that unhelpful wall between evangelicals and science. One of the more visible wall busters is Francis Collins, a highly respected geneticist and evangelical Christian who is director of the National Institutes of Health. Collins is an advocate for the view that scripture-bound Christians can reconcile themselves to the reality of evolution by simply accepting it as part of God's wondrous creation.

Perhaps even more compelling are the example and witness of a well-known technology guru who is founding editor of a respected publication no one would ever associate with evangelical Christians—*Wired* magazine. With a credibility of one who is himself an evangelical, Kevin Kelly powerfully articulates what is so self-defeating about evangelical anti-scientism. Reading Kelly's take on evangelicals and science, one cannot help but be struck by how remarkable it is that a religious movement committed to the public expression of God's goodness would resist contributing to fields that offer so many benefits to people. Kelly reflects on the situation:

> The insights of evolutionary science today continue to help us find oil in the earth, manipulate genes in organisms, and overcome ancient diseases. On the other hand the insights of creationism spur no advances in know-how. Therefore this quaint view will simply disappear. Several generations from now, most evangelical and even most "fundamentalist, literal-scriptures, Bible-believing" Christians will endorse the facts and perspective of cosmic evolution and wonder what the fuss was about in the past.
>
> But in the meantime, the denial of the reality of evolution by evangelical churches is hugely detrimental to themselves and to the rest of American society. It harms the rest of society because the strong evangelical influence on textbooks and public education in some states means the true strength and role of evolution in the world at large is not made clear, and even hidden. But more importantly, the denial of evolution harms the greater church as well. The denial of evolution is the prime reason why there are so few leading scientists professing orthodox Christian Protestantism. Evangelical schools and churches steer their best students away from a full embrace of the biggest

unifying idea in science—cosmic evolution—and toward technical, social, and business professionalism. Thus the evangelical church is cut off from the leading edge of our society. Their refusal to adopt the full scientific framework means that only non-evangelicals can lead in inventing our progress. . . .

Both the radical atheists and fundamentalist Christians are drinking the cup of the same error: that evolution = no god. In a weird way the radical atheists and fundamentalists are agreeing with each other, and feeding each other this unnecessary mistake: that evolution must be godless. [19]

Francis Collins and others use such terms as *theistic evolution* and *evolutionary creation* to articulate a view that picks no unnecessary fights between science and Bible belief. (These are unnecessary fights that some hard-core atheists pick too, of course. As Kelly rightly suggests, demonstrating the scientific validity of evolution does not prove the nonexistence of God or nullify the many good things that religion gives to people.) God, in the view of Collins and others, creates through evolution. Kelly, in his aforementioned reflection piece, uses a more stirring term for the concept: *divine evolution.*

Do not underestimate the enormity of the leap this line of thinking requires on the part of Christians whose whole lives have been spent swimming in the waters of biblical literalism, with the conviction that if any part of the Bible is accepted as not factually accurate—not *literally* true—the whole edifice crumbles. For an example of the phenomenon, consider the conflicts that have surfaced within evangelicalism in recent years as some conservative Bible scholars have begun pressing a highly provocative point: that science's growing understanding of human genetics makes it impossible to continue believing and claiming that all human beings spring from a common ancestor; Adam and Eve, in other words, could not literally be the mother and father of all people, per the account found in the book of Genesis. From a fundamentalist-leaning standpoint, such a concession can be earth-shaking, utterly unacceptable. It appears to spoil the story of the Fall and original sin and to undercut a precept crucial to orthodox Christian theology: that humanity needs the savior, Jesus Christ, to atone for that universally borne sin.

No real Adam and Eve? This can be highly upsetting to conservative Bible believers. But as one Christian intellectual puts it, "This stuff is unavoidable. Evangelicals have to either face up to it or they have to stick their head in the sand. And if they do that, they will lose whatever intellectual currency or respectability they have."[20]

To one of conservative Christianity's leading spokesmen, Albert Mohler of the Southern Baptist Theological Seminary, "intellectual respectability" is an acceptable loss. "That's simply the price we'll have to pay," Mohler says. "The moment you say 'We have to abandon this theology in order to have the respect of the world,' you end up with neither biblical orthodoxy nor the respect of the world."[21]

If anti-science orthodoxy costs Jesus a fair hearing by a skeptical public, as I believe it does, Mohler's dismissal of intellectual respectability is ill advised. As I opined in *USA Today*, Bible-based rejection of science is not a winning play for Christians intent on sharing their good news. The validity of the religion's ultimate truth claims—the case for transforming lives and societies through the love taught and modeled by Jesus—does not depend on proving that the stories in the Bible are factually accurate. In a way, Mohler, like the makers of the creation-science museum and so many other biblical literalists, plays into the cynics' and anti-religionists' hands by appearing to make it a cinch to debunk Christianity.

Showing the way through this thicket are evangelical thinkers such as Peter Enns, a Bible scholar who is challenging anti-science literalists to accept more nuanced ways of understanding what the Bible teaches about planetary and human origins. In his 2012 book *The Evolution of Adam: What the Bible Does and Doesn't Say about Human Origins*, Enns asserts that what may appear to be irreconcilable conflicts between evolution and Christianity are not due to science and its discoveries, but to believers expecting too much of the biblical texts. They were written for ancient people, Enns points out, and while they may speak profound truth to eternal questions and struggles, they need not be regarded as factual textbooks all these thousands of years later. "Once those ancient settings are adequately understood," Enns writes, "there will be less of an urgency to align scientific models and biblical literature."[22]

Enns, like Kevin Kelly, sees a grim future of marginalization for Christianity if evangelicals—Christianity's most public and ardent champions—cannot free their collective leg from the anti-science trap in which it's been caught. "Often Christians focus on the need to be faithful to the past, to make sure that present belief matches that of previous generations," Enns writes. "I support the sentiment in general, but we must be just as burdened to be faithful to the future, to ensure that we are doing all we can to deliver a viable faith to future generations. That, too, is a high calling—even if it is unsettling, destabilizing, and perhaps frightening. . . . It is a journey that must be taken, for the alternatives are not pleasant."[23]

It's easy to see how the point applies well beyond science. Whether it's a requirement for a high mass of JPMs—Jesus references per minute—in a pop song or iron-strong, doubt-free faith for the hero or heroine in a Christian novel, whether it's "Christian news" that takes only an embattled conservative perspective and portrays evangelicals as the good guys and Islamists and secularists as the bad guys, the pattern holds: opposition, non-participation in the cultural mainstream, and self-imposed disqualification from avenues of our shared national life where good things happen to improve the human condition—and, frankly, where many glaring needs go begging for attention.

One can extend this concept of walls to other aspects of evangelical culture that are likewise undergoing promising change. Take, for example, the phenomenon of evangelicals condemning the "godless" public schools and teaching their children at home instead. Better by far to remember that real human beings remain at those schools, struggling to teach and learn against difficult odds, and that there's something Christ-like about dropping the culture-wars grievances and actually helping the kids—which, as explored in previous chapters, indeed is beginning to happen.

This over-the-walls concept plays out in important ways around issues of race and class, too, and around the consumerism featured prominently in the megachurch communities that have become such a prominent feature of America's suburban and exurban landscapes. Paul Louis Metzger is a new-paradigm evangelical raising a prophetic voice against these materialistic, consumerist currents in American evangelicalism—and against hypocritical tendencies among secular progressives in his home base of Portland to skip too quickly over hard, unresolved issues of race in the rush to become greener, more bicycle-friendly, more walkable, and more livable. How livable is the city, Metzger asks, if you're nonwhite and poor and the affordable housing you once lived in has been razed for something trendier? Not questions that proudly progressive Portlanders like to hear, but that need to be asked lest the city become too enamored of its own reflection.

Metzger, a prolific author and a theology professor at Multnomah Biblical Seminary in the city's northeast corner, decries a tendency in his own evangelical culture to make American consumerism its guiding light, rather than Jesus. In his book *Consuming Jesus*,[24] Metzger takes particular issue with the infusion of consumerist marketing values into the fabric of megachurches. When growing the church by attracting and pleasing members is the main point, it's only natural to make Christianity as easy and convenient as possible, Metzger writes. The problem, he says, is that Christianity should be *hard*. Following Jesus ought to mean entering into uncomfortable interactions with people of other races and classes, in those "other" places in and around the city that are not comfortable and trendy—and entering not as know-it-all heroes and saviors but as vulnerable and humble learners in a relationship of mutual need. More than a concept, this describes the relationships that Metzger, who is white, has forged with Portland's black church community. In a similar vein, consider the case of David Moriah, an evangelical in New Jersey, who, after years of belonging to white Baptist congregations, joined a historically significant black church in Trenton and today remains one of two active white members (the other being his wife), and a deacon to boot.[25]

Discussing Christians and consumerism with me for a *USA Today* column, Metzger observed, "Many thriving prosperity-gospel churches appear to have thoroughly embraced the American ideal of upward mobility and material well-being." So much so, we agreed, that one starts to wonder if these churches' leaders think Jesus was a savvy entrepreneur on the rise, who would have become rich had his career not been cut short.[26]

In recent times, the Christmas season has furnished a reliable annual demonstration of how culture-war mind-sets of grievance and battle can spur some evangelicals to obsess over Christianity's diminished upper hand while distracting them from the buy-buy-buy consumerism that poses the more serious threat to the "reason for the season." Are merchants and media figures insulting the nation's Christians by saying "Happy Holidays" as opposed to "Merry Christmas"? Has another manger scene been banned from a public space somewhere? There's a war on Christmas, they cry—a war on *Christians*!

Meanwhile, the culture hears scarcely a word from these defenders of Christianity about materialism's takeover of a holiday that is supposed to celebrate a savior who taught selflessness and the rejection of shallow materialistic values. That worthy conversation is denied the water and light it deserves; higher grow the walls.

Would that prophetic voices like Metzger's receive the hearing they merit as the years roll on. These are insights and examples worthy of attention from evangelicals and non-evangelicals alike—ideas that call both Christianity and the country to their higher ideals.

To those with a less charitable inclination toward their evangelical fellow citizens, the notion of Christians relegating themselves to the backwaters and sidelines of American culture might seem the real "good news" about Christianity in our country. "Good riddance!" is the likely response of the anti-religion flame-throwers like Richard Dawkins and Sam Harris, authors of the atheist manifestos *The God Delusion* and *The End of Faith*, respectively, and those who subscribe to the point of view that Christians are a blight on the postmodern landscape. To the prospect of Christians reintroducing themselves to spheres of culture they had shunned, leeriness and opposition seem the likely response. What good could possibly come of *this*?

    Quite a bit, actually.

    Let's not idealize the mainstream culture that more evangelicals have set their hearts on rejoining. The worlds of secular music, art, and media certainly offer some finely wrought works. But there is plenty of corrosive schlock, too—shows and songs and books and Web content that are poorly done, insulting to our intelligence and sensibilities, and, often, outright demeaning. The airwaves are poisoned by loud-volume anger and mean-spirited mockery. Television pumps out consumerist messages that prey on our possessive, me-first proclivities, working against our ability to reach healthy states of satisfaction and gratefulness. Politics aims to manipulate us through our fear and anger. The Internet? Land on the right video at the right site and you might get some "fatherly advice" from a rapper on how to manipulate middle school–aged girls into giving you sex.[27]

    This is what evangelicals are getting at when they talk about "brokenness" in the world, and they are on to something. A lot *is* broken.

    Nor should we idealize science and carry on as though it, too, is beyond any constructive new influences of the kind that idealistic, good-hearted religionists might bring. For all its contributions to life-saving medicine and life-enhancing technologies, science has unleashed devastating nightmares (see "Hiroshima, Japan") and is more than capable of spawning more, and worse. The years and decades ahead promise leaps of science and technology that boggle the mind. And while it's easy to imagine them yielding great benefit, they also offer horror scenarios: possibilities like nuclear weapons in the hands of revenge-thirsty terrorists; children farmed for their cells or organs; laboratory-hatched germs with properties conducive to fast, far-flung, and deadly distribution; and genetics technologies that put in people's hands the ability to create designer children—perfect, seemingly, in every way, if you can look past the ominous consequences for children of technologically inferior makings. It's not just the wizardry that boggles the mind but also the magnitude of the ethical dilemmas and opportunities for evil.

"Good riddance" to Christians who disqualify themselves from participation in the arts and sciences and other venues of our shared national life? Sure, if the Christians in question are the loud-mouth condemners who come to mind for many when they hear the word *evangelical*. But if they are Christians of a different orientation, seeking to offer their intelligence, talent, heart, and sweat, "good riddance" is no good at all.

Just as new-paradigm evangelicals challenge their confinement to a walled-off church culture, open-minded secularists ought to challenge those made-up minds that cling to the idea that religion's retreat or banishment is humanity's brightest hope. When it comes to idealism, to commitments to holding ethical lines against abuse and exploitation in its many forms, this roiling culture needs all the help it can get, whatever the sources. This train of thought does not require those of a non-religious bent to concede that Christians are somehow "better" than everyone else. It's clear to anyone with eyes that plenty of ethically committed non-Christians are striving mightily and selflessly, with their art and activism, with their entrepreneurial and technological wiles, to create something finer between these shores, and well outside of them as well. And you won't hear the new evangelicals contesting that reality—a reality they, too, have seen and have come to appreciate.

Young Christians, David Kinnaman reports, resent how the church has demonized everything outside its figurative boundaries. "As they explore 'the world,' they come to believe (rightly or wrongly) that the world is not nearly as hopeless or awful as they've been told. They discover movies, music, and other art and media that sometimes describe the reality of human experience much better than the church does."[28] Many who leave the evangelical church do so not as an act of rejecting God, Kinnaman finds, but as an act of *following* God. "They sense God moving," he writes, "outside the walls of the church."[29]

The emerging new Christians, writes evangelical change leader Gabe Lyons, "resist the urge to condemn everything that isn't explicitly Christian. They have a capacity to find goodness, truth, and beauty in most any creation."[30]

As they do in most any *person*. And this is where we see some of the most promising new openings toward a post-culture-war world in which in Jesus is no longer a dividing line, but in which people committed to making bad situations better are willing to work alongside one another—*with* one another—regardless of their allies' and partners' theological perspectives or the type of church they attend, if any.

For secularists who still have their backs up about evangelicals, an important and disarming insight emerges from this shift in the dynamic. The new evangelicals don't see "the rest of us" as bad people living in the darkness, too stubborn or too selfish to accept Jesus in the old evangelical way. They admire a great deal of what has been created beyond church walls in that vast terrain known as "secular culture." They admire the people who created it and are open to working with them. They are, in other words, people whom secular progressives can deal with, can work with.

In a post-9/11 world churning with threats, challenges, and animosities, bursting with new ideas, creations, and possibilities, the new evangelicals are not content to stay in a room watching old tapes of a fantasy-hero "Bible-man" preaching the need to limit contact with those bad influences out there. They want out. They want to be part of, and contribute to, what's on the other side.

The rest of us would do well to welcome them and accept the gifts they bring.

Chapter Ten

September 12

The immensity and muscle of the Big American West hit you hard when you stand on the campus of Focus on the Family and scan the western horizon. The eye moves first to Pikes Peak, snow-dusted and, at 14,114 feet, one of the tallest mountains in the continental United States. In an uneven line running left to right across the foothills, you track the military installations: Fort Carson, an army base; NORAD, also known as the North American Aerospace Defense Command; and, farthest to the north, the United States Air Force Academy.

A stout Christianity fuses with the mountains and military might represented here. Sprawling Colorado Springs is so stacked with headquarters of evangelical Christian organizations that media observers have dubbed it, variously, the evangelical Vatican, the Christian Mecca, Ground Zero for the Christian Right, and a utopia-in-progress for conservative evangelicals.

Towering above all these Christian ministries in scope, reach, fame, and infamy is Focus on the Family, founded to promote the gospel and cultivate skilled parenting and committed marriages, but now better known in progressive circles for its starring role in culture-war politics. Mention Focus on the Family to a dyed-in-the-wool liberal, and all manner of political associations come to mind, none of them positive. The way Focus is referenced in progressive discourse and media, it's as if a few new words have been added to its name. The "Anti-Choice Focus on the Family," you'll see it called, or the "Anti-Gay Focus on the Family." You'll sometimes even see that most damning of qualifiers attached to its name: "hate group."

Demographic data will tell you that Colorado Springs residents are, in fact, more multidimensional than that "evangelical Vatican" nickname would suggest and less than 100 percent enamored of Focus on the Family. The percentage of the population belonging to a church, for instance, lags behind the national average.[1] Then there are those bumper stickers sported by locals who do not appreciate the ministry organization that people around the country associate with their city. In the words of those pithy stickers, "Focus on your own damn family."

This is where I find myself on a late March morning, visiting Focus on the Family, looking to see if the new currents in American evangelicalism have reached all the way to this high-elevation heart of conservative Christendom.

As my tour of the Focus campus commences, my ultra-friendly guide impresses me with the statistics that roll off her tongue. Diane Ingolia informs me that the ministry's family counselors assist some 7,000 people a day in the direct consultations they do by e-mail and letters and over the telephone. That is a lot of people, as are the roughly 250,000 people who visit Focus each year—a figure that makes Focus one of the top tourist destinations in the city. Focus operates in 140 countries, Ingolia points out, and delivers its literature in twenty-six different languages.[2]

My guide invites me to take a seat in a small theater and shows me a brief video featuring Jim Daly, the man who took over as the public face of Focus when founder and longtime president and chairman James Dobson resigned in 2009. I see Daly on the screen cavorting with his young sons and talking earnestly about the importance of family—"These are the things that are meaningful in life!" When it's finished, Ingolia adds a word about the new Focus leader. Having been an orphan in his youth, shuttling between foster homes and living on his own for a time, "Jim knows what it's like," she says, "to put Kool-Aid on your cereal because you don't have any milk."[3]

Ingolia takes me around the oak-laden administration building with the sophisticated TV and radio setups—Daly can be seen through the glass walls of the radio studio, recording a program—and she shows me the massive event space with the stage sporting old-fashioned leather-and-wood winter sports gear. Across the way, Ingolia guides me through a sprawling children's area that could rival many amusement parks. It features an elaborate, twisting slide, an ice cream parlor, and room after colorful room offering kids' activities all relating in some way to the characters and storylines from Focus's radio theater series, *Adventures in Odyssey*. She shows me a station where kids can fill out and submit prayer request forms. "Some," she says, "are heartbreaking."

As my guide leads the way out of the children's area and into the massive bookstore, she happily points out that a gift from "the Prince family" had enabled Focus to give the store a much-needed expansion several years before. I snap to attention when I realize who she's talking about—the Prince family, as in Erik Prince, whose private security force, Blackwater, played a highly controversial role in the Iraq war that still makes progressives seethe and whose late billionaire father, Edgar Prince, was a Christian Right figure who helped found the Family Research Council.[4]

When Focus founder James Dobson and his organization decided to move to this spot from Southern California in the early 1990s, they wanted to establish a more suitable home for their ever-expanding operation—room to grow in a place where the land was plentiful and its cost low. Who knew that Christians would start making pilgrimages? The fact that they did, and that they continue to do so by the hundreds of thousands, tells you something about the role Focus on the Family has come to play in conservative Christian homes across the country, where the ministry's radio broadcasts and copious literature are as familiar as the families' Bibles, and nearly as trusted.

Focus registers on a whole different frequency on the liberal side of the cultural tracks, of course. As I prepare for my sit-down with Jim Daly, I realize how toxic the organization has become to many progressives and secularists. I contemplate how toxic it was to *me* before I started hearing about the new tone and tempo of Focus under Daly's leadership, and before I met Daly at a conference and had several amiable exchanges with him.

A few months before my trip to Colorado Springs, TOMS Shoes, a much-admired shoe seller and charity that has given away more than a million pairs of footwear to poor children, found itself in the teeth of a controversy and facing a boycott for a move that founder Blake Mycoskie would deem a regrettable but innocent mistake. His transgression? Speaking at a Focus on the Family event and exploring with the ministry the possibility of setting up a partnership by which Focus would take advantage of its network in South Africa and serve as a distributor of TOMS giveaway shoes on the African continent. (The proposed arrangement was scrapped when the parties realized that the volume exceeded Focus's capacity.[5]) When word seeped out that Mycoskie had consorted with this supposed enemy from Colorado, progressive criticism came hard and fast.

"TOMS Shoes Founder Working with Christian, Anti-Gay Focus on the Family," blared a headline on the *Village Voice* website. TOMS, the ensuing article reported, "has been working closely with Focus on the Family, which does not exactly work with the brand's totally chill image. Focus on the Family is an evangelical nonprofit and the things that come along with that— hating gay people, evolution, abortion—clash mightily with the beliefs of most hippie, hipster, bearded, crunchy, countercultural(-ish), what-have-you types that have embraced the feel-good mission of TOMS and what everyone thought they stood for."[6]

The gay-rights website RENWL ran a headline that asked, incredulously, "TOMS Shoes Partnered with Gay Hate Religious Group Focus on the Family?" Yes, it did, replied the ensuing article. "We're so overcome with shock we can barely find the words to describe our profound disappointment with Mycoskie," the article continued. "We've met him a couple of times. [He] didn't come off all religiony or anything like that."[7]

With talk of a boycott rising on the Internet and in social-media networks, Mycoskie pled innocent ignorance and disavowed Focus on the Family: "Had I known the full extent of Focus on the Family's beliefs, I would not have accepted the invitation to speak at their event. It was an oversight on my part and the company's part and one we regret. . . . Let me clearly state that both TOMS, and I as the founder, are passionate believers in equal human and civil rights for all."[8]

Reviewing the flare-up the night before my Focus visit, reading article after article about the price TOMS Shoes paid for its dalliance with Focus on the Family, I reminded myself of how much animosity has built up over the years—animosity over Dobson and his Christian Right allies and the way in which they scapegoated and demonized gays, lesbians, feminists, and abortion supporters for so long. It's understandable that many in progressive America are still reciprocating with some demonizing of their own, even though Focus has entered a new, post-Dobson era. I typed a gallows-humor joke in my notes: What backlash would *this* Tom face—would *I* face—for journeying to Colorado Springs not solely with curiosity and questions but with something of an olive branch as well?

When Focus's vice president for communications Gary Schneeberger[9] escorts me into Jim Daly's office on a Friday afternoon, Daly is just hours away from a weekend focusing on a family that has just grown larger. Beginning that very night, his wife and he will have under their roof two orphans they have just taken in from the foster-care system, bringing to four the number of under-twelve boys they are raising. (The two foster children would remain with Daly for six months.) Daly needed no schooling on the experience of being a foster kid. Through a calamitous combination of divorce, death, alcoholism, and abandonment involving his parents and stepfather, Daly became an orphan at age ten. Between then and adulthood, he took a Kafka-esque ride from one dysfunctional foster-care arrangement to another. One reason his evangelical faith burns so bright is that his bornagain experience in high school, under the tutelage of a devout Christian mentor and in the embrace of a Fellowship of Christian Athletes group, was one of the first times Daly had been nurtured by people whom he could trust and whose support he could count on.

Burly, quick with a smile and funny stories about his kids, Daly exudes none of the stern judgmentalism that Focus detractors associate with his predecessor, Dobson. Even when you know his theological and social beliefs are unabashedly conservative (and yours are not), Daly has an air about him that makes him nonthreatening, likeable. I had noticed this when I met him the previous year, and it strikes me again as our conversation gets under way around the conference table in his spacious office.

I quickly learn that this Friday is not only day one of his and his wife's new foster-parenting adventure but also the twenty-third anniversary of his going to work for Focus on the Family. Daly, a few months shy of his fifty-first birthday on the day of our meeting, left a lucrative career in the paper industry to join Focus, working as a field director for Asia, Africa, and Australia before being named vice president of the international division. Dobson handpicked him to become president in 2005, but it was not until Dobson left Focus completely four years later that Daly and his imprint began to emerge, that Focus started taking small steps to drag itself out of the culture wars.

We start by talking about the relationship between Daly's own brutal childhood and his career as a leading promoter of committed marriage and parenting. "That's what motivates me," he says. "I want every child to have a mom and dad. I want Focus to do the best job possible providing resources and tools for parents to do a good job in their marriage and as parents. And Focus does that well, certainly from a Christian perspective."[10]

Not that I have ever met Dobson, but I explain that I always imagined him disapproving of me. I don't get that from Daly. His story has a disarming effect. My childhood was rocky, too, I tell him—alcoholic father, parents divorcing when I was very young—although "it was a cakewalk compared with yours," I say.

Daly appreciates the point. "Being born in the sixties as I was, and with what happened with my mom and dad, I think that gives me empathy, a sense of, 'Guess what. We're all broken.'"

Born in the 1960s—born, in other words, during a time of great social upheaval that included a surge in divorce rates and the beginning of the erosion of a certain kind of Christian consensus in this country. Daly points out that he understands why his predecessor and the Christian Right standard bearers of the older generation—the Dobsons, the Falwells, the Robertsons—adopted a culture-war stance. "They were born and they were raised in an America that was different than today's America," Daly says. "They were seeing the erosion of things, the lack of cultural concurrence around certain moral values. They were seeing it fracturing, moving in different directions. And their response to that was, 'We've got to hunker down. We've got to gather the troops. We've got to win the battle.' And you ended up with a lot of culture-war speak."

Focus on the Family got caught up in all that, I offer.

"Oh, definitely, definitely," Daly agrees. "I have an appreciation for what [those older evangelical leaders] lived through and what they experienced. Now it is a new generation. There is a younger Christian leadership now, and we have a different perspective, a different application of the gospel, because we have lived in a different period of time. It is *not* a war to us. It's more of an attempt to share the good news. I can't remember who said this, but I love the idea that God is 'in our corner.' And I'm not just talking about just Christians. God is in our corner as human beings, and he is the creator of *all* this. The Bible shows how to live your life in a way that brings you peace, brings you a sense of mission and calling, and a reason for existence. I think when we human beings live by that, broadly speaking, we do well. And the social sciences—I know it's debatable, but when you look at what the social sciences teach us, the manual usually proves to be true. Couples who pray together, they tend to have happier marriages, the kids do well, all those kinds of things."

Ah, yes, couples. This conversation was bound to delve into this matter—more specifically, into what constitutes a legitimate couple for the purposes of rearing children and cultivating a healthy society—and into the pitched disagreement between Focus on the Family and the gay community and its allies. I bring up comments Daly had made to conservative *World* magazine about Christians "losing" on the gay marriage issue and the imperative for Christians to recalculate "where we are in the culture."

Indeed, I ask, where *are* Christians in the culture?

"It's so difficult," Daly responds, "because of the way this issue has been positioned. It's 'us against them,' and that's what I really don't like. What I'm trying to say, what the emerging Christian leadership is trying to say, is that we recognize homosexuals as human beings, made in God's image, deserving of our respect. We absolutely agree that any kind of bullying, done for whatever reason, is unacceptable. Yet at the same time, we are trying to say that we have a different opinion on God's design for family. From where we sit and how we read scripture it seems self-evident that we're talking about marriage being between a man and a woman for the obvious procreation of the next generation. That's a general statement, and I know that inflames people today, but we're just trying to live that out and say, 'Here's our opinion.'"

It's an opinion, I point out, that steams a lot of people. The TOMS Shoes controversy flashes through my mind, and I recall the way Focus on the Family detractors are often quick to attach that "hate group" label to Focus's name. As I asked in one of my *USA Today* columns, does opposition to gay marriage automatically constitute hate? I've come to conclude that indeed it does if this opposition comes with a raft of malignant misinformation and false accusations—charges that gays tend toward pedophilia, that gays indoctrinate children, that gays provoked God's wrath in the form of 9/11. These and other outrageous forms of blaming and character assassination have indeed been inflicted on our discourse and our gay fellow citizens. Yet in preparing for my journey to Colorado Springs, I had become convinced that Focus had made progress in extricating itself from that nasty business and that the Southern Poverty Law Center was correct in withholding the "hate" label from the new Focus on the Family.

I tell Daly that as much as I support marriage equality, I agree that it's simply wrong that some from the progressive, secular crowd are so indiscriminate in sticking that "hate" label on him and his organization. "I think the advocates for gay rights have been too fast and loose with that term," I say. "It's really harmed the dialogue. . . . It has got to be frustrating to be told that you're a hate-monger."

It goes with the territory, Daly responds. Yet he concedes that it stung to find himself on a list of three dozen social conservatives targeted for censure by the gay-rights advocacy group GLAAD. As part of its Commentator Accountability Project, GLAAD charged that the frequently interviewed people on the list brought no expertise to the discourse, just "extreme animus towards the entire LGBT community."[11]

Judging from much of the progressive rhetoric on the Internet, I suggest, tongue in cheek, there's apparently a new rule requiring that every reference to Focus on the Family must be preceded by the adjective "anti-choice," "anti-gay," or "anti-woman," as if that's the only thing to know about Focus on the Family.

"Bigot—don't forget that one," Daly adds ironically.

"I think that's wrong and unfair," I say. "I would not want to be subjected to that, and I'm sure you don't. How does that affect you? What can you do to get past that?"

Daly responds, "For me, it doesn't really go very deep, because I know who I am and I know what I am. I do sigh when I hear that kind of thing, though, because it puts yet another brick in the barrier, the wall, and that's unfortunate. I wish people could sit down and tour the place. It's like John Weiss here at the *Independent*."

Daly is referring to the publisher of the left-leaning *Colorado Springs Independent*, the city's alternative weekly. The newspaper has often been sharply critical of Focus, and its readers voted to give the organization the Claim to Shame award in the newspaper's "Best of 2010" issue.[12] (Maintaining their sense of humor, Schneeberger and community relations director Rajeev Shaw attended the awards event and accepted the dubious prize, donning tuxedos for the occasion.[13]) As Daly explains to me, relations took a positive turn when *Independent* publisher Weiss invited him to a coffee meeting. When they started talking, Weiss admitted he was under the impression that 90-something percent of Focus's work was political (a misimpression that I, too, was under at one point). Daly explained that it was the reverse; well over 90 percent of the ministry's work is nonpolitical. Out of that conversation, the Focus president and *Independent* publisher agreed to join forces to rally the community for a cause that they could both wholeheartedly endorse: appreciation and support for foster-case families.[14] Focus and the *Independent* would team up again in 2012 after the Waldo Canyon wildfire destroyed 350 homes in their city, sponsoring a benefit concert that netted more than $288,000 for the victims.[15]

Yet despite feel-good exceptions of this sort, the caricature view of Focus prevails in many progressive minds, analogous to the way numerous Christian conservatives view Planned Parenthood as an evil abortion provider, choosing to forget, or to never learn, that the preponderance of its work is dedicated to providing non-controversial forms of health care to women. Daly admits that living with the stereotype is frustrating but that Focus itself helped create the problem. It now has a life and momentum of its own now, he sighs.

"I have a desire to talk to people who are pro-choice," Daly says. "They have a perspective that I may disagree with, but they're not evil people, and I think it's a terrible mistake the Christian community has made in attaching a label of evil to a moderate culture that is dealing with things, not recognizing that there are these fair-minded people we could actually talk with. I have many friends who fit that category. . . . And so I have more hope that there is a wonderful middle section of the country that is not polarized, where we actually can come together and talk about solutions."

"That goes in the other direction, too," I suggest. If the president of Focus on the Family is going to invite dialogue with pro-choice progressives, the latter should reciprocate. If Focus on the Family is going to contribute to the greater good through noncontroversial projects like supporting foster families—or helping TOMS get shoes to poor children in need—it simply will not do for progressives to shoot it down, as if Focus on the Family is only, and can only be, a rights-stealing, hate-spreading blight.

"This whole TOMS Shoes thing—think about that," I say. "You were interested in helping this guy distribute shoes in Africa, yet the association with this radioactive Focus on the Family put him in the firing lines. The reaction was ridiculous, unjustified." Then, to see TOMS leader Blake Mycoskie disavow Focus and ask it not to air the radio interview it had recorded with him? Imagine the TOMS Shoes buying spree that would have ensued after the three million Focus listeners heard the interview and the message, and imagine the number of children who would have received much-needed free shoes via that admirable TOMS formula: one giveaway pair for each pair sold. The disavowal, the request not to air the Mycoskie interview—that had to hurt, I say.

"Oh, it did," Daly confirms. "The activists who put the pressure on him—what they are not held accountable for is the fact that half a million, maybe a million kids, didn't get shoes. And it seems like everybody is okay with that."

It's indicative, I say, of the hypocrisy of which "my side" in the national arguments is capable. "It really goes against what are supposed to be the hallmarks of the secular, progressive community," I elaborate. "You know—rational, clear thinkers, open-minded, inclusive. The behavior around this TOMS Shoes controversy is just the opposite of those values. What happened is not cool."

I had some challenging comments and questions for Daly. I brought up a recent development by which Focus became the sponsor of the Day of Dialogue in U.S. high schools, a counterpoint to the Day of Silence held to support gay students. "Convince me that's not disrespectful toward the kids who started the Day of Silence and find it deeply meaningful," I say.

Daly expresses surprising ambivalence about the Day of Dialogue and suggests he took it on reluctantly. He insisted on changing its name from the original "Day of Truth" to the "Day of Dialogue" and on toning down the language "so there's not a sense of disrespect." He describes his thought process: "Now that we have it, let's at least try to shape it into something that's constructive for the culture. We may not have hit the mark yet, and I get that, and I'm trying to see that we shape it in such a way that it can be constructive. . . . Having discussion among people who don't necessarily agree—that's really the idea behind the Day of Dialogue."

I bring up something that I have struggled to understand for a long time. "This next question," I tell Daly, "comes out of reflecting on my family life as an adult. I'm in a long-term marriage, and now my daughter is a mother, a stay-at-home mother, with a husband and two little kids. I'm hard pressed to figure out how the advance of gay rights has harmed my family and my daughter's family. So maybe you could educate me as to ways that this may be happening that I don't see."

Daly responds with his typical nondefensiveness. "This is one of the more difficult questions for us, to be honest with you," he begins. "I think it is difficult because there is a sense of fairness that is deeply rooted in the American psyche. And I think most people would agree that what two adults do really is between them and their God, if they have one. The point being, it's a very *private* matter."

Daly goes on to articulate his philosophy—one he has articulated many times before—about the family format he believes most conducive to healthy child rearing, and about the government's responsibility to enact laws and policies that foster that format. That format, he believes, is a father and a mother, who complement one another with the different personalities and parenting styles intrinsic to their gender. "Even a gay couple, they still need the products of male-femaleness in order to have a child," Daly says. "It can't be created without those unique attributes of sperm and egg. So that's the broader answer in terms of God's design for marriage."

As he elaborates, it's clear that my question—How is gay marriage a threat to my family, to any family?—defies an easy and convincing answer. Also clear is that from the standpoint of Focus on the Family it is not the most pertinent question. The issue is this: What are the long-term ramifications for *society* as the culture norms and family types continue to evolve?

My thoughts race back to a sharp challenge Daly faced the previous year at the conference where I'd first met him. A pundit with passionate regard for gay rights pressed him hard to support gay adoption and to include gay and lesbian couples in Focus's orphan-adoption campaign. Daly had refused to budge. His message: Focus was going to approach adoption its way, but avenues were open to gay rights advocacy groups to organize adoption campaigns of their own; he was not going to get in their way.[16] His answer did not satisfy the pundit who was grilling him; nor will his stance please other passionate advocates for gay rights. Nor is it entirely true that Focus is not standing in the way of gay couples adopting; its political affiliate, Citizen Link, remains active in state-level legislative battles to confine adoption to heterosexual couples. This stance harms not only the gay couples affected and the children who fail to get adopted as a result but also efforts by Focus to reposition itself outside of the culture wars. Yet despite this, and despite my view that Daly probably goes too far with his idealized view of male-female, father-mother dualities, I am willing to give him credit for refocusing evangelical churches on something positive they can do for orphans—namely, adopt them and love them.

Pivoting now, I express my annoyance with the over-the-top anti-religion rhetoric that proliferates in some progressive circles and on the Internet. I cite a few of my "favorites" for Daly and his communications vice president: the notion that someone's Christian religion is no more deserving of respect than a child having an imaginary friend; that all Christians are right-wing idiots; that Christianity, because of its worship of a resurrected savior, is a zombie religion. All that mockery—it's just not right, I say. "It has to suck to be subject to all that, and I'm sorry that you are."

Daly nods in appreciation of the point I'm making. I've said my piece.

Ninety minutes later I'm flying back to Portland while Daly is heading home to his newly expanded family. As I reflect on the interaction over the ensuing days, I realize that optimists should not go overboard in proclaiming a transformed Focus on the Family, just as conservatives should not despair of Focus selling out to the liberals—of "going soft," as some of them put it to Jim Daly. Kinder tone? Yes. But Focus's bedrock conservative principles remain the same. And even though Jim Daly is a friendly man with a respectful tone, it will take a long time for his organization to shed the baggage of decades of culture war.

Also, Focus has to be held to account for the network of state-level family councils it helped create, many of which continue to show a political face that is sometimes more snarl than smile. To be sure, when the Florida Family Association launches a drive to boycott companies that advertise on a cable-television program that has the audacity to portray American Muslims in a non-condemning light, as was the case with TLC and its *All-American Muslim* reality show,[17] Focus on the Family does not deserve the blame, per se. And the relationship between Focus and the network of state-level councils has evolved away from Focus exerting any direct or substantive control.[18] "There is a continuum," Schneeberger explains, when it comes to how far these several dozen councils have gone to adopt the tone and style of "Focus 2.0."[19] Yet the conduct of the state councils is part of the Focus legacy, part of what James Dobson wrought, as are the often-distorted right-wing polemics pumped out by the Washington-based Family Research Council, now separate from Focus on the Family but owing its birth to James Dobson and the political directions in which he led Focus on the Family during his long tenure. Progressives are not about to grant instant, blanket absolution. Nor should they.

By the same token, conservatives worried that Focus on the Family has sold out to "the left" can rest assured. Yes, Daly did praise Barack Obama for being a model family man. Yes, Daly does have the temerity to talk with progressives and secularists and to stand with a politically diverse mix of evangelical leaders in calling for a more humane immigration policy.[20] But Focus is hardly going the way of the American Civil Liberties Union. If hardliners cannot tolerate Daly's ready smile and willingness to be friendly with unwashed liberals, if they cannot abide his giving credit to a Democratic president for being a devoted father and husband, they would seem to be in need of a Bible refresher course.

What might liberals and/or secularists make of the changing tone and tactics at Focus on the Family, and all they represent for the changing face of public evangelicalism? Some will hold to the belief that until Focus affirms full marriage equality for gays and lesbians, it must remain in the enemy category and one should never breathe a positive word about anything it does. While I understand that line of thought, I suggest a different response. The good done by Focus on the Family is still *good*, whether it's motivating church members to put their pro-life money where their mouths are and adopt foster kids, whether it's consoling and counseling a panicked parent whose marriage is in crisis, or whether it's trying to promote TOMS Shoes and the footwear it provides to needy children. Those are still *good* even if the organization takes other stands and actions with which progressives disagree. It's time to affirm and encourage the noncontroversial, nondivisive directions in which it also moves. In our mental drawings of the people at Focus on the Family, it's time to erase the horns and tails.

Wayne Besen, executive director of the gay-rights advocacy group Truth Wins Out, is hardly on the verge of becoming Focus on the Family's biggest fan or donor. But despite deep disagreement with Focus, he told me that he senses, and appreciates, the change taking place in Colorado Springs. "I do support the new direction of Focus on the Family," he says. "It's far from adequate or complete. But they have taken it from a 'culture war' to a heated cultural discussion, which is much better for everyone involved. It's not as quick as we would like, but it's progress."[21]

Three weeks after my visit to Focus on the Family, the group Soulforce made a return visit to the Colorado Springs campus as part of its Equality Ride 2012. Soulforce, which describes its mission as advancing freedom from religious and political oppression for sexual minorities, had come to Focus several times in previous years as well. On those occasions, Focus officials denied them the meetings and apologies they demanded. The Soulforce people staged protests; some were arrested. But this time, they came not with demands but with a request for dialogue, and Focus responded with hospitality.

On the Sunday preceding the official visit, a dozen or so Equality Riders had lunch with Schneeberger and his wife, Karla. They sat in the restaurant and talked for two hours. The next day, the eighteen-member Soulforce group, mostly in their twenties, all gay and lesbian, met with Focus people for three and a half hours. Coming out of the getting-to-know-you meeting, both sides agreed to be careful about the words they would use to describe one another in the future.[22]

"Focus is carefully combing through the language we use in talking about these 'hot- button' topics to ensure that we stand for God's truth, yes, but do so with Christ's heart," Schneeberger told me after the meeting. "The Soulforce people indicated that there are times they've been too harsh with their rhetoric, too quick to accuse us of 'hate.'

"It was a very good meeting to have. No one on either side walked away with a different worldview, but we did leave each other with hugs and well wishes and, hopefully, fewer faulty assumptions about each other."[23]

To reprise Wayne Besen of Truth Wins Out, what's happening at Focus on the Family *is* progress—something to affirm, something to take heart in, something to build on. Unless another Thirty Years' (Culture) War is more to your liking.

"My generation, in elementary school when 9/11 occurred, is now on the precipice of adulthood, poised to enter a world more turbulent, more divided, and more insecure than ever before." So wrote a University of Pennsylvania undergraduate, Meher Rehman, in her university's alumni magazine on the tenth anniversary of the 9/11 terrorist attacks.

"We remember vividly where we were on 9/11 because we remember the moment when that new reality, so sharp and so bitter, entered our lives," she continued. "Today, we are still struggling to try to make sense of the instant our world altered."[24]

Rehman, who spent much of her childhood in Pakistan and Saudi Arabia, was attending an American school in the latter country on 9/11, the day the world took a dark turn. She recalls Saudi youths hurling rocks at the bright yellow school bus in which she rode—a symbol of the United States—in the days following the 9/11 disaster. "I still reflect on the moment that distorted the decade that followed," she wrote. "The gulf that opened up on that Tuesday morning has grown. In nearly an instant, the world changed, and a single morning's event changed everyone's perceptions of 'Muslim' and 'American.' Everyone picked sides, everyone paid a cost."

Despite a brief unity respite that many of us sensed in America on September 12, 2001, and during that brief period of best behavior that followed, politics soon returned in this country, and with a vengeance. Which were *you*? Christian or secularist? Conservative or liberal? Bush supporter or Bush detractor? Muslim basher or Muslim defender? Iraq war supporter or Iraq war critic? Which relationships were *you* obliged to sever, or at least push to your periphery, because some people in your life had chosen the other side?

We had to choose, it seemed. We picked our sides. And we have been paying a cost.

But well over a decade has passed now. It's the day after. It's "September the Twelfth" of a whole different sort. The time has come for a reassessment of what divides and unites us. "The post-9/11 wars are over or ending," *New York Times* columnist Roger Cohen writes. "They were not entirely lost but nor were they won."[25] Ending, too, is the post-9/11 "war" we have fought stateside. It has consumed too much energy for too long. Time is passing, and the terrain is shifting right under the warriors' feet. Attention and history are turning elsewhere, to other causes and other terms of engagement. The old culture war may continue for some time, but on an ever-smaller stage, most likely, and with ever-decreasing relevance.

Which side *did* we pick? Who really *is* on your side, on my side, when we take careful stock of things? Does any of this make sense anymore?

This is not a cue to break into a rendition of "We Are the World." There remain many threats to resist and much to defend. There are still deep fissures cutting apart the landscape of American religion, politics, and culture. But here's the thing: When the scales fall from our eyes, we can sense that the lines of division do not run exactly where we thought they did. Perhaps that crack on the surface—the crack between religious people and the non-religious, for instance—misdirected our attention. The deeper divide, the real fissure, aligns each of us with teammates and allies who might surprise us.

I thought I knew my side. When I first began speaking out publicly on the national controversies around religion in public life, my side was the one made up of progressive secularists and liberal and moderate religionists. My opponents were the evangelicals—as I understood them. For me, the bundling-up of evangelical Christianity with an arrogant patriotism, an aggressive war on Iraq, and conservative politics were too much to bear. I could not remain silent. As a new-on-the-scene commentator, I came out firing against the worst in the other side—the hijacking of Jesus for partisan political purposes, the offensive silliness of evangelicals' invoking Jesus in their strivings to win in sports and business, the remaking of God as a mascot for America (and the GOP). Quickly came the angry e-mails and letters. Why was I such an anti-Christian bigot? Did I realize I was bound for hell? Why did I hate God and the USA? The divide I saw was the evangelicals on one side, they with their exclusive beliefs and their Jesus-or-the-highway mentality, and all of us "non-evangelicals"—the rest of us—on the other.

I had my teammates: the secularists, the liberal religionists, the interfaith-cooperation promoters, the embattled Muslims. But I have proven to be an increasingly poor team player as the years have passed. Not that I am now against those teammates—quite the opposite—but I have been promiscuous in my relationships. My opposition research, my search for misdeeds and misstatements and misunderstandings, for misuses of religion that I could pounce on and expose, had an unintended consequence. Out there searching, I stumbled upon evangelical people and projects that I admired. I crossed paths with evangelical Christians who shared my critique, who wanted no part of the stereotypes, who were crazy for Christ and pained to find their Jesus disguised, disgraced, and domesticated. I came upon evangelical Christian after evangelical Christian doing something inspiring and going a second mile, and then a third, to do something good for people and society.

Because of the way I have spoken up for these evangelicals, because of the way I have criticized those on "my side" who are indiscriminate in demonizing all evangelicals, I have been accused of being an evangelical myself. If you stick up for certain people in one group, you must be part of that group—or so the thought process goes. When asked, I always make it clear that I do not share the theological convictions of evangelicals, that my own beliefs are far to the left on the theological spectrum. But that does not mean that I cannot give credit where credit is due or that I cannot acknowledge what we have in common.

Yes, there are important fissures that gash the religious/cultural/political landscape. But they are not found in the places I thought, and they do not run in the directions I assumed. The important divide is not between religious and non-religious people, or between the Christians and the Muslims, or between the evangelicals and everyone else.

Eboo Patel, the founder and leader of the Interfaith Youth Core, has a compelling description of the dividing line that matters. It's the line that separates "religious totalitarians," as Patel calls them, from respecters of pluralism, tolerance, and interfaith cooperation.[26] Patel, a Muslim from Chicago, dedicates his organization to uniting college students of varying faiths and religious traditions, atheists and agnostics included, in projects they can work on together, shoulder to shoulder, to advance cross-cultural understanding and serve people in need.

Indeed, there is a "faith line," Patel argues. But it's not the line that separates the Christians from the Muslims or the devoutly religious from those of a secular bent. The line, Patel says, is that which "divides the forces of hope and inclusiveness from the forces of fear and intolerance."[27]

Religious totalitarians. This is an apt term that Patel uses to describe those in the latter category, those who carry on as though they and only they are right, and as though people of other beliefs or persuasions must be feared, repelled, and ultimately defeated for good to reign and peace to prevail. While Patel mainly uses this phrase in the context of Christian-Muslim tensions and relations, it takes no leap of imagination to see how it applies to other conflicts as well, particularly the one central to this book: the evident divide between America's evangelicals and the liberally oriented secularists with whom those evangelicals have most often been at odds.

Sadly, we have totalitarians of the non-religious variety as well. Consider the call that rose from the speaker platform at the Reason Rally held on the National Mall in Washington in the spring of 2012: "Ridicule and show contempt" for the doctrines and sacraments of religious people, famed atheist Richard Dawkins urged. Author of the atheist manifesto *The God Delusion*, Dawkins declared to the crowd of twenty thousand, "I do not despise religious people. I despise what they stand for."[28]

Sad that someone of Dawkins's intellect, someone who held a faculty position at England's prestigious Oxford University, would have his critical-thinking faculties fail him in his assessments of religion. Disappointing that someone of his intellectual capacity can muster so little nuance for his critique of religion.

Dawkins despises what religion "stands for"? Which religions, we might ask? Which mainstreams and tributaries within each of them? Which people, and which teachings and behaviors, within those currents and traditions? Given that the world's two predominant religions, Islam and Christianity, "stand for" love of one's neighbor, Dawkins would seem to have some explaining to do. Does he despise the strivings of both of these faiths to inculcate this love in their adherents? For all the failures of faith to live up to his noble and hard-to-implement principle, followers can be found acting it out in innumerable small and large ways every day, against the grain of selfishness and shallowness inside each of us. Dawkins despises *this*?

These one-size-fits-all condemnations of religion—whether from Richard Dawkins or from the late Christopher Hitchens of "religion poisons everything" fame[29] or from Sam Harris, with his call for "the end of faith,"[30] or from star comedians like Bill Maher who skewer religion and religious people for laughs or from everyday wags on the Internet who jump on religious people and religious ideas as if they are all bad and only bad—sound like a project to defeat all religion. They look eerily similar to the totalitarianism of which Eboo Patel speaks.

But criticism of atheism is obliged to exhibit the fairness of thought that the high-profile atheists flame-throwers find so difficult to summon. The point being: Let us recognize that not all atheists are like this. Like religionists, *non*-religious people come in many shapes and sizes. The culture includes "friendly atheists" like the blogger and activist Hemant Mehta, who encourages atheists to team up with religionists for good causes. The landscape features such purveyors of "positive atheism" as national organizer Margaret Downey, who, like the new-paradigm evangelicals, wants her movement to be associated with what it's for (learning, knowledge, education, and so on) rather than what it's against (belief in God and the granting of social privilege for those who claim that mantle). And we have the "new humanism" and its catchy slogan: good without God. "There is a new brand of secular humanists," writes Paul Raushenbush, religion editor of the *Huffington Post*, "that is requesting a place at the religion table instead of trying to overturn it."[31]

You might be surprised by some of the non-evangelicals who are lining up to vouch for these crazy, irrational Christians who are so worthy of "contempt." Take, for instance, the celebrated actor and activist George Clooney, who has praised the work of evangelical ministry organizations in Sudan. After returning from an activist trip to the new South Sudan in 2012, Clooney gave firsthand reports about Sudanese attacks and abuses against the South Sudanese—and praise for the Christian organizations and people he found there, helping ease the suffering and calling attention to the humanitarian crisis.[32] Take, for instance, Portland's Sam Adams, a gay man who, while mayor from 2008 to 2012, entered a broad partnership with the region's evangelical churches to serve the city's least fortunate. Wouldn't evangelical disapproval of Adams's sexual orientation preclude such cooperation? This disapproval "is not lost on me," Adams says. "But we also have massive agreement about needing to help people."[33]

A writer for the arch-progressive Internet news outlet Nation of Change calls for more left-leaning secularists to think this way—to update their sorting process, as it were. "Perhaps the left-oriented political press should be more welcoming of voices from Christianity who have a different point of view from what is presented by the fundamentalist lobbying arm of their religion," wrote Dekker Dreyer. "Embracing the liberal voices from [the Christian] community and giving them a platform might help to close the rift between secular America and believers—a rift that a select few conservative political organizations have fought so hard, and spent so much, to widen."[34]

These are voices worth hearing, advices worth heeding. Building on Dreyer's point about liberal religious voices, the embrace of centrist religion-ists is important too—even the embrace of actions and commitments by conservatives when they contribute to the greater good.

As discussed in the last chapter, Kevin Kelly offers a rich insight when he points out that the fundamentalists of the atheist and Christian variety com-mit the same error in equating evolution with the non-existence of God. It's striking how much these forces agree with one another, resemble one an-other, and depend on one another to keep the game rigged in the customary fashion—not just when it comes to evolution but also on matters of politics and culture. They are, in important ways, the same: their oppositional stance and black-and-white thinking; the blinders they wear that allow them only to see the stupidest, most appalling behaviors of the other; the zeal with which they hold up the worst in their ideological enemy like a foul-looking piñata, their sticks ever at the ready. The Family Research Council *needs* the likes of Richard Dawkins and Bill Maher to continue with their anti-religion di-atribes, *needs* them to continue furnishing the cases in point that Christian Right organizations trade on in convincing their supporters that their faith and freedom are under assault from the God-hating, anti-Christian menace. In the same manner, those of the Dawkins/Maher persuasion, those with their books and articles and television programs that specialize in finding, expos-ing, and ridiculing the most noxious and scary deeds of right-wing Christian figures, absolutely *need* the likes of the Family Research Council and the American Family Association to continue lobbing their anti-gay, anti-liberal bombshells—just to provide more grist for the mill, more material for the "can you believe these guys?" program segments. The fundamentalists, the totalitarians, are committed to maintaining the falsehood there is only one kind of Christianity, only one kind of atheism.

They can have each other. But they cannot be allowed to monopolize the microphones any longer.

The appearance of the new evangelicals, the subject of this book, trip up these old dynamics and understandings in the most encouraging ways. Not to romanticize them and their movement. They are not angels. They are not super-human. They, too, possess limited energy and finite capacities to sniff out and avoid the pitfalls of popularity, anger, impatience, power. And they, too, like all change creators, face resistance and reaction. They are a solu-tion—a solution to important problems facing their religion and their coun-try—but all solutions have problems, and their corrective courses have their share. Yet their emergence on the scene cannot be ignored or cynically dismissed if you want to understand American culture and politics or if you want to write off evangelical Christianity. It forces a refiguring of the equations, a recalibration of the equipment. It compels an overdue exercise of disaggregation. As in:

You have a problem with evangelical Christians? Which ones?

At the level that matters, the quarrels that vex American society are not between Christians and non-Christians, between religionists and atheists, between evangelicals and everyone else. The line that matters now is the one separating the "we're always right/you're always wrong" arguers from unity-seeking, goodwill-mongering action takers of whatever religious persuasion, or none, ready to go to work to address a society's aching needs.

What is increasingly and undeniably clear is that the culture warriors do not speak for all evangelical Christians or all dyed-in-the-wool secularists, respectively. There are plenty of people—believers and unbelievers, churched and unchurched, washed in the blood of Christ and agnostic to the bone—who are able and willing to do the necessary work of disaggregating, of eschewing one-size-fits-all labeling and demonizing, and of joining forces with *whomever* to get something done.

For some non-religious progressives, it might be discomfiting to imagine going to social transformation battle with "Jesus nuts" who publicly pray, who sing praise songs to their God and savior when they congregate, who believe Jesus really did rise from the dead and really will come again. Yet you might be surprised to find, depending on the given issue, how many share the dreams and commitments of progressive hearts. You might be surprised to find out who and how many, depending on the particularities of the task at hand, are on *your* team—and how much energy, heart, and sophistication they bring.

Meet the Christian non-totalitarians, the evangelical pluralists, who are at peace with people of different beliefs and feel no compulsion to defeat them, who are willing to go to work with anyone to accomplish good things for people and communities, who want only to know if you're ready to support that struggling school, feed those starving kids, free that sex slave, protect those innocents under threat of war or poverty, and bring an overdue dose of humility and decency to politics.

Opening up on the changing landscape of "post-Christian" America, in a culture where the 9/11 wars and a 9/11 world are fading in the rearview mirror, is a new territory where fellow travelers of goodwill are coming together. This is a "place" you might call the common good.

The young evangelical writer Jonathan Merritt calls his co-religionists to a metaphorical space that leaves the culture wars behind, that transcends the traps of politicized, right-wing Christianity that snared so many of their fathers and mothers. "We aren't forced to choose a human-formed party with a systemized divide-and-conquer agenda," Merritt writes. "We can stand in the gap and claim loyalty only to Jesus."[35]

The "gap" beckons those outside of Merritt's evangelical tradition as well. This is a place where open-minded good-doers of any persuasion are welcome, are needed. This is not a safe, boring space in the mushy middle for the wishy-washy and commitment-phobic. It's more like a no-man's-land, offering none of the safety and comfort of permanent membership in one camp or the other but plenty of bracing fresh air for those who can handle some new company and the sound of the occasional missile passing overhead.

Not that you'd know it from the old culture-war framework and rhetoric, but you'll find plenty of company there. Not that you'll see much evidence of it in the latest news from the political campaign trails and legislative halls, but there seems to be more of a crowd forming there in that gap.

May it grow.

Notes

1. REPLACING STYROFOAM JESUS

1. "Jesus statue struck by lightning," WHIO TV, Dayton, Ohio, June 15, 2010. (Video of the segment can be found at http://www.whiotv.com/videos/news/monroe-solid-rock-jesus-statue-will-be-rebuilt/v7CJ.)

2. Some scholars believe a more apt term would be "post-Christendom," with "Christendom" conveying the idea of a Christian nation or "kingdom" featuring a fusion of Christianity and government.

3. The comment was made by Dr. Bob Roberts Jr. at the Q conference in 2011, in a talk titled "Going Glocal."

4. Phyllis Tickle, *The Great Emergence: How Christianity Is Changing and Why* (Ada, MI: Baker, 2008).

5. I am referring here to the feet-washing I witnessed at Night Strike, a weekly service exercise in which Christian volunteers interact with homeless people in Portland. For my observations and reflections on Night Strike, see Tom Krattenmaker, "A Witness to What Faith Can Be," *USA Today*, December 17, 2006.

6. Albert Mohler, "Transforming Culture: Christian Truth Confronts Post-Christian America," AlbertMohler.com, July 15, 2004, www.albertmohler.com/2004/07/15/transforming-culture-christian-truth-confronts-post-christian-america.

7. John Connolly, "Dr. James Dobson Calls for Future Generations to Rise to the Call of Pro-Life Leadership," LifeSiteNews.com, March 13, 2008, http://www.lifesitenews.com/news/archive/ldn/2008/mar/08031305.

8. Jerry Falwell, "The Emerging Church: Straying from the Gospel," WorldNetDaily, April 14, 2007, http://www.wnd.com/2007/04/41101.

9. Tom Krattenmaker, "The Evangelicals You Don't Know," *USA Today*, June 2, 2008. (Although no longer available on the *USA Today* website, a copy of the article can be accessed at http://tomkrattenmaker.com/?p=65.)

10. In this instance and through most of this book, I use "secular" and "secularist" in the colloquial sense, as synonymous with not religious or not under the authority of a church or religion. For an insightful exploration of "secularism" as a model of church-state relations, see

Jacques Berlinerblau, *How to Be Secular: A Call to Arms for Religious Freedom*, Boston: Houghton Mifflin Harcourt, 2012.

11. Nicholas Kristof, "Evangelicals without Blowhards," *New York Times*, July 30, 2011.

12. Wes Granberg-Michaelson, "Wes Granberg-Michaelson Answers, 'What Is an Evangelical?'" Sojourners website, http://sojo.net/blogs/2012/01/06/wes-granberg-michaelson-answers-what-evangelical.

13. Marcia Pally, *The New Evangelicals: Expanding the Vision of the Common Good* (Grand Rapids, MI: Eerdmans, 2011), 179.

14. David Kinnaman, *You Lost Me: Why Young Christians Are Leaving Church . . . and Rethinking Faith* (Ada, MI: Baker, 2011), 28.

15. "2 years after fire, Jesus statue returns," WLWT.com, June 18, 2012, www.wlwt.com/news/local-news/butler-county/2-years-after-fire-Jesus-statue-returns/-/13601510/15142450/-/70nvhkz/-/index.html.

16. Anugrah Kumar, "'Touchdown Jesus' Statue in Ohio to Return Soon," *Christian Post*, September 18, 2011, www.christianpost.com/news/touchdown-jesus-statue-in-ohio-to-return-soon-55843.

17. Shane Claiborne, "The Emerging Church Brand: The Good, the Bad, and the Messy," Red Letter Christians website, June 1, 2011, http://www.redletterchristians.org/the-emerging-church-brand-the-good-the-bad-and-the-messy/.

18. Jason Pitzl-Waters, "Caught in Another Faith's Crisis," Patheos.com, April 5, 2012, http://www.patheos.com/blogs/wildhunt/2012/04/caught-in-another-faiths-crisis.html.

19. Krattenmaker, "Can cause of social justice tame our culture wars?" *USA Today*, June 27, 2011.

2. JESUS' FAVORITE CITY

1. The remarks were made in a panel titled "The Church and the City" at the 2011 Q conference, held April 27–29 in Portland, Oregon. A video of the panel can be found on the Q Ideas website at http://www.qideas.org/video/q-panel-church-and-the-city.aspx.

2. Kevin Palau, Luis Palau Association, interview conducted in Portland, Oregon, August 2011.

3. "The Church and the City" panel, 2011 Q conference.

4. George Will, "Ray Lahood, Transformed," *The Daily Beast*, May 15, 2009, http://www.thedailybeast.com/newsweek/2009/05/15/ray-lahood-transformed.html.

5. Jahnabi Barooah, "Most and Least Religious Cities in America," *Huffington Post*, May 18, 2012, www.huffingtonpost.com/2012/05/18/most-and-least-religious-cities_n_1522644.html?ref=religion#s821198&title=1_Mississippi_59.

6. The photo appeared on the cover of *Willamette Week*, May 20, 2009.

7. Milan Homola, Compassion Connect, interview conducted at Compassion Rockwood event held at Portland Lutheran School, May 22, 2010.

8. Milan Homola, Compassion Connect, interview.

9. Aaron Mesh, "Undercover Jesus," *Willamette Week*, May 20, 2009, http://www.wweek.com/portland/article-10543-undercover_jesus.html.

10. "Gordon Robertson Elected CEO of the Christian Broadcasting Network, Inc.," press release posted at Pat Robertson.com, December 3, 2007, http://www.patrobertson.com/PressReleases/Gordon_Robertson_CEO_CBN.asp.

11. Mesh, "Undercover Jesus," *Willamette Week*, May 20, 2009.

12. Sabrina Tavernise, "Whites Account for Under Half of Births in U.S.," *New York Times*, May 17, 2012.

13. "Religion Among the Millennials," The Pew Forum on Religion & Public Life, report released February 17, 2010. The report can be found online at http://www.pewforum.org/Age/Religion-Among-the-Millennials.aspx.

14. "Old vs. Young," David Leonhardt, *New York Times*, June 22, 2012, http://www.nytimes.com/2012/06/24/opinion/sunday/the-generation-gap-is-back.html.

15. Tom Breen, "Religion waning among Americans, study shows," Associated Press, August 27, 2011. A copy of the article can be accessed at http://www.sltrib.com/sltrib/lifestyle/52464056-80/religious-chaves-percent-religion.html.csp.

16. Brett McCracken, "The Perils of 'Wannabe Cool' Christianity," *Wall Street Journal*, August 13, 2010.

17. "Religion among the Millennials," Pew Forum on Religion & Public Life, February 17, 2010.

18. "Survey: Only Four-in-Ten Correctly Identify Romney as Mormon," a report by Public Religion Research, July 25, 2011, http://publicreligion.org/research/2011/07/obama-romney-religion-2012.

19. "Religion among the Millennials," Pew Forum on Religion & Public Life, February 17, 2010.

20. Ibid.

21. David Brody, "Obama to CBN News: We're no Longer Just a Christian Nation," *CBN News*, July 30, 2007, http://www.cbn.com/CBNnews/204016.aspx.

22. Barry Kosmin and Ariela Keysar, "American Religious Identification Survey 2008," Trinity College, Hartford, Connecticut, released March 2009. The report can be accessed online at http://commons.trincoll.edu/aris/files/2011/08/ARIS_Report_2008.pdf.

23. From the summary of a report titled "Religious identification in the U.S.: How American adults view themselves," published by ReligiousTolerance.org at http://www.religioustolerance.org/chr_prac2.htm.

24. "U.S. Religious Landscape Survey," Pew Forum on Religion & Public Life, February 2008, http://religions.pewforum.org/pdf/report-religious-landscape-study-full.pdf, 5. See also "'Nones' on the Rise," Pew Forum on Religion & Public life, October 9, 2012, http://www.pewforum.org/unaffiliated/nones-on-the-rise.aspx.

25. Gabe Lyons, "Engaging Post-Christian Culture: Our Mission in a New Context," a Q study guide published by Zondervan, Grand Rapids, Michigan, 2010. A PDF copy of the booklet can be accessed online at http://media.zondervan.com/media/samples/pdf/9780310325222_samptxt.pdf.

26. Mark Silk, "And what about non-liberal Christianity, Ross?" Religion News Service, July 16, 2012, http://www.religionnews.com/blogs/mark-silk/and-what-about-non-liberal-christianity-ross.

27. Jon Meacham, with Eliza Gray, "The End of Christian America," *Newsweek*, April 13, 2009. A copy of the article can be found online at http://www.thedailybeast.com/newsweek/2009/04/03/the-end-of-christian-america.html.

28. Kevin Palau, personal interview, August 2011.

29. "The Church and the City" panel, 2011 Q conference. The Palau quotation also appears in the following blog post: Rusty Wright, "Gay Mayor, Christians in Surprising Alliance," RustyWright.com, June 27, 2011, http://rustywright.com/articles/gay-mayor-christians-in-surprising-alliance.

30. Ibid.

31. Ibid.

32. Ibid.

33. Ibid.

34. Tim Stafford, "Servant Evangelism," *Christianity Today*, November 2008. The article can be found online at http://www.christianitytoday.com/ct/2008/november/13.42.html.

35. *"Reader's Digest* Names Portland's Season of Service Best Service Project in America," news release issues by Luis Palau Association, June 2009. The release can be found online at http://www.reuters.com/article/2009/06/15/idUS173552+15-Jun-2009+PRN20090615.

36. "10 Reasons to Love Our Country," *Reader's Digest*, July 2009. A slideshow version of the article can be found online at www.rd.com/slideshows/10-reasons-to-love-our-country.

37. Kevin Palau, personal interview, August 2011.

38. The reader comment appears in the online version of the following article: Tom Krattenmaker, "Evangelicals walk a fine line in public schools," *The Oregonian*, March 8, 2009. The column can be found online at www.oregonlive.com/opinion/index.ssf/2009/03/evangelicals_walk_a_fine_line.html.

39. Tom Krattenmaker, "A witness to what faith can be," *USA Today*, December 18, 2006, http://www.usatoday.com/news/opinion/editorials/2006-12-17-portland-faith-edit_x.htm.

40. Milan Homola, Compassion Connect, interview conducted at Compassion Rockwood event held at Portland Lutheran School, May 22, 2010.

41. Documentation of the Christian Right's low standing in public opinion can be found in several references contained in Robert D. Putnam and David E. Campbell, *American Grace: How Religion Divides and Unites Us* (New York: Simon & Schuster, 2010).

42. The comment can be found beneath, Tom Krattenmaker, "The New Evangelical Alliance Waiting to Happen," *Huffington Post*, July 19, 2011, http://www.huffingtonpost.com/tom-krattenmaker/the-new-evangelical-allia_b_899415.html. (The article initially appeared in *USA Today* on June 27, 2011, under the headline "Can cause of social justice tame our culture wars?")

43. Forrest Wilder, "A Wingnut and a Prayer," *Texas Monthly*, August 3, 2011.

44. Dan Amira, "Evolution Is Just a 'Theory That's Out There,' According to Rick Perry," *New York* magazine, August 18, 2011, http://nymag.com/daily/intel/2011/08/rick_perry_evolution_theory.html.

45. Shane Claiborne, "What If Jesus Meant All That Stuff?" *Esquire*, November 18, 2009, http://www.esquire.com/features/best-and-brightest-2009/shane-claiborne-1209.

3. ALL BAIT, NO SWITCH

1. Jim Henderson, personal interview conducted in Portland, Oregon, April 2, 2010.

2. An explanation of that stage production, *Stories from the Shack*, and the term "interactive spectacle art" can be found in an article on the Andrew Himes website. See Andrew Himes, "Stories from the Shack—Jim Henderson and Wm. Paul Young," AndrewHimes.net, April 28, 2011, http://andrewhimes.net/content/stories-shack-jim-henderson-and-wm-paul-young.

3. Personal interview, April 2, 2010.

4. Matthew 28:19–20.

5. Personal interview, April 2, 2010.

6. Maureen Dowd, "Moral Dystopia," *New York Times*, June 16, 2012, http://www.nytimes.com/2012/06/17/opinion/sunday/dowd-moral-dystopia.html.

7. David Kinnaman, *You Lost Me: Why Young Christians Are Leaving Church . . . and Rethinking Faith* (Ada, MI: Baker, 2011), 42.

8. Ibid., 55.

9. Tom Krattenmaker, "Q Gathering 2010: Heralding the Arrival of a Post-Christian America," *Huffington Post*, May 11, 2010, http://www.huffingtonpost.com/tom-krattenmaker/q-conference-2010-heraldi_b_571089.html.

10. Jonathan Merritt, blog post at "Evangelism: Answering the Questions No One Is Asking," JonathanMerritt.com, March 12, 2012, http://www.jonathanmerritt.com/blogs/news/evangelismansweringthequestionsnooneisasking.html.

11. A news release about the survey can be found on the LifeWay website. See Chris Turner, "Ultimate purpose and meaning: Some say they pursue it, others do not," December 27, 2011, http://www.lifeway.com/ArticleView?storeId=10054&catalogId=10001&langId=-1&article=Research-Ultimate-purpose-and-meaning.

12. Merritt, "Evangelism."

13. Andrew Wilson, *If God Then What? Wondering Aloud about Truth, Origins and Redemption* (Downer's Grove, IL: InterVarsity, 2012). Wilson's questions can also be found in an article at the Patheos.com website. See Scot McKnight, "If God Then What 2—Seven Really Good Questions," Patheos.com, March 14, 2012, http://www.patheos.com/blogs/jesuscreed/2012/03/14/if-god-then-what-2-andrew-wilson.

14. Personal interview, April 2, 2010.

15. Tom Krattenmaker, "Atheism: A positive pillar," *USA Today*, November 17, 2008.

16. Jim Henderson, Todd Hunter, and Craig Spinks, *The Outsider Interviews: A New Generation Speaks Out on Christianity* (Ada, MI: Baker, 2010).

17. Tom Krattenmaker, "How to sell Christianity? Ask an atheist," *USA Today*, June 27, 2010; the column can be found online at http://www.usatoday.com/news/opinion/forum/2010-06-28-column28_ST_N.htm.

18. N. T. Wright, *Surprised by Hope: Rethinking Heaven, the Resurrection, and the Mission of the Church* (New York: HarperCollins, 2009), 225.

19. Wright, *Surprised by Hope*, 226.

20. *This American Life*, November 6, 2009; an archive recording of the program can be found on the *This American Life* website at http://www.thisamericanlife.org/radio-archives/episode/394/bait-and-switch. (The segment featuring Dickerson and Henderson is "Act Two: Raw Sex.")

21. *This American Life,* November 6, 2009.

22. This reference comes from a page on the website of the Institute for the Theology of Culture: New Wine, New Wineskins at Multnomah Biblical Seminary, http://new-wineskins.org/about/purpose/.

23. Tony Kriz, *Neighbors and Wise Men* (Nashville: Thomas Nelson, 2012), 78.

24. The line can be found on the "About" page at the website of the New Wine, New Wineskins Institute (see http://new-wineskins.org/about/purpose/). The theme is developed in such works as Paul Louis Metzger's *Connecting Christ: How to Discuss Jesus in a World of Diverse Paths* (Nashville: Thomas Nelson, 2012), 50.

25. The teachings are found on the "About Jim" page of the "Jim Henderson Presents" website. See http://jimhendersonpresents.com/about-jim.

26. Ernesto Tinajero, "Who Is the Messiah of Evangelical Politicians?" Sojo.net, August 31, 2011, http://sojo.net/blogs/2011/08/31/who-messiah-evangelical-politicians.

27. Telephone interview conducted April 2010.

28. The remarks were made in a panel titled "The Church and the City," at the 2011 Q conference, held April 27–29 in Portland, Oregon. A video of the panel can be found on the Q Ideas website at http://www.qideas.org/video/q-panel-church-and-the-city.aspx.

29. Interview conducted by e-mail, August 28, 2011. (Mehta had previously chaired the Student Secular Alliance board of directors.)

30. Personal correspondence sent to Kevin Palau and Tom Krattenmaker on February 27, 2010.

31. Tom Krattenmaker, "Christopher Hitchens: Adamant atheist is a hard-core believer," *The Oregonian*, January 17, 2010, http://www.oregonlive.com/opinion/index.ssf/2010/01/christopher_hitchens_adamant_a.html.

32. An example of this phenomenon can be found in a Salon.com interview with *End of Faith* author Sam Harris published in 2006. See Steve Paulson, "The Disbeliever," Salon.com, July 7, 2006, http://www.salon.com/2006/07/07/harris_24.

33. Wright, *Surprised by Hope*, 227.

4. UNCHRISTIAN NATION

1. David Brody, "Obama to CBN News: We're No Longer Just a Christian Nation," CBN News, July 30, 2007, http://www.cbn.com/CBNnews/204016.aspx.

2. "Fox News figures outraged over Obama's 'Christian nation,'" Media Matters for America, April 9, 2009, http://mediamatters.org/research/200904090033.

3. Gabe Lyons, Q Ideas, personal interview conducted in New York, November 14, 2011.

4. Ibid.

5. Ibid.

6. Ibid.

7. Ibid.

8. Ibid.

9. David Kinnaman and Gabe Lyons, *unChristian: What a New Generation Really Thinks about Christianity . . . and Why It Matters* (Grand Rapids, MI: Baker, 2007), 12.

10. Ibid., 13.

11. Ibid.

12. "Violence-Related Firearm Deaths among Residents of Metropolitan Areas and Cities, United States, 2006–2007," Centers for Disease Control and Prevention, May 13, 2011, http://www.cdc.gov/mmwr/preview/mmwrhtml/mm6018a1.htm?s_cid=mm6018a1_w. Note: Placing the Virginia Tech shootings in this context was not my original idea but was gleaned from a column by Bob Herbert in the *New York Times* on April 19, 2007, "A Volatile Young Man, Humiliation and a Gun," http://www.nytimes.com/2007/04/19/opinion/19herbert.html.

13. Yana Kunichoff, "Arizona Shooting Sets Off Debate on Violent Political Rhetoric," *Truthout*, January 8, 2011, http://archive.truthout.org/congresswoman-gifford-six-others-killed-gunman66671.

14. Jeff Muskus, "Sarah Palin's PAC Puts Gun Sights on Democrats She's Targeting in 2010," *Huffington Post*, January 9, 2011, http://www.huffingtonpost.com/2010/03/24/sarah-palins-pac-puts-gun_n_511433.html.

15. "Survey: Only 1-in-5 Give 'Moral State of the Union' High Marks," Public Religion Research, January 20, 2011, http://publicreligion.org/research/2011/01/only-1-in-5-give-moral-state-of-the-union-high-marks.

16. Jim Wallis, "Evangelical Consistency and the 2012 Elections," *Huffington Post*, December 1, 2011, http://www.huffingtonpost.com/jim-wallis/evangelical-consistency-a_b_1123046.html.

17. David Kinnaman and Gabe Lyons, *unChristian*, 24.

18. Ibid., 25.

19. Ibid., 26.

20. Tom Krattenmaker, "Q Gathering 2010: Heralding the Arrival of a Post-Christian America," *Huffington Post*, May 11, 2010, http://www.huffingtonpost.com/tom-krattenmaker/q-conference-2010-heraldi_b_571089.html.

21. Timothy Keller, comments made in video streamed on the Q Ideas website, February 2011; the video can be found online at http://www.qideas.org/webcast.

22. Gabe Lyons, *The Next Christians: The Good News About the End of Christian America* (New York: Doubleday, 2010), 53.

23. Ibid., 73.

24. Ibid., 93.

25. Ibid., 174.

26. James Scott Jr., "Book Review: Gabe Lyons' 'The Next Christians' is dismissive arrogance," April 23, 2011, http://extraordinarylivingbydrscotty.blogspot.com/2011/04/book-review-gabe-lyons-next-christians.html.

27. Shane Claiborne, personal interview, November 15, 2011.

28. Ross Douthat, "A Tough Season for Believers," *New York Times*, December 19, 2010, http://www.nytimes.com/2010/12/20/opinion/20douthat.html.

29. Gabe Lyons, "A Third Way for the 'Christian Nation' Debate," *Huffington Post*, October 26, 2010, http://www.huffingtonpost.com/gabe-lyons/third-way-christian-nation-debate_b_773744.html.

5. CONFESSION BOOTH

1. Tony Kriz, in comments for the film *Lord, Save Us from Your Followers*; an extended version of his on-camera interview for the film can be found on the front page of tonykriz.com.

2. Ibid.

3. Donald Miller, *Blue Like Jazz: Nonreligious Thoughts on Christian Spirituality* (Nashville: Thomas Nelson, 2003), 117, 118.

4. Tony Kriz, tonykriz.com.

5. Ibid.

6. Dan Merchant, personal interview in Lake Oswego, Oregon, September 14, 2011.

7. Ibid.

8. *Lord, Save Us from Your Followers: Why Is the Gospel of Love Dividing America?* (Nashville: Thomas Nelson, 2008).

9. Ibid.

10. Dan Merchant, personal interview.

11. Tom Krattenmaker, "Playing the God Card," *USA Today*, January 29, 2006, http://www.usatoday.com/news/opinion/editorials/2006-01-29-god-card_x.htm.

12. Then-president George W. Bush made these comments, and comments to this effect, on numerous occasions, most notably in his acceptance address at the 2004 National Republican

Convention. A copy of that speech can be found at www.presidentialrhetoric.com/campaign/rncspeeches/bush.html.

13. Tim Egan, "Soldier's Choice," *New York Times*, December 22, 2011, http://opinionator.blogs.nytimes.com/2011/12/22/soldiers-choice.

14. Bachmann made the remarks in a campaign speech in Sarasota, Florida, on August 28, 2011. A video of Bachmann making the remarks can found, as well as comments by a campaign official insisting they were in jest, at www.huffingtonpost.com/2011/08/29/michele-bachmann-hurricane-irene_n_940209.html.

15. Tom Krattenmaker, "A War on Christians? No," *USA Today*, March 26, 2006, http://www.usatoday.com/news/opinion/editorials/2006-03-26-religion_x.htm.

16. Molly Worthen, "Brothers' Keepers," *Foreign Policy*, August 2, 2011; a copy of the article can be found online at www.foreignpolicy.com/articles/2011/08/02/brothers_keepers?page=full.

17. Molly Worthen, "Brothers' Keepers."

18. For a thorough analysis of evangelicals' advance to positions of power and influence in American life, see D. Michael Lindsay, *Faith in the Halls of Power: How Evangelicals Joined the American Elite* (New York: Oxford University Press, 2007).

19. Matthew 25:40, New International Version.

20. "Obama or God: Who Said It?" American Bible Society news release, November 23, 2009. A copy of the release can be found online at http://www.harrisinteractive.com/vault/Client_News_AmericanBibleSociety_2009_11.pdf.

21. Ibid.

22. Richard Stearns and Lamar Vest, "Christians Losing Their Way," Washingtonpost.com, December 14, 2009, http://newsweek.washingtonpost.com/onfaith/guestvoices/2009/12/call_for_christians_to_help_poor.html.

23. Stearns and Vest, "Christians Losing Their Way."

24. Tom Krattenmaker, "A Model of Faith," *USA Today*, June 4, 2006, http://www.usatoday.com/news/opinion/editorials/2006-06-04-on-religion_x.htm.

25. Matthew 7:16, New International Version.

26. Ben Sand, personal interview in Portland, Oregon, September 7, 2011.

27. Ibid.

28. Ibid.

29. Frank Bruni, "True Believers, All of Us," *New York Times*, August 6, 2011, http://www.nytimes.com/2011/08/07/opinion/sunday/Bruni-True-Believers-All-of-Us.html.

30. "Robert Asks Christians to Pray for Israel," *CBN News*, September 27, 2011, http://www.cbn.com/cbnnews/insideisrael/2011/September/Robertson-Asks-Prayers-for-Israel-/.

31. Paul Louis Metzger, "Editor's Introduction," *Cultural Encounters* 7, no. 2. The article can be found online at http://new-wineskins.org/journal/volumes/7/#number-1.

32. David P. Gushee and Glen H. Stassen, "An Open Letter to America's Christian Zionists," published at the website of the New Evangelical Partnership for the Common Good, September 19, 2011. The piece can be found online at http://newevangelicalpartnership.org/?q=node/139.

33. Joel Connelly, "Genuflecting to the Christian Right in GOP campaign," *Seattle Post-Intelligencer*, August 14, 2011, http://www.seattlepi.com/local/connelly/article/Genuflecting-to-the-Christian-Right-in-GOP-1924922.php.

34. Ibid.

35. David Brooks, "The Politics of Solipsism," *New York Times*, May 5, 2011, http://www.nytimes.com/2011/05/06/opinion/06brooks.html.

36. Todd Strandberg, "Bible Prophecy and Environmentalism," Rapture Ready, http://www.raptureready.com/rr-environmental.html.

37. N. T. Wright, *Surprised by Hope*, 197.

38. Shane Claiborne, "What If Jesus Meant All That Stuff?" *Esquire*, November 18, 2009, http://www.esquire.com/features/best-and-brightest-2009/shane-claiborne-1209.

6. BREAKING FORMATION

1. Lisa Sharon Harper and D. C. Innes, *Left, Right, & Christ: Evangelical Faith in Politics* (Boise, ID: Russell Media, 2011), 34. (Note: The passage comes from a portion of the book in which the two co-authors take turns telling their own faith-and-politics stories.)

2. Ibid., 34, 35.

3. Ibid., 35.

4. Ibid., 35.

5. Ibid., 35.

6. Alan Jacobs, "Come On, You Call This a Manifesto?" *Wall Street Journal*, May 6, 2008, http://online.wsj.com/article/SB121029045957979237.html.

7. Benjy Sarlin, "Paul Ryan Confronted by Bible-Wielding Protester Decrying Ayn Rand." TalkingPointsMemo.com, June 3, 2011, http://tpmdc.talkingpointsmemo.com/2011/06/paul-ryan-confronted-by-bible-wielding-protester-decrying-ayn-rand.php.

8. "Mobile Billboard, Florida Pastors: GOP Presidential Candidates Must Protect Poor and Vulnerable," news release issued by Faith in Public Life, September 22, 2011, http://faithinpubliclife.org/content/press/2011/09/mobile_billboard_florida_pasto.html.

9. Kemberly Richardson, "Local religious leaders join Wall Street protest," website of WABC television, New York, October 9, 2011, http://abclocal.go.com/wabc/story?section=news/local/new_york&id=8385099.

10. Frances Fox Piven, "The War on the Home Front," TomDispatch.com, November 6, 2011, http://www.tomdispatch.com/blog/175463/tomgram%3A_frances_fox_piven%2C_the_war_on_the_home_front.

11. Jennifer Butler, "The Golden Calf and Occupy Wall Street," *Huffington Post*, October 13, 2011, http://www.huffingtonpost.com/rev-jennifer-butler/golden-calf-occupy-wall-street_b_1009455.html.

12. Amanda Nover, "Young Americans: Their Faith, Attitudes, and Values," a report by the Center for Information and Research on Civic Learning and Engagement, April 2010. The report can be found online at http://www.civicyouth.org/PopUps/FactSheets/Religion_Fact_Sheet_Final.pdf.

13. Ibid. Note that support for Obama among younger white evangelicals was significantly lower in the 2012 election, according to polling by Public Religion Research and Georgetown University's Berkley Center for Religion, Peace, and World Affairs. PRRI president Robert P. Jones told me the strong preference for GOP nominee Mitt Romney did not represent evangelical millennials' permanent return to the Christian Right/Republican fold but was, rather, due to disappointment with Obama and other particularities of the 2012 race. See "Diverse, Disillusioned, and Divided: Millennial Values and Voter Engagement in the 2012 Election," Public Religion Research, October 4, 2012, http://publicreligion.org/research/2012/10/millennial-values-voter-engagement-2012.

14. Dan Cox, "Young White Evangelicals: Less Republican, Still Conservative," Pew Forum, September 28, 2007.

15. "Survey: Committed to Availability, Conflicted about Morality—What the Millennial Generation Tells Us about the Future of the Abortion Debate and the Culture Wars," a report by Public Religion Research Institute, June 9, 2011, http://publicreligion.org/research/2011/06/committed-to-availability-conflicted-about-morality-what-the-millennial-generation-tells-us-about-the-future-of-the-abortion-debate-and-the-culture-wars.

16. "News Release: Millennial Generation Committed to Availability, Conflicted about Morality of Abortion," Public Religion Research Institute, June 9, 2011, http://publicreligion.org/newsroom/2011/06/millennial-generation-committed-to-availability-conflicted-about-morality-of-abortion.

17. The study did not include a large enough sample of evangelical millennials to say with certainty whether this "both/and" finding holds among the young evangelical cohort, Jones indicated in an e-mail exchange with me. However, judging from the wider patterns, he expressed confidence that the trend would generally prevail with this group.

18. Robert P. Jones, *Progressive & Religious: How Christian, Jewish, Muslim, and Buddhist Leaders are Moving beyond the Culture Wars and Transforming American Public Life* (Lanham, MD: Rowman & Littlefield, 2008), 1–2.

19. Karen Tumulty and Nia-Malika Henderson, "Republicans hope to spark political revival among evangelicals for 2012 race," *Washington Post*, June 2, 2011, http://www.washingtonpost.com/politics/republicans-hope-to-spark-political-revival-among-evangelicals-for-2012-race/2011/06/02/AGacjbHH_story.html.

20. Ibid.

21. Ibid.

22. Personal interview conducted by e-mail, June 3, 2011.

23. Jonathan Merritt, *Green Like God: Unlocking the Divine Plan for our Planet* (New York: Faith Words, 2010), 2.

24. Ibid., 2.

25. Ibid., 90.

26. Tom Krattenmaker, "Torture and evangelicals: Faith takes a back seat," *The Oregonian*, October 18, 2008, www.oregonlive.com/opinion/index.ssf/2008/10/torture_and_evangelicals.html.

27. Ibid.

28. Ibid.

29. Randall Balmer, *The Making of Evangelicalism: From Revivalism to Politics and Beyond* (Waco, TX: Baylor University, 2010), 70.

30. "Few Say Religion Shapes Immigration, Environment Views," a report by the Pew Forum on Religion & Public Life, September 17, 2010, http://pewforum.org/Politics-and-Elections/Few-Say-Religion-Shapes-Immigration-Environment-Views.aspx.

31. E. J. Dionne, "Election 2012's great religious divide," *Washington Post*, November 6, 2011, www.washingtonpost.com/opinions/election-2012s-great-religious-divide/2011/11/06/gIQAiRbdtM_story.html.

32. Greg Garrett, "An Open Letter to Joel Osteen," Patheos.com, May 9, 2012, http://www.patheos.com/Progressive-Christian/Open-Letter-to-Joel-Osteen-Greg-Garrett-05-10-2012.html.

33. Jonathan Merritt, *A Faith of Our Own: Following Jesus beyond the Culture Wars* (New York: Faith Words, 2012), 60.

34. Ibid., 62.

35. Dana Milbank, "For the religious right, faith without works," *Washington Post*, January 20, 2010, www.washingtonpost.com/opinions/religious-right-has-lost-its-political-influence/2012/01/20/gIQAsnMrDQ_story.html.

36. This scene unfolded at a Republican presidential candidates forum held September 12, 2011, in Tampa, Florida. A video of this particular exchange can be found at http://www.youtube.com/watch?v=yva0VSN1_T4.

37. Tom Krattenmaker, "Re-branding the Right," Swarthmore College *Bulletin* magazine, January 2012; the article can be found online at http://media.swarthmore.edu/bulletin/?p=804.

38. Shane Claiborne, personal interview conducted in Philadelphia, November 15, 2011.

39. Jim Wallis, "What is 'Biblical Politics'?" Sojourners.com, September 15, 2011, http://sojo.net/blogs/2011/09/15/what-biblical-politics.

7. THROUGH THE LOGS IN THEIR EYES

1. The photograph, although appearing with *Time*'s coverage of OneWheaton's activities at Homecoming in October 2011, was actually taken the previous spring. The article can be found at http://www.time.com/time/nation/article/0,8599,2096426,00.html.

2. Elizabeth Dias, "Wheaton's (Unofficial) Homecoming for Gay Evangelicals," *Time*, October 7, 2011.

3. The text of the letter appeared in an article by Mike Clawson, "Support (Finally!) for Gays at the 'Harvard' of Christian Colleges," Patheos.com, April 29, 2011, www.patheos.com/blogs/friendlyatheist/2011/04/29/support-finally-for-gays-at-the-harvard-of-christian-colleges.

4. Dias, "Wheaton's (Unofficial) Homecoming for Gay Evangelicals."

5. Clawson, "Support (Finally!) for Gays at the "Harvard" of Christian Colleges."

6. "Gay Marriage," a fact sheet published by the nonpartisan group ProCon.org at http://gaymarriage.procon.org/view.resource.php?resourceID=004857.

7. "Most Say Homosexuality Should Be Accepted by Society," a report by Pew Research Center for the People & the Press, May 13, 2011, http://www.people-press.org/2011/05/13/most-say-homosexuality-should-be-accepted-by-society.

8. "Majority of Americans support same-sex marriage," news release issued by Public Religion Research Institute, May 18, 2011, http://publicreligion.org/newsroom/2011/05/majority-of-americans-support-same-sex-marriage.

9. Leviticus 18:22, King James Version.

10. "Wheaton College Is Nation's Least LGBT-Friendly School, for Second Time in Three Years," *Huffington Post*, August 3, 2011, www.huffingtonpost.com/2011/08/03/wheaton-college-again-ran_n_917342.html.

11. "Message from President Ryken Regarding OneWheaton," news release issued by Wheaton College, May 3, 2011, www.wheaton.edu/Media-Center/News/2011/05/Message-from-President-Ryken-Regarding-OneWheaton.

12. Ibid.

13. Clawson, "Support (Finally!) for Gays at the "Harvard" of Christian Colleges."

14. David Kinnaman and Gabe Lyons, *unChristian: What a New Generation Really Thinks about Christianity . . . and Why It Matters* (Grand Rapids, MI: Baker, 2007), 101.

15. Bruce Nolan, "Gay Marriage Divides Evangelicals Along Generation Gap," Religion News Service, September 7, 2011. The article can be found online at http://www.huffingtonpost.com/2011/09/07/gay-marriage-evangelicals_n_952888.html.

16. Marvin Olasky, "Refocused: As marriage crumbles, says Focus on the Family's Jim Daly, Christians can try to uphold the biblical family as a model to the world," *World* magazine, June 4, 2011, http://www.worldmag.com/articles/18060.

17. Kinnaman and Lyons, *unChristian*, 92.

18. David Kinnaman, *You Lost Me: Why Young Christians Are Leaving Church . . . and Rethinking Faith* (Ada, MI: Baker, 2011), 171.

19. "Mass Exodus: How the Church Is Losing the Youth," a segment on the Chrisitan Broadcasting Network, January 21, 2012. The segment can be found online at http://www.cbn.com/cbnnews/us/2011/November/Mass-Exodus-How-the-Church-Is-Losing-the-Youth. (Note: The comments quoted here appear in the "extended interview," which is linked further down the page.)

20. Randall Balmer, *Thy Kingdom Come: How the Religious Right Distorts the Faith and Threatens America* (New York: Basic, 2006), 24–25.

21. Ibid., 26.

22. For one of numerous sources exploring this phenomenon, see Ronald J. Sider, *The Scandal of the Evangelical Conscience: Why Are Christians Living Just Like the Rest of the World?* (Grand Rapids, MI: Eerdmans, 2006).

23. Greg Boyd, *The Myth of a Christian Nation: How the Quest for Power Is Destroying the Church* (Grand Rapids, MI: Zondervan, 2005), 138.

24. Amy Sullivan, "Why Does Michigan's Anti-Bullying Bill Protect Religious Tormenters?" *Time*, November 4, 2011, http://swampland.time.com/2011/11/04/why-does-michigans-anti-bullying-bill-protect-religious-tormenters.

25. Evelyn Schlatter, "18 Anti-Gay Groups and Their Propaganda," a report by the Southern Poverty Law Center Intelligence Report, Winter 2010. The report can be found online at www.splcenter.org/get-informed/intelligence-report/browse-all-issues/2010/winter/the-hard-liners.

26. Ibid.

27. Dan Gilgoff, "Christian group pulls support for event challenging homosexuality," CNN Belief Blog, October 6, 2010, http://religion.blogs.cnn.com/2010/10/06/christian-group-pulls-support-for-event-challenging-homosexuality.

28. Charles Colson, "Upsetting the Apple Cart: The 'Offensive' Manhattan Declaration," Breakpoint.org, December 2, 2010, http://www.breakpoint.org/bpcommentaries/entry/13/15962.

29. Ki Mae Heussner, "'Anti-Gay' iPhone App Pulled from Apple Store," ABCNews.com, November 30, 2010, http://abcnews.go.com/Technology/anti-gay-iphone-app-pulled-apple-store/story?id=12274937#.T-3rocXNknU.

30. Peter Schmidt, "Federal Judge Upholds Dismissal of Counseling Student Who Balked at Treating Gay Clients," *Chronicle of Higher Education*, July 27, 2010.

31. Laurie Goodstein, "Bishops Say Rules on Gay Parents Limit Freedom of Religion," *New York Times*, December 28, 2011.

32. Marcia Pally, *The New Evangelicals: Expanding the Vision of the Common Good* (Grand Rapids, MI: Eerdmans, 2011), 235.

33. Nick Sementelli, "Why Does MSNBC Invite Hateful, Anti-Gay Spokespeople Who Tell Lies on TV to Represent Christians?" Faith in Public Life, January 12, 2012, www.faithinpubliclife.org/blog/why-does-msnbc-invite-hateful-anti-gay-liars-on-tv-to-represent-christians.

34. Jody May-Chang and Jill Kuraitis, "The Story Behind the American Family Association's Bryan Fischer," Southern Poverty Law Center Intelligence Report, Winter 2010, www.splcenter.org/get-informed/intelligence-report/browse-all-issues/2011/winter/the-story-behind-afas-bryan-fischer.

35. Marcia Pally, *The New Evangelicals*, 144.

36. Jennifer Knust, *Unprotected Texts: The Bible's Surprising Contradictions about Sex and Desire* (New York: HarperOne, 2011), 17.

37. Ibid., 244.

38. Romans 2:1.

39. John 8:7.

40. Matthew 7:3, English Standard Version. (The word "plank" is used in various other translations.)

41. Bakker has made this point on numerous occasions and in numerous contexts. See, for example, Rebecca Lee, "Punk Pastor Preaches Tolerance, Compassion," ABCNews.com, December 8, 2006, http://abcnews.go.com/WNT/Story?id=2711472&page=2#.T_sSMfXNknU.

42. Tom Krattenmaker, "On gay rights, keep fighting or adapt?" *USA Today*, February 15, 2011, http://www.usatoday.com/news/opinion/forum/2011-02-14-column14_ST_N.htm.

43. Marcia Pally, *The New Evangelicals*, 183.

44. For example, a *Rolling Stone* magazine article on anti-gay bullying and related suicides in a Minnesota community circulated widely in progressive circles and in progressive media in early 2012. See Sabrina Rubin Erdely, "One Town's War on Gay Teens," *Rolling Stone*, February 2, 2012. (The article can be found online at http://www.rollingstone.com/politics/news/one-towns-war-on-gay-teens-20120202#ixzz1lXjKcXla.)

45. Heather Sells, "Christian's Outreach to Gays: I'm Sorry," CBN News, September 19, 2010, www.cbn.com/cbnnews/us/2010/August/Missionarys-Message-to-Gays-Im-Sorry-/.

46. Michael Lindenberger, "An Evangelical's Concession on Gays," Time.com, March 16, 2007, http://www.time.com/time/nation/article/0,8599,1599987,00.html.

47. Cyd Zeigler, "Michael Irvin: The Playmaker Preaches," *Out* magazine, July 11, 2011, http://www.out.com/entertainment/sports/2011/07/10/michael-irvin-playmaker-preaches.

48. Erik Eckholm, "Even on Religious Campuses, Students Fight for Gay Identity," *New York Times*, April 18, 2011, http://www.nytimes.com/2011/04/19/us/19gays.html.

49. Tim King, "Love Comes First," Sojo.net, May 9, 2011, http://blog.sojo.net/2011/05/09/love-comes-first.

50. Paul Waldman, "The Culture War Ain't What It Used to Be," *The American Prospect*, December 20, 2010, http://prospect.org/article/culture-war-aint-what-it-used-be.

8. PRO-LIFE . . . SERIOUSLY

1. Stephanie Tama-Sweet, personal interview and e-mail exchange, March 2012.

2. Lena H. Sun, "Virginia ultrasound bill joins other states' measures," *Washington Post*, February 26, 2012, www.washingtonpost.com/national/health-science/virginia-ultrasound-bill-joins-other-states-measures/2012/02/24/gIQAervUcR_story.html.

3. Stephanie Tama-Sweet, personal interview, March 2012.

4. Randall Balmer, *The Making of Evangelicalism: From Revivalism to Politics and Beyond* (Waco, TX: Baylor University, 2010), 61.

5. Ibid., 61.

6. Ibid., 65–66.

7. Lydia Saad, "U.S. Abortion Attitudes Closely Divided," a report by the Gallup polling agency, August 4, 2009, www.gallup.com/poll/122033/u.s.-abortion-attitudes-closely-divided.aspx.

8. Ibid.

9. "Committed to Availability, Conflicted about Morality: What the Millennial Generation Tells Us about the Future of the Abortion Debate and the Culture Wars," a report by Public Religion Research Institute, June 6, 2011, http://publicreligion.org/site/wp-content/uploads/2011/06/Millenials-Abortion-and-Religion-Survey-Report.pdf.

10. Ibid.

11. Kate Nocera, "Poll: Public tired of abortion debate," Politico.com, June 2, 2011, http://www.politico.com/news/stories/0611/56154.html.

12. Tom Krattenmaker, "Abortion's middle ground? Reducing them," *USA Today*, May 2, 2010, http://www.usatoday.com/news/opinion/forum/2010-05-03-column03_ST_N.htm.

13. "Morbidity and Mortality Weekly Report," Centers of Disease Control, Surveillance Summary, November 25, 2011, http://www.cdc.gov/mmwr/preview/mmwrhtml/ss6015a1.htm?s_cid=ss6015a1_w#Tab12.

14. Ibid.

15. Karen Schuberg, "Abortion Kills More Black Americans than the Seven Leading Causes of Death Combined, Says CDC Data," CNSNews.com, October 22, 2009, http://cnsnews.com/node/55956.

16. "Births: Preliminary Data for 2006," National Vital Statistics Report, Centers for Disease Control, December 5, 2007, http://www.cdc.gov/nchs/data/nvsr/nvsr56/nvsr56_07.pdf.

17. Catherine Davis, personal interview conducted by telephone, April 2010.

18. Christian Piatt, "When Legislating Morality Falls Short," *Huffington Post*, November 21, 2011, www.huffingtonpost.com/christian-piatt/when-legislating-morality_b_1095167.html.

19. Nathan Clarke, "Christian or Lobbyist? Yes!" ChristianityToday.com, October 20, 2011, http://www.christianitytoday.com/thisisourcity/portland/lobbyistyes.html.

20. Ibid.

21. Tama-Sweet, personal interview, March 2012.

22. Shoshon Tama-Sweet, comments made in Christianity Today video released on line on October 21, 2011. The video can be found at http://www.christianitytoday.com/thisisourcity/portland/shoshon.html.

23. "Freedom Sunday: Churches Fight Child Trafficking," CBN News, February 26, 2012, http://www.cbn.com/cbnnews/us/2012/February/Freedom-Sunday-Churches-Fight-Child-Trafficking.

24. Kelly Rosati, Focus on the Family, personal interview, March 23, 2012.

25. Statistics provided by Gary Schneeberger of Focus on the Family in an e-mail interview, April 2012.

26. "Dignity of Human Life" statement, print publication of Focus on the Family, 2012.

27. Mitchell Hescox, "A Christian perspective on the costs of mercury to human health and well-being," testimony given before the Energy and Power Subcommittee of the Energy and Commerce Committee of the U.S. House of Representatives, February 8, 2012. The text of Hescox's statement can be found at http://energycommerce.house.gov/sites/republicans.energycommerce.house.gov/files/Hearings/EP/20120208/HHRG-112-IF03-WState-MHescox-20120208.pdf.

28. Marcia Pally, *The New Evangelicals: Expanding the Vision of the Common Good* (Grand Rapids, MI: Eerdmans, 2011), 141.

29. Steven Kull et al., "Faith and Global Policy Challenges: How Spiritual Values Shape Views on Poverty, Nuclear Risks, and Environmental Degradation," a study by the Center for International and Security Studies at the University of Maryland and its Program on International Policy Attitudes, December 2011, http://cissm.umd.edu/papers/files/faith_and_global_policy_challenges__final.pdf.

30. "Climate Change and Poverty," released by Faith in Public Life, April 2009, http://www.faithinpubliclife.org/poll/climate-change-and-poverty-3.

31. Nicholas Kristof, "Learning from the Sin of Sodom," *New York Times*, February 27, 2010, http://www.nytimes.com/2010/02/28/opinion/28kristof.html.

32. Shoshon Tama-Sweet, personal interview, March 2012.

33. Ibid.

34. Jon Cohen, Peyton M. Craighill, and Scott Clement, "New Hampshire primary: 10 key exit poll results," WashingtonPost.com, January 11, 2012, http://www.washingtonpost.com/blogs/behind-the-numbers/post/new-hampshire-primary-10-key-exit-poll-results/2012/01/03/gIQAM2oopP_blog.html.

35. Stephanie Tama-Sweet, e-mail interview, April 2012.

36. Shoshon Tama-Sweet, e-mail interview, April 2012.

9. FROM BEHIND CHURCH WALLS

1. Julie Clawson, "We've Changed, But How?" Sojourners website, September 9, 2011, http://blog.sojo.net/blogs/2011/09/09/weve-changed-how.

2. Ibid.

3. Ibid.

4. Andrew Himes, *The Sword of the Lord: The Roots of Fundamentalism in an American Family* (Seattle: Chiara, 2010), 203.

5. Julie Clawson, "I'm a heretic, so what?" JulieClawson.com, February 14, 2010, http://julieclawson.com/2010/02/14/im-a-heretic-so-what.

6. "*Harry Potter* Books Spark Rise in Satanism Among Children," *The Onion*, July 26, 2000. The article can be found online at http://www.theonion.com/articles/harry-potter-books-spark-rise-in-satanism-among-ch,2413.

7. Shane Claiborne, "The Christian Industrial Complex," Red Letter Christians website, December 24, 2011, http://www.redletterchristians.org/the-christian-industrial-complex.

8. Andy Crouch, *Culture Making: Recovering Our Creative Calling* (Westmont, IL: Intervarsity, 2008).

9. Brett McCracken, "A very hipster Christmas," WashingtonPost.com, December 21, 2010, http://onfaith.washingtonpost.com/onfaith/guestvoices/2010/12/a_very_hipster_christmas.html.

10. Dan Merchant, personal interview in Lake Oswego, Oregon, September 14, 2011.

11. Micheal Flaherty, comments at the Faith Angle Forum, April 4, 2011. A transcript of the session in which Flaherty participated can be found at www.eppc.org/programs/faithangleforum/news/newsID.4461,programID.37/news_detail.asp.

12. Ibid.

13. I witnessed the performance at a *Christianity Today* event held in Portland, Oregon, in October 2011. A video of Potter's performance can be found online at http://www.christianitytoday.com/thisisourcity/portland/celebratesportland.html.

14. "Public Divided on Origins of Life," a report by the Pew Forum on Religion & Public Life, August 30, 2005, http://www.pewforum.org/Politics-and-Elections/Public-Divided-on-Origins-of-Life.aspx.

15. "Public Praises Science; Scientists Fault Public, Media," a report by the Pew Research Center for the People & the Press, July 9, 2009, http://www.people-press.org/2009/07/09/section-5-evolution-climate-change-and-other-issues.

16. "Survey: Climate Change and Evolution in the 2012 Elections," Public Religion Research Institute, September 22, 2011, http://publicreligion.org/research/2011/09/climate-change-evolution-2012.

17. David Kinnaman, *You Lost Me: Why Young Christians Are Leaving Church . . . and Rethinking Faith* (Ada, MI: Baker, 2011), 81.

18. Ibid.

19. Kevin Kelly, "Jesus and Divine Evolution," the Technium website, May 1, 2011, www.kk.org/thetechnium/archives/2011/05/jesus_and_divin.php.

20. The comments were made by Daniel Harlow, a religion professor at Calvin College. See Barbara Bradley Hagerty, "Evangelicals Question the Existence of Adam and Eve," National Public Radio website, August 9, 2011, www.npr.org/2011/08/09/138957812/evangelicals-question-the-existence-of-adam-and-eve.

21. Ibid.

22. Peter Enns, *The Evolution of Adam: What the Bible Does and Doesn't Say about Human Origins* (Grand Rapids, MI: Brazos, 2012), xvii–xviii.

23. Ibid., 147–48.

24. Paul Louis Metzger, *Consuming Jesus: Beyond Race and Class Divisions in a Consumer Church* (Grand Rapids, MI: Eerdmans, 2007).

25. Tom Krattenmaker, "Church closes racial divide," *USA Today*, April 29, 2012, http://www.usatoday.com/news/opinion/forum/story/2012-04-29/religion-racial-divide/54629552/1.

26. Tom Krattenmaker, "You can't buy the real gifts of Christmas," *USA Today*, December 21, 2009.

27. I refer here to an incident involving the rapper Too $hort in a video at the website of XXL magazine. For more on the ensuing controversy, see Stephen Willis, "Rapper's Explicit 'Advice' Sparks Outrage," HipHopBlog.com, February 14, 2012, http://www.hiphopblog.com/news-mainmenu-35/30286-too-horts-xxl-controversy.html.

28. Kinnaman, *You Lost Me*, 97.

29. Ibid., 77.

30. Gabe Lyons, *The Next Christians: The Good News about the End of Christian America* (New York: Doubleday, 2010), 80.

10. SEPTEMBER 12

1. Roughly 37 percent of the population of Colorado Springs is affiliated with a church, according to statistics published at CityData.com, as against the overall national rate of 50 percent. See Colorado Springs demographic profile at CityData.com, www.city-data.com/city/Colorado-Springs-Colorado.html.

2. Diane Ingolia, personal interview at Focus on the Family, March 23, 2012.

3. Ibid.

4. Jim Schaefer, M. L. Elrick, and Todd Spangler, "Ready for Battle," Detroit Free Press, October 7, 2007, http://www.freep.com/article/20071007/NEWS06/710070665/Ready-battle.

5. Jeannine Hunter, "TOMS Shoes founder apologizes for Focus on the Family connection," WashingtonPost.com, July 14, 2011, www.washingtonpost.com/blogs/under-god/post/

toms-shoes-founder-apologizes-for-focus-on-family-connection/2011/07/13/gIQAPuN4DI_
blog.html.

6. Joe Coscarelli, "Blake Mycoskie, TOMS Shoes Founder, Working with Christian, Anti-Gay Focus on the Family," VillageVoice.com, July 8, 2011, http://blogs.villagevoice.com/runninscared/2011/07/blake_mycoskie_toms_focus_on_the_family.php.

7. "Toms Shoes Partnered with Gay Hate Religious Group Focus On Family?" RENWL.org, July 8, 2011, http://www.zimbio.com/Blake+Mycoskie/articles/TAu57Bajd_V/Toms+Shoes+Partnered+Gay+Hate+Religious+Group.

8. Sarah Pulliam Bailey, "TOMS Shoes Founder Distances Himself from Focus on the Family," Christianity Today Politics Blog, July 9, 2011, http://blog.christianitytoday.com/ctpolitics/2011/07/toms_founder_di.html#.ThnX64-Dlmk.facebook.

9. Several months after this interaction, Gary Schneeberger left Focus on the Family for communications position at Grace Hill Media in Los Angeles (Gary Schneeberger, e-mail interview, October 2012).

10. Jim Daly, Focus on the Family, personal interview, March 23, 2012.

11. "Commentator Accountability Project," GLAAD.org, http://www.glaad.org/cap.

12. "Best of 2010," *Colorado Springs Independent*, October 21, 2010. The reference can be found online at http://www.csindy.com/coloradosprings/personalities/Content?oid=1886246.

13. Gary Schneeberger, Focus on the Family, personal interview.

14. Jim Daly, Focus on the Family, personal interview.

15. Gary Schneeberger, Focus on the Family, e-mail interview, June 2012.

16. The exchange took place at the "Retreat from Marriage" session at the 2011 Faith Angle Forum in Miami, Florida. A transcript of the session can be found online at http://www.eppc.org/programs/faithangleforum/news/newsID.4455,programID.37/news_detail.asp.

17. Samuel G. Freedman, "Waging a One-Man War on American Muslims," *New York Times*, December 16, 2011, http://www.nytimes.com/2011/12/17/us/on-religion-a-one-man-war-on-american-muslims.html.

18. For example, as Focus communications vice president Gary Schneeberger explained to me, state-level councils have their own boards and do not officially answer to Focus on the Family.

19. Gary Schneeberger, Focus on the Family, e-mail interview, April 2012.

20. In the summer of 2012, Daly was one of nearly 150 evangelical leaders from across the political spectrum to sign an "Evangelical Statement of Principles for Immigration Reform." See Jim Wallis, "How to Change Politics," *Sojourners* (September–October 2012), http://sojo.net/magazine/2012/09/how-change-politics.

21. Wayne Besen, Truth Wins Out, e-mail interview, April 2012.

22. Gary Schneeberger, Focus on the Family, e-mail interview, April 2012.

23. Ibid.

24. Meher Rehman, "The Foreign Student: How 9/11 shaped my fourth-grade year in Saudi Arabia," *Pennsylvania Gazette* (March/April 2012). The article can be found online at http://www.upenn.edu/gazette/0312/student.html.

25. Roger Cohen, "In Search of Sustainable Swagger," *New York Times*, April 2, 2012, http://www.nytimes.com/2012/04/03/opinion/cohen-in-search-of-a-sustainable-swagger.html.

26. Patel has used the term in numerous articles and interviews. For example, see a transcript of an interview Patel did for the "Voices of Antisemitism" podcast series of the U.S. Holocaust Memorial Museum at http://www.ushmm.org/museum/exhibit/focus/antisemitism/voices/transcript/index.php?content=20070510.

27. Eboo Patel, "Nine years after 9/11, a debate about Islam," WashingtonPost.com, October 4, 2010, http://onfaith.washingtonpost.com/onfaith/eboo_patel/2010/10/how_to_build_a_fear_bomb.html.

28. Cathy Lynn Grossman, "Richard Dawkins to atheist rally: 'Show contempt' for faith," USAToday.com, March 24, 2012, http://content.usatoday.com/communities/Religion/post/2012/03/-atheists-richard-dawkins-reason-rally/1#.UABqE_VdDU0.

29. The phrase comes from the subtitle of Hitchens's book, *God Is Not Great: How Religion Poisons Everything* (New York: Hachette, 2007).

30. The phrase comes from the title of Harris's book, *The End of Faith: Religion, Terror, and the Future of Reason* (New York: W. W. Norton, 2004).

31. Paul Brandeis Raushenbush, "Religion Stories of 2011: The Top 11," *Huffington Post*, December 6, 2011, http://www.huffingtonpost.com/2011/12/06/religion-stories-of-2011-_n_1131566.html.

32. John Jessup, "Clooney: Christian Ministries Key to Helping in Sudan," CBN News, March 15, 2012, www.cbn.com/cbnnews/world/2012/March/Clooney-Christian-Ministries-Key-to-Helping-in-Sudan-/.

33. Dan Harris, "Evangelicals Team with Portland's Gay Mayor for Charity," ABCNews.com, December 25, 2011, http://abcnews.go.com/US/evangelicals-team-portlands-gay-mayor-charity/story?id=15218876#.T6FCg-tYukN.

34. Dekker Dreyer, "Where Are the Progressive Christians?" NationofChange.org, July 13, 2012, http://www.nationofchange.org/where-are-progressive-christians-1330960317.

35. Jonathan Merritt, "Why I'm a Christian Independent," *Relevant* magazine website, March 1, 2012, http://www.relevantmagazine.com/life/current-events/op-ed-blog/28455-why-im-a-christian-independent.

Index